Kewa Tales

KEWA TALES

Edited by John LeRoy

University of British Columbia Press
Vancouver
1985

Kewa Tales

© The University of British Columbia Press 1985

This book has been published with the help of a grant from the Social Science Federation of Canada, using funds provided by the Social Sciences and Humanities Research Council of Canada, and a grant from the Canada Council.

Canadian Cataloguing in Publication Data

Main entry under title:
Kewa Tales

ISBN 0-7748-0218-9

1. Tales - Papua New Guinea.
2. Kewa (Papua New Guinea people) - Folklore.
I. LeRoy, John D., 1944-
GR385.P36K48 1985   398.2'0995'3   C85-091136-2

ISBN 0-7748-0218-9
Printed in Canada

Contents

CHAPTER 3   OF JEALOUS SPOUSES AND SIBLINGS

CHAPTER 4   OF MARRIAGES TO GHOSTS

CHAPTER 5   OF TRICKSTERS, LITTLE-MEN, AND OLD MEN

CHAPTER 6   OF SKIN CHANGING AND OTHER
              TRANSFORMATIONS

CHAPTER 7   OF BROKEN PROMISES AND ANGRY GHOSTS

Illustrations

Photographs by John LeRoy

Preface

The Kewa of Papua New Guinea have as part of their living cultural tradition an extensive body of folktales. A number of these tales are collected here, preceded by a brief introduction.

The tales stand well on their own. Like the familiar European folktales, they have one foot outside their historical and cultural base. Just where this pan-cultural foothold lies cannot be discussed here. Suffice it to say that because it exists, the tales in this book can be read independently of the major analytical and interpretive efforts that scholars continue to devote to tales and myths. Yet, coming as they do from a remote corner of the earth, Kewa tales need to be understood in context. In the introduction, I make a few brief comments about the tales and then give a quick sketch of Kewa culture. The main part of the book consists of the tales themselves, arranged by subject in seven chapters: fratricidal conflicts between brothers; misadventures of a brother and sister; the rivalry between sisters-in-law; the marriage of a young woman to an animal or ghost; attacks on villages by a frail but malicious hermit or by a troop of old men; young men and women who change their skins; the fateful breaking of a promise, and finally, and as a secondary theme in many other tales, narrow escapes from dangerous ghosts. Appendix 1 lists the narrators' names; Appendix 2 gives a synopsis of the tales' formal structure.

For further information on either the tales or the culture, the reader should consult the companion volume *Fabricated World: An Interpretation of Kewa Tales,* a study of the tales from an anthropological and literary point of view. It describes the formal patterning of the plots, takes note of symbolic structures, and comments on the connections between the tales and Kewa culture.

As an editor, my main word of thanks must go to the thirty-eight Kewa men and women who told these tales. I shall thank them all collectively, since their names and the tales they narrated are given in Appendix 1. I want more generally to thank the Kewa people of Karapere, Iapi, Koiari, and Kerabi for generously accommodating my fieldwork. My special thanks go to Adano and Malu of Karapere for their assistance in this project.

In addition, I am grateful to the Institute of Papua New Guinea Studies and to the Department of Anthropology and Sociology of the University of Papua New Guinea for sponsorship and help during two periods of fieldwork. A research grant from the Social Sciences and Humanities Research Council of Canada helped defray the cost of preparing the materials for publication.

Introduction

The tales collected here are one of two types of traditional narratives that Kewa people tell. They call them *lidi* (or *iti* or *rida*, depending on the dialect). The other type they call *ramani* or *rema*, which I translate as "legend." The main difference between the two types is that the Kewa deem legends to be true, whereas tales they admit to be fictitious. The difference is one between narrative as "oral history," on the one hand, and as "oral literature," on the other. In many instances, though, it is difficult for an outsider to distinguish between the two, especially if he happens to rely on Western notions about truth and fiction. Legends deemed veracious often seem no less improbable than some tales, and often they share the same unlikely cast of characters, such as sky people and ghosts. Occasionally, it is true, the Kewa may disagree among themselves about whether a particular story is a *lidi* or a *ramani*, but in my experience this happens infrequently (or perhaps only infrequently is it important to decide).

The term *myth* is used loosely both within and outside academic circles. From one point of view the tales collected here are indeed myths; they are false narratives. But the term *myth* generally connotes a false narrative that is considered to be true, at least by those who believe in it (its falsity being evident only to the outsider who ostensibly knows better than the believer). By this standard, Kewa tales cannot be myths, since everyone admits they are fictitious. This explains my choice of *tale* as a gloss, since this English term readily connotes "literature" rather than "erroneous belief." Here two further comments can be added. One has to do with scholarly conventions. Probably most of what anthropologists continue to call "myths" are in fact tales, if the criterion of avowed fictionality is applied. Folklorists readily use the term *tale* for these narratives, and it may be that anthropologists avoid it for that reason. (The choice of the term may tell us more about disciplinary boundaries than about the texts.) A second point concerns the narratives themselves. When people call *lidi* untrue, they have in mind what the stories literally say. But a good case can be made (though the Kewa do not make it) for tales conveying truths of a figurative kind, and then they would indeed be myths or have a mythic function. In fact, one could argue plausibly that literal untruths often have semiotic value, as pointers to deeper metaphorical or allegorical truths. According to this line of thinking, tales deal with "essential" truths. Legends on the other hand recount contingent ones at best.

Most of the tales brought together in this book were collected between December 1976 and April 1977 in the village of Karapere (Kuare Census Division, Kagua District, Southern Highlands Province); others were collected between June and December 1971 in Koiari (Fore-Tsimberigi C.D.) and between January and May 1972 in Iapi (West Sugu C.D.). The procedure was to tape-record the stories as they were told in the vernacular by men and women who came to narrate them at my house. Tales are traditionally told in the evening, and most of the recordings were done at that time. No effort was made to structure the storytelling sessions, or to elicit certain kinds of stories. I am therefore fairly confident that the present collection represents a good crossection of the *lidi* genre.

After recording I translated the stories into English, working sentence by sentence from the taped original. In this timeconsuming task I was greatly assisted by a local person with facility in pidgin English, since he was able to help me over my problems with the vernacular. The English version is, however, a translation from the Kewa and not from the pidgin, which was used mainly to speed up what would have otherwise been an unconscionably long task.

There is little point in striving for a literal translation, if by this is meant a word-for-word rendition of Kewa into English. The grammatical and idiomatic structures of the two languages are altogether different. Instead I have striven for a balance between too free or too literal a translation, one which both reads easily in English and preserves the sense of the original.

Considerable variation will be noted in length, detail, and clarity. Length may be either a structural feature (longer narratives stringing together a few distinct episodes) or a matter of style and texture (longer narratives being richer in detail, dialogue, and other expansions). Richness of detail need not make for greater clarity, which is equally a matter of structural coherence. Some of the tales included here are very clear, both in structure and texture. Others seem muddy, either too terse or too disjointed. I have resisted the temptation to omit or interpolate these, for two reasons. Structural clarity must always be somewhat subjective, and what at one moment seems confused may later prove clear. Moreover, clarity may be less a feature of a tale in itself than a consequence of how many other textual versions there are to support it. And this has to be a contingent matter, a result of accidental encounters. There may well be tales which I did not collect that clarify the obscure ones here.

Tales do in fact clarify one another, provided one looks for clarity not in the whole tale but in the constituent episodes. Interested readers might try reading "across" tales by following a particular episode – say, about two brothers and their rivalry – from one tale to the next, using appendix 2 as a guide. This will be an especially useful reading strategy when an episode or a whole tale is found confusing. For example, the somewhat eliptical tale 48, "The Pig Girl," becomes much clearer if it is read in conjunction with other narratives of the same type. (These are tales with sequence 6, and especially tales 29, 30, 35, 39, 46 and 47). This "intertextual" approach forms the basis for the interpretive study in *Fabricated World*.

As for the style of delivery, little needs to be said. As expected, narrators differ considerably. Some speak in a lively and entertaining fashion, punctuating their discourse with gesture or modulating their tone of voice; others adopt a flatter and less expressive style, their hands left folded on the lap. Kewa tales begin matter-of-factly. At the narrator's discretion there may be a brief introductory phrase like "Now I'll tell a tale about" or "Here's my tale." Otherwise the opening statement identifies the initial actors: "There were a brother and sister," "Many youths," "Rube and his wife." The closing of the tale is marked by a distinct motif: the effect or consequence of the tale. Usually this is the origin of a natural feature, often some bird, animal, or plant; or it may be the origin of some property of the real world. Occasionally a narrator will say something like "Now I am closing my tale."

There is nothing wrong with narrators calling attention to the act of narration this way. Occasionally they insert the phrase "as they say in tales" (*lidi tapalame yade*) just before some unreal exaggeration or other obvious falsity: maybe an awesome feat of strength, such as making a huge food garden single-handedly; or some impossibly adroit action, such as crossing a stream on a single stalk of sugar

cane; or a sudden compression of time such as an infant's reap-
pearance as a youth or maiden.

A more prominent feature of many *lidi* is a brief song, usually
only a couple of lines, sung by a principal character. In a few cases
these songs are uttered as secret or urgent communications between tale characters. Others are songs sung by males to express
pleasure or exaltation; these are modelled on the Kewa dance songs
known as *yasa* or *mata*. But in most cases they are women's songs of
sorrow, loss, and mourning. In the stories these are called just
"weeping" or "lamenting," but they follow closely the Kewa songs
called *remali* or *rupale* – slow, dirge-like songs, sung softly and sadly.
Usually these occur close to the end of the story.

The Kewa language has a rich repertoire of imitative words that
is fully exploited in *lidi* and which lends them a vividness lost in the
translations. Attacker and victim tussle in a house, *kiii gau kiii gau;*
an old man falls down a deep well, *kili kili tata tata;* water boils or
bubbles, *kulu kulu kala kala.* Similar but less easily explained is the
noise heralding the approach of an evil old man or old woman, that
is to say a "ghost." Narratives render this sound variously as *buu,
duu, ruu, dau, dui* or the like, and it appears to be something
between an explosive sound and a dull, resonant roar – perhaps like
the English world *boom.*

I have supplied titles for the tales, although the Kewa do not do
so, and they may be useful. These titles can only give an approximate
idea of what the tale is about, especially when a tale interlinks
several different episodes. The ordering of the tales in this volume
respects the order in which they are introduced in *Fabricated World.*
Since episodes, not whole tales, are the object of study in that
volume, some stories will appear to be out of order. This is most
apparent toward the end of the list, in chapters 8 and 9. Some of the
prime examples of "skin changing," "transformation," "broken promises," and "angry ghosts" occur in tales included in preceding chapters. Here, too, Appendix 2 will prove useful to readers who would
like an accurate analysis of tale content.

Occasionally I have inserted explanations of Kewa words or
phrases, enclosing them within parentheses. These are not inter-
pretations so much as translations, required when the vernacular
has been retained in the text.

I want also to say something about formal patterning in the tales
collected here. These remarks will not only explain to the reader the

numerical notations in the page margins, but they should also enhance his understanding and enjoyment of the tales. A very noticeable feature of folktales is the way blocks of narrative content recur with variations from tale to tale and get combined with different such blocks. Kewa *lidi* are very episodic in this sense. Despite the fact that a single story line runs from start to finish, a tale is constructed of detachable blocks or episodes which recombine variously. This feature may not be evident upon a first reading of a few (unmarked) texts, but it becomes progressively clear as one reads and rereads the collection. The marginal numbers indicate this episodic structure.

Although this structure is explained at length in *Fabricated World,* a condensed review of it may prove helpful here. The resemblances among episodes in different tales form the basis of a formal or formalist description. It is formal in the sense that the resemblances exist in the overall design of the episode, its general theme, rather than in the particular contents ("variations"). This common theme can be expressed in just a few sentences (two to four), or "functions" as they have been called, formulated in terms sufficiently abstract to "cover" all the variations. Each set of two to four sentences forms a "sequence," of which there are (in my estimate) eleven. To clarify this: episodes in different tales which resemble one another are formally described as a sequence of sentences (functions). Or to put it differently, particular tales may be said to expand on and specify abstract functions.

If this still confuses, an example may help. Here is a summary of what I call a narrative episode. It belongs to tale 1 (and happens to form nearly the whole tale).

> There are two brothers. Palolo is a cultivator and Aleka is a hunter. Aleka goes out hunting and kills some possums, which he cooks. A dog comes, instructs him to enlarge his cooking pit, and then brings him a pig. Aleka cooks the pig and offers the dog some pork, but the dog repeatedly refuses. Finally it accepts the pig snout and departs. After Aleka obtains pork in this manner several times, Palolo insists upon taking his place. But Palolo becomes impatient with the dog and kills it. Aleka discovers that the dog is really a man, mourned now by his sister. Aleka promises the sister he will retaliate, and he does so by killing Palolo.

Now, nine other tales contain episodes with much the same thematic structure. Three simple sentences, or functions, are sufficient to represent this pattern:

i.   A brother benefits from a source.
ii.   Another brother misuses the source.
iii. There is an act of retaliation.

These three functions constitute sequence 1, titled "Two Brothers."
In my notational system, the sequences are numbered from 1 to 11,
while the constituent functions of each are numbered i to iv. Thus
the notation *1i* means "sequence one, function one," *1ii* means "sequence one, function two," and so forth. These numbers are placed
in the margin where the corresponding part of the text begins
(sometimes this must be approximate), and the next appearance of a
number indicates where this portion ends and another one begins.
In some cases the same portion of text can be part of two or (rarely)
three different sequences when they overlap. Then two or three
numbers are placed in the margin. The *O* at the beginning stands for
"opening" (or it may be construed as a zero). Not itself a sequence, it
sets the scene and names the initial dramatis personae. Occasionally,
a *?* will be found instead of a sequence number. This means that the
corresponding text fits into none of my sequences.

Most of the typical scenarios or episodes in Kewa tales concern
human actors, often kinsmen, and it is therefore very tempting to
look for correspondences between narrative themes and social
structures, specifically kinship and marriage. The following is a very
brief indication of the narrative content of the eleven sequences,
along with the social correspondences I identify for each. The latter
are enclosed within parentheses to indicate their provisional nature.
To be convincing, they would have to be developed in much greater
detail.
    Sequence 1, "Two Brothers," recounts a fraternal conflict over
some item of value that one of two brothers discovers and the other
one spoils. (This sequence takes up the issue of whether brothers
can truly cooperate as equals or are, more realistically, bound to
differ and dispute.)
    Sequence 2, "Brother and Sister," tells of a deception and argu-
ment between a brother and sister, who separate from one another
and thereafter rejoin. (These episodes debate the proper moral distance between the two siblings by illustrating two untenable extremes, excessive closeness and excessive distance.)
    Sequence 3, "Ghost Attack," recounts how a malevolent "old
man" or "old woman" attacks the hero or heroine, how he or she
escapes, usually with some supernatural assistance, and sometimes

kills the attacker. (As the sequence title indicates, these episodes correlate with the belief in ghostly intervention in human life, particularly in illness and death caused by ghosts.)

Sequence 4, "Brother, Sister, and Wife," tells of a dispute between two sisters-in-law, one good, the other evil. The evil one kills the good one, or tries to; the brother (husband) retaliates or intervenes. (The rivalry between the two women can be seen as depicting how, in real life, a wife takes the place of a sister in the clan and in the household—an idea that bridewealth exchanges sharpen considerably—and how, in the imagination at least, the displacement indicates competing interests.)

Sequence 5, "Abuwapale the Provider," recounts how a man finds a magical source of ceremonial wealth in the form of a nubile young woman and how he loses this wealth when he breaks a promise he makes to her. (The key to understanding this sequence is to see the miraculous woman as a symbol of the sister; the wealth she brings stands for the bridewealth that comes to a brother upon his sister's marriage.)

Sequence 6, "Ghost Marriage" is about a young woman's brief meeting with a youth. He comes to her, sometimes in animal form; he departs; and she undertakes a long journey to rejoin him. (These tales can be taken to represent what marriage entails for a young woman in Kewa society: a permanent departure and a new residence among unfamiliar people.) Four tales in this set develop a further episode, sequence 6A, involving the ghost of the youth's dead sister.

Sequence 7, "Poor-man, Little-man, Old Man," recounts how several siblings or whole clans are decimated by a nefarious trickster or by a pair or group of old men until a hero or heroine finally outwits him or them. (Tales of this type develop ideas about the threat to society from within or from its margins, particularly the denial or devaluation of ceremonial wealth.)

Sequence 8, "Skin Changer," relates how a young man or young woman of rather dusty and dismal countenance deceives his or her spouse by mysteriously appearing at ceremonies as a resplendent dancer. (This sequence develops ideas about one's different experiences in domestic and ceremonial situations.)

Sequence 9, "Restorative or Regenerative Transformation," recounts the symbolic death and rebirth of a principal character or some related symbolic transformation. (Here it is difficult to specify a correspondence in social life without taking into account the specific narrative context. In many instances an alteration of one's social self seems to be meant.)

Sequence 10, "Interdiction," develops the familiar narrative theme about the benefit of keeping a promise and the consequence of breaking it. (Here again the social correlates are difficult to specify, but quite arguably the episode reflects two promisory or contractual relationships in Kewa life: between spouses and between ancestor and descendent.)

Sequence 11, "Result," which routinely occurs in Kewa tales as the final episode, tells how some object or property of the natural or cultural world has come into being through events in the tale. Although this sequence is primarily a formal literary device for ending the narrative, its content may be significant: natural and cultural objects originate from death or death-related actions. But whether this tells us something about the world of the Kewa—as opposed to the world of their tales—is a matter for debate.

It is one thing to identify a narrative structure like the sequence and quite another to suggest a close correspondence or correlation between it and some external social or cultural structure. What does it mean, really, to say that a tale or myth "corresponds" to cultural reality? At least three different explanations are possible.*

One explanation is that narratives correspond to cultural realities in a strict sense, that narratives and life respond directly to one another the way, for example, that one's knowledge of the environment corresponds with one's place in the production process or the way some piece of everyday discourse ("listen to what happened this morning") corresponds with what it refers to. If this were true, narratives would always be firmly rooted in their cultural soil, not just lie scattered on its surface. And "collecting" them would imply more than just picking them up; it would mean pulling them out of their context, the cultural matrix supporting them. According to this view, the tale bears evidence of its cultural roots by expressing, for example, some focal concern or maybe some social conflict in the culture. Or, assuming that the tale might have originated in some real-life event and later become fictionalized, that event should have happened (or should possibly happen) right where the tale is told. This we can call a reflectionist view; narratives mirror cultural reality. And in its stronger version it is also a functionalist view: narratives not only reflect reality but re-enforce and validate it. One might include here the Marxist variant as well, that narrative serves as ideology which screens out certain realities to protect the position of a dominant group.

---

*For a discussion of theories of narrative, see *Fabricated World.*

A second explanation is that tales or myths are free-floating, fully detached from the particular circumstances of their origin. They have become the product and property of a collective or even a universal mind. This larger mind may be called the intellect, the psyche, or the creative spirit. Narrative is seen to have meaning in direct proportion to the observer's knowledge of how the mind thinks, feels, or creates, independently of particular cultural conditions. This "mentalist" theory of narrative takes the notion of cultural correspondences much more lightly than the first theory. What will be of interest in the narrative is not so much the particular meanings it might have for the people who tell it as the logical or archetypal regularities it evinces. Cultural correlates such as those listed above will be worth studying only because these local "ethnic ideas" give us a clue to the more basic, elemental ideas behind them. Examples of this second type of theory are the Freudian and Jungian approaches and, sometimes, structuralism.

A third answer takes a position between the extremes. Tales have a close connection to the cultural circumstances of their origin, but they cannot be reduced to them. They also give evidence of mental, psychic, or aesthetic structures, but they are irreducible to these as well. Rather, they are like certain "abnormal" forms of language such as metaphor, parable, and poem; and their intent is to re-describe and re-create the world around us. This entertains and instructs; we see something new, and we smile or frown. The odd, make-believe characters and plots, crucial to our enjoyment, pose no obstacle to insight; they are in fact its vehicle. Often the fantastic is a decoy to lure in an unsuspected truth. It may also sharpen our perception or widen it. (Take a metaphor like "He is a wolf!" This is not a statement we would take literally, but nor is it one we would dismiss. The same goes for tales, which are themselves metaphors, extended and elaborated.) According to this third view, tales bear the stamp of the world outside and of the mind within. This "interactive" view of narrative makes good sense. It is, however, a difficult one to manage, for the tendency is to steer too close to the Scylla of cultural determinants or to the Charybdis of mental forms.

To sum up, the first two explanations serve well as partial theories. It makes good sense to see *some* aspects of tales and myths as rooted in social structures, for how else can we explain the utter strangeness of narratives from an exotic culture? Clearly, we cannot explain it simply in terms of fantasy or imaginative whim; we have to reckon with a wholly different constellation of institutions, rules, and purposes. But from a different point of view, it makes equally good sense to see *some* aspects of narrative as evidence of the lawful operation of the mind itself, irrespective of culture. Otherwise, how can we explain the fact that, despite their different signs and symbols, we still find exotic texts not only meaningful but, sometimes at least, oddly familiar? When the institutional arrangements in two cultures, theirs and ours, are so different, the meeting point must be the mind.

The third explanation provides the best understanding of the narrative as a whole. There is a reason that narratives appear strangely familiar. The reason is not the obvious cultural rootedness, which incidentally they share with all human things, for this would make them familiar to us only in an intellectual sense, when we treat them as data. Nor can the reason be the oneness of the human mind, for tales are familiar to us not just as mental forms but specifically as tales, as a form of literature. The strangely familiar comes from the way tales, and literature generally, redescribe and remake reality—a phenomenon that can be recognized even when the reality to be remade is vastly different from our own. Tales like the ones collected here are models or visions of the world that we can know and enjoy, despite the fact that the world they envision is not our world, precisely because our own myths and literatures remodel our own world in much the same way. In short, what is strangely familiar to us is the way different literatures recreate different realities in similar ways.

In a brief introduction such as this we need not take the idea further. But we now see the twofold path interpretation must proceed along: an investigation into the tales' cultural context and into their own narrative conventions and structures. Something has been said so far about the narrative structure, but nothing as yet about the culture. So let us turn to it.

The Kewa are a people numbering about forty thousand and inhabiting a portion of the Southern Highlands Province of Papua New Guinea. The name *Kewa* is not one they ever use for themselves, for traditionally they have never thought of themselves as a distinct and unified culture. In fact *kewa* was a term a community would apply to others lying to the south of it, whether they were Kewa or not. But for convenience we can think of "the Kewa" as a culture with its own language and traditions; and nowadays it is developing a sense of its own political being as well, as distinct from its neighbours the Melpa, Wiru, Sau, and Mendi.

The land of the Kewa is a plateau of moderate elevation (about 1,500 metres above sea level). The bedrock is sedimentary for the most part, dominantly limestone in the south, sandstone and lime-stone in the north. The limestone areas are frequently pitted with depressions and wells, "karst features," which find frequent reference in Kewa tales. (For the Kewa term, *neka,* I substitute "well" or "hole.") The plateau is forested in its southern, lower portion, and more open and grassy to the north. Land is plentiful (the population density is four to forty persons per square kilometre), and on it the Kewa raise their staple crop, sweet potato, in open gardens near their homesteads. As well, they cultivate many secondary crops in smaller, more remote gardens in the forest, and raise domestic pigs for their ceremonial exchanges, for periodic feasts and, increasingly these days, for cash. They also hunt for possums, wild pigs and casso-waries and gather a variety of bush foods and materials. The home-steads are either clustered into villages (in the forests) or scattered (in the grasslands). In the past, when feuding still prevailed, self-defence required some degree of nucleation; today it seems that privacy and autonomy have become more important, and dwellings are dispersed. Regardless of the settlement pattern, the custom was for men of the community to reside with their sons in a single men's house, while women and children occupied separate dwellings scat-tered around it. But as domestic concerns gain significance and col-lective ones recede, the men's house is nowadays losing the import-ance it once had.

Women cultivate the sweet potato gardens after men have cleared away the trees or sod. Men cultivate the vegetable gardens, where they raise crops such as taro, plantains, sugar cane, cucum-bers, and greens. Both men and women generally care for the family's pigs, but most of this work falls to the women, who feed them substandard potatoes from the daily harvest. Pigs nominally belong to men, but it is an unwise husband who refuses to consult his wife about his plans for them.

Described thus as a daily round of subsistence activity, little seems to have changed in the fifty years or so of contact with the West. In other respects, though, little of Kewa society has been left unchanged. The first outside exploration of the Kewa heartland was in 1935. In that year Hides and O'Malley crossed through the western and southern valleys before making their way down to the south coast. But it was only in the 1950s that contact really began, and by 1960 most areas were well under colonial control. During the 1960s the last outbreaks of feuding were quelled, colonial law grew to be better understood and respected, village censuses be-came more accurate, airstrips and government stations were ex-tended, missionaries gained a tighter foothold, and money pene-trated the traditional exchange economy. So even while people continued to till the soil and care for their pigs in the traditional style, their world was shifting. Feuds and wars, endemic at one time, are now past. Missionary activity eliminated the major religious rituals. From the government and missions came a new means of exchange, Australian currency. Contact also brought schools, labor contracts, cash crops, roads and trucks, and local government councils: all these have altered the tenor of daily village life.

Just how much the narrative tradition has changed is difficult to say, but probably very little has indeed been altered. With few exceptions, the tales show no sign of "contamination" from the Western presence. There is ample reason to assume that they will retain their traditional shape so long as people continue to tell them. But how long that will be is uncertain.

Kewa society is organized by the extension of kinship and marriage rules outward into virtually all other domains of activity: politics, economics, religion. Like other Highland people, the Kewa trace descent through males. They are organized into patrilineal clans (*ruru*), many of which have split into sections and dispersed into different communities. Sons grow up to succeed their fathers, living on the same *ruru* land; daughters generally leave home and join their husbands after marriage. Brothers, either true or classificatory (i.e., of the same clan-section), reside together, while married sisters rarely do. It follows that a main axis of Kewa social organization is brotherhood, both genealogically and morally. A local *ruru* can be thought of most simply as a group of brothers (although it includes men of different generations, as well as their unmarried daughters). The link between siblings of the same sex, whether true or classificatory, is a strong one, but only brothers are able to affirm it in practice in an ongoing way.

Kewa may not marry within their own *ruru* or to anyone known to be a blood relative. This leaves many potential mates, but in fact the choices narrow further. Fathers, uncles, and older brothers of groom and bride-to-be must negotiate a bridewealth payment, and the negotiation can be protracted and difficult. A sum of four pigs, perhaps twenty mother-of-pearl shells, and a hundred dollars or so in cash is no small matter. Nor of course is the well-being of a daughter, for whose loss the payment is partial compensation. Moreover, parties to the exchange know that the transaction is not a one-shot affair. A man and his brother-in-law will continue to give and take from one another so long as they live, or so long as they remain on good terms, and a good relationship will be continued in the next generation by their sons, who will be cross-cousins to each other.

Exchange of wealth items and foodstuffs unites brothers-in-law, but unlike brothers the two are not each other's equals. A man will always be in debt to his wife's brother. His continued gifts of pigs, pork, and shells – well in excess of any return gifts – express the inequality between the two in-laws; never do they allay it. The wife's brother's claim over his sister's husband is given sanction by witchcraft: anger over an unpaid debt can cause harm to the debtor, or to his close kin. Whether brothers-in-law are on the best of terms or on the worst, they stringently observe a taboo on pronouncing one another's name in public, and on hearing the name as well, requiring everyone's cooperation, of course.

The relationship between husband and wife generally remains distant and difficult until their later years, by which time they will have built up a solid mutual trust, and social pressures will have tapered off by then as well (the husband will be less active in exchange and therefore less likely to antagonize his brother-in-law, who will have moderated his own demands, and the husband will no longer fear intentional or inadvertent poisoning by his wife's menstrual blood). Until then, a certain amount of distrust seems to be the norm. A husband resents a wife who promotes her brothers' interests too often, or who expresses her dissatisfactions by shirking her duties in the sweet-potato gardens. A wife, for her part, resents a husband who, in concert with his *ruru* mates, tries too hard to control her activities and movements or who is ineffective in hunting or producing.

The giving and taking of major items of exchange – pigs, pearl shells, and nowadays money – are a constant focus for debate by men. Exchange usually is the topic of discussions in the men's house or at a crossroads. The immediate, practical reason for all this talk is that there is always something going on that involves wealth: a pig kill to plan or review, some bridewealth in which to share, blood money to pay or seek (even today), and countless other occasions of greater or lesser scale and significance. Behind it all, though, is a concern with maintaining a healthy self-image and a sound social order, which is to say a social order wherein people act dependably and predictably. In Kewa terms, trustworthy people have "good *kone*," that is, good attitudes, good thoughts, and good actions. Conversely, people who do not act according to one's expectations are people with "bad *kone*." Exchanging, sharing, and lending wealth items serve as a measure of these inner qualities, and what measures up best is not so much a selfless altruism as a shrewd balancing of self-seeking and helping.

The periodic pig kill is a good place to see *kone* enacted. Held every six years or so, these three-day ceremonies represent a major investment of time and resources. Above a hundred pigs are killed, scores of guests invited, and pork and shells are exchanged in a complicated lattice-work of interlinked clans. Preparations for the event start a good half-year ahead of time, and during these intervening months the host village sponsors festive gatherings (referred to as singings in the narratives) attended by villagers and guests dressed in their finest shells, feathers and furs, and body paint. Now that the feuds and the major cults have disappeared, these singings, and of course the final pig kill itself, figure as peak experiences in these post-contact years.

The planning and management of pig kills, and previously of the fighting and ritual activity, is done by village leaders or "big-men," acting in concert with their circles of supporters. Becoming a big-man requires a special set of skills and a special character: skills primarily in raising and tending crops, but also in performing magic; and character in dealing not only with other men but with one's wife or wives (big-men are usually polygynous). In addition, one should have the patrilineal ancestors in one's favour, and one's supporters respectful of one's powers, whether verbal, physical, or hidden (witchcraft). Men with these requisites are able to parlay reciprocal exchanges (ideally of equivalent values) into profit-making occasions, "profit" here meaning temporary accumulations of pigs, shells, and money that can be deployed and displayed with great éclat.

On the other end of the social scale are those who remain nearly inactive during ceremonial exchanges, either because they have never been able to accumulate enough social prestige or because they are simply disinclined to do so. Some such men are so inactive as never to marry (marriage being, after all, a necessary prerequisite to achieving wealth and renown). These "little-men" or "poor-men" (*alisi* or *riaboali*–the two are generally interchangeable) are good-naturedly tolerated, but they are also the butt of a certain amount of contempt.

With one or two big-men and perhaps a little-man or two in a village of several hundred, most men fall into the category that we would label ordinary. Similar differences in social standing are not found among women, who rarely take part in village politics. True, a woman can sometimes be important behind the scenes, promoting the interests of her husband or brothers. But only exceptionally, when she is quite old and respected or when she is deputizing for an absent husband, is she seen on the public stage. Excluded from the traditional forum, women nowadays form the nucleus of church support.

"Witchcraft" for the Kewa is not a dark and nefarious art. It is rather an admission of what is taken to be a self-evident fact: one is angry, distraught, or resentful because of something another person did; and then some misfortune happens – maybe to oneself, maybe to the other, or maybe to a close relative of either. The logic, *post hoc ergo propter hoc*, may be unsound but the effect is dramatic; holding social troubles responsible for physical misfortunes both satisfies a psychological need (to live in a predictable world) and a social one (to ensure conformity). Conformity is at issue because any kind of bad *kone* – "bad thought" – can manifest itself as witchcraft and adversely affect others (or oneself). So one will try to avoid provoking bad thought or, once it has arisen, try to root it out. This means paying back debts, sharing wealth with those who are entitled to it, doing one's part in domestic or collective undertakings, and the like.

"Ghosts" of dead relatives play much the same kind of role as bad thought, and indeed the distinction between "ghost attack" and "witchcraft" may often be a difficult one to make. "Real" ghosts are rarely glimpsed, though they may manifest themselves sometimes as animals and birds of the bush. But they make themselves felt by causing misfortunes of various kinds, just like human "witches." And ghosts, too, act for a reason; they are angry because of what others have done, either to themselves (when they were not yet ghosts, but still living men or women) or to their living descendents. So they attack the wrongdoers or, as the Kewa say, strike and "bite" them: an idea to which *lidi* give literal expression. Ghosts in fact loom quite large in Kewa tales, perhaps because they are so easily materialized, rendered phenomenal that is, by the imagination. Witchcraft, on the other hand, being so much an inner state, is absent from them.

These brief comments conclude our bird's-eye view of Kewa tales and culture, enough only to acquaint the reader generally with the tales he holds in his hands and with the culture where they were and still are told.

Told why? The answers to this question could outnumber the tales in this book. Over the last hundred years, scholars have proposed that myths and tales give evidence of errors in language, personify the forces of nature or the cosmos, express animistic beliefs, serve as instruments of social cohesion, yield psychic comfort, bear messages from the unconscious, socialize children, and mediate logical contradictions. But the simplest answer (though deceptively so) is that tales entertain. They draw one in the way a more sober, abstract language cannot. Matthew Prior puts it well: "Examples draw where precept fails, / And sermons are less read than tales." And so it should be. Enough instructing and introducing, then, and let the tales have their say.

CHAPTER 1

Of Good and Bad Brothers

Tale 1: The Provident Wild Dog

0   There were two brothers, Aleka and Palolo. Palolo's work was to cultivate the food gardens, and Aleka's was to hunt for game. Palolo's garden was extensive; it bordered Koparu Stream on one side, Ami Stream on another, and reached as far as Raipala Hill. As for Aleka, he found abundant game of all kinds in the forest. Indeed, he often brought back so many possums that those at the bottom of his netbag would begin to rot. He did not cook the game back at the house but in a forest hut called Akiliadaga. Having cooked the food there, he would carry it back to the house and the two brothers would eat it there.

1i   One day, then, Aleka came to Akiliadaga after a successful hunt. He split some firewood, collected cooking stones, and got other things ready for a small earth oven, sufficient for his possums. Having laid firewood across the pit and piled the stones on top, he was about to light a fire underneath when he heard a twig snap. A little dog trotted up, wagging its tail. It was carrying another piece of firewood in its mouth. It dropped the firewood beside the cooking pit and looked up at Aleka.

Aleka thought about this and then began to enlarge the pit, fetching more wood and stones, more cooking leaves, more possums from his netbag. He understood that the dog was instructing him to do this, for the dog was pointing its head at the wood, the leaves, and other objects. When he had finished, the cooking pit was quite large. Apparently satisfied, the dog trotted off. Aleka waited, not knowing what to expect.

Presently the dog returned. In its mouth was one end of a pig tether; the other end was tied to the foot of a large pig. Having led the pig to Aleka, the dog dropped the tether and quickly fetched a heavy length of wood. The dog was telling Aleka to club the pig. He did so, then singed the pig's bristles and began to butcher it.

As he was cutting up the pig, he sliced off the ears and offered them to the dog to eat, but the dog refused them. Having covered up the earth oven and left it to cook, Aleka prepared the entrails. They cooked quickly. When they were ready, he offered them to the dog, but again he met refusal. Aleka then roasted the liver and held out half of it for the dog to take, but again there was no response. The same thing happened after he had opened the earth oven and taken out the cooked pork and possums. He divided all the cuts of meat and offered half to the dog, but still the dog refused. Forequarter, hindquarter, ribs, backbones, belly—each time some pork was offered, the dog silently refused it with a slight movement of its head. Finally, Aleka offered the pig's snout and this time the dog accepted, dipping its muzzle in assent. It took this worthless piece of meat in its mouth and withdrew. Aleka carried the rest of the cooked meat back to the house.

Each time Aleka went to Akiliadaga, the dog came with a pig, and each time it accepted only the snout.

1ii One day Palolo told his brother that he was tired of working in the gardens. He, too, would like to go out and find game. At first Aleka refused, but when Palolo insisted he had to give in. He told his brother exactly what to do and instructed him to proceed carefully. Palolo set off.

Palolo hunted successfully and brought many possums to Akiliadaga, and so it happened that the little dog came to him, just as it had to his brother, bringing firewood, then a large pig, and then a club. Palolo killed and cooked the pig, and, just as his brother had done the first time, offered the dog cuts of the meat. Ears, entrails, liver, the better cuts of pork—all were refused. Finally the dog accepted the pig snout. When it did so, Aleka became furious. "What sort of thing is that to want?" he exclaimed, and picking up the tongs he had used to move the hot stones, he struck the dog. Whimpering and bleeding, the dog retreated. Palolo gathered the meat in a netbag and made his way back to the house.

1iii When Aleka saw that his brother had brought the snout along with the rest of the animal, he sensed trouble. He scolded his brother, "I told you to be careful and to follow what I did. But you did not listen. Well, stay here and eat this food you have brought. I must find out what you have done."

He hurried to Akiliadaga, and there he found a trail of drops of blood. He followed it a long way to a wide ceremonial ground, surrounded by stands of plantains and sugar cane growing thickly underneath tall casuarinas and pines. To one side he saw a long men's house. The body of a tall man, with massive hair, was lying on a platform beside the house. Close by a woman was sitting cross-legged on the ground. She was weeping this lament: "Oh, my good brother, just this once did I not tether the red and white pig, and now it is lost. Oh, my brother."

Aleka approached the dead man's sister and promised to avenge her brother's death. Then he returned home, fitted an arrow to his bowstring, bent the bow, and killed his brother. Next he broke a branch of a red cordyline plant called *potawe* and planted it in the ground.

11i-ii   Aleka was acting according to a custom that we, too, follow. When an enemy kills one of us and then one of the enemy is killed in return, a red cordlyine branch is given. Had Palolo not acted badly, we might still be able to go to the forest and be given pigs by that little dog. But Palolo did not listen to his brother's advice, and Aleka had to do this *ali potawe* custom that we do even now.

Tale 2: The Pigs from the Forest Pool

0   Now I will tell how pigs originated. Lobai's two sons, Agura and Ledepa, lived at Kusayo, where they hunted grasshoppers in the kunai grass fields. The first brother, Agura, used to get very many, while Ledepa killed only a few. They had no food other than the grasshoppers they caught.

1i   One day Agura went to Asapili, a nearby kunai patch. There he found many grasshoppers and began to hunt them. While doing so, he saw a place where wild pigs seemed to have trampled, rooted in the kunai, and dropped their feces. It looked as though sweet potato leaves were growing there, too. He had never seen the new growths of sweet potato, plantain, or sugar cane before. Yet right there, in the excrement of the wild pigs, grew many sweet potato runners, shoots of *padi* and *rani* greens, and sugar cane.

Agura cut some *yadawape* sword-grass stalks and made a fence around this place. Then he dug up the earth and planted out these shoots. Having done all this very quickly, the way things happen in tales, he returned home. He said nothing about his discovery to his brother, and the two stayed there at Kusayo and continued to catch grasshoppers.

After two months of this, Agura went back to the garden and saw that much sweet potato, greens, and sugar cane was growing there. Agura had not said anything about this to his brother because he had not seen these things before. Now for the first time, he put his hand into the earth and found a sweet potato. He took four of them. Then he cut a few lengths of pole and tied up the yam stems and the sugar cane. Next he cleared some more undergrowth and planted more sweet potato cuttings. In Okayo through to Wata he made this garden, down to the Yaku Stream. Then he carried some of the food back to the house; but he did not tell his brother how he had come by it, nor did he share it. He cooked the food in the hearth and found it very good. He also ate the sugar cane and greens he had brought home.

After another two months he went back and saw even more food in the garden. Some of the sweet potatoes were sending up new runners. He dug up some tubers, took them home, and ate them himself. Once again he gave none to his brother.

1i   Now this other brother, Ledepa, had little to eat, only the one or two grasshoppers which he would eat before going to sleep. Ledepa sat and pondered about this. In the morning he started out on the path that led to Kolapi and Tidane; he came to Kilipimi, Kepelea, Kolapi, and down to Mapi. There he climbed a tree and looked around. Not far away he saw a kunai patch. "There must be many grasshoppers down there," he thought. "I will go and have a look." So he went there, and indeed there were many which he shot with his bow and arrows. "Before it was not like this!" he thought with pleasure. He shot more and more.

In the sunken middle of this kunai field, he found a pool with a tall hoop pine growing at its edge. He saw that the pool was very dark, dark as the feathers of a grown cassowary. When he approached it, he grew frightened, for he had not seen such a thing before and feared it would engulf him.

Ledepa walked over to the base of the hoop pine, and there, visible in the short grass, he saw the hoofprints of pigs. He looked around: everywhere he saw tracks left by pigs of all sizes. All of them seemed to have been walking around near the base of that pine tree. It looked as though they ate underneath this tree and then went back into the pool. The area around the tree was clear and clean of all debris, and fine grasses grew around it.

Ledepa reflected, "Before, my father used to tell me about how people would kill their many pigs and then dance. They used to do *tama* dances during these occasions."

Just then a little bird sitting in the pine called out, "Do a *tama* dance, do a *tama* dance!" So Ledepa started to dance underneath the tree. As he did so, a long-tusked pig emerged from the water and came to the edge of the pool, to the *wiru* pine where the youth was standing. Ledepa first considered shooting the pig with his bow and arrow, but then he thought of killing it with a blow from a club. He was worried that the pig might bite him, though. Finally, he decided on the arrow. When he took one of his arrows and just pointed it at the pig's flank, the animal rolled over onto its side.

Ledepa cut a length of vine, peeled away its sheath, and tied together the pig's feet. He wondered whether he should kill it right there or take it back and kill it outside his house. In the end he decided to take it back to Kolapi. It was in Kolapi, he remembered, that people used to kill their pigs a long time before, and nearby grew many good edible greens to cook with the pork. Back then, people had made a *winya remo* ancestral cult house there, close to the Yaro River.

At Kolapi he collected some red cooking stones for his earth oven. Then he killed his pig. Next he cut lengths of bamboo, gathered cooking leaves, butchered the pig, and put the pieces into the oven to cook. The intestines and belly fat he kept aside and cooked separately in the bamboo tubes. These small parts cooked quickly, and he ate them first, having thrown aside the grasshoppers he had shot earlier.

The rest of the pig cooked quickly, the way things happen in tales. Ledepa made a small house close to the base of a pandanus tree. Its walls he made of bark so there were no holes, and inside he made a platform to store the cooked pork. That done, he opened the oven and began to eat. He had never had so much to eat before, and he was indeed pleased.

Then he burned some strong firewood and went to sleep. When he awoke, he saw that some of the pork which he cooked had begun to smell bad. There was so much of it still uneaten. So he recooked it. Then he shouldered a whole side of pork and left for home.

When he reached the house, he found his brother sitting there. "Did you take and kill someone else's pig?" asked Agura.

"You never gave me your food," replied Ledepa, "but I will share with you this pork that someone gave me when I was walking along a path." And he gave his brother half of what he had brought, while he cooked and ate the rest.

Agura again asked, "Where does this pig come from?" But Ledepa did not tell him. "I don't know," he said. "I got it when I was walking home." Then he added, "Maybe it belongs to someone else, and maybe he will come and kill us."

Four months passed. One day Ledepa put on fine ornaments and returned to the pool and its pine tree. He did a *tama* dance as before, and a large pig came out of the water. And as before, he tied the pig with vines, killed it in Kolapi, cooked it, and carried it back to the two brothers' house. Again he gave half of it to his brother, while half he kept for himself.

Agura still wanted an answer: "Twice now you have brought large pigs home. Where did you find them?"

"Well, I have many pigs but I will collect them and kill them; I cannot show you their source," Ledepa replied.

Nearby, at Kuare, people were preparing a pig kill. The Akoali, Yeki, Poramerepa, and Kamarepa clans were sponsoring it. Ledepa intended to take part; he planted pig stakes in a long row from Nemare to Kaimare. So far, he had not offered any of his pigs to his brother Agura. But now he told him, "I was angry with you once before, because you did not give me food. Now, though, I will divide my pigs." He divided the line of pig stakes in half: pigs tied to the stakes on the Nemare side Agura would kill, and those on the Kaimare side he himself would kill. Thus the two brothers killed those many pigs, more of them than all the other men, who had only a few.

Afterwards Agura once again asked Ledepa, "Brother, where did you get all those pigs?"

"I will not show you where they are from," replied Ledepa. "But when I bring them back I will give you half. Don't we eat them often?"

"Yes," said Agura, "I've seen that. But I want to know where they come from."

1ii Finally Ledepa gave in and told his brother. "Go to Tamoka," he said, "where there is an open field and a pond. I went there looking for grasshoppers. Near the pond is a place with red cordylines planted around it. Go and do a *tama* dance there. Take only one pig, kill it, and bring it."

Agura did this, and a long-tusked pig came out of the pool. "Take some rope, carry it to Kolapi and kill it there," Ledepa had said. But Agura did not do this; he killed the pig right there at the side of the pool. Again and again he did a *tama* dance and killed a pig. The once full pool went down and down.

Agura, you see, was angry with his younger brother, who had for so long kept him from coming to this source of pigs. That is why he did this, killing many pigs, cooking only a few, and leaving the rest to rot. He depleted the pool, except for a small puddle of water. In it Agura saw a huge sow, a pig as large as a house. This last pig, he killed as well, and the pool was now empty. Then he butchered the first pig he had killed, cooked it there, and carried a side back to Kolapi.

1iii Back home, Ledepa asked him, "Why have you been away so long? What have you been doing?"

"Oh," replied Agura, "I took all the pigs and killed them."

"Is our pool still there?" asked Ledepa.

"There is no more pool," was his brother's reply.

Ledepa then picked up his bow and an arrow and killed his brother.

11i   Well, I am finishing this story now. We might still take pigs from this pool had not this man killed them all. Now there are no more of them. This brother, who never shared his food with the other one, killed so many pigs he had to leave most to rot.

11ii   Today we have few pigs, and when one man steals another's pig, or when two men fight because one man's pig has broken into another's garden, we revive this occurrence at the pool where pigs spread from. When Ledepa killed his brother, he was compensating for those pigs. Now these thefts of pigs and fights over them continue.

Tale 3: The Pigs from the Sky*

0   Two brothers built a house down in the kunai fields where there used to be a lake. They made a very good dwelling place there, surrounded by trees, banana, black palms, and various red-leafed plants. One brother made a vegetable garden on the Yekita ridge and planted food crops there. (In another version, this brother is married.) The other always stayed in the house and ate the food which his brother regularly brought for him.

1i   Sometimes when the cultivator brother was in his gardens, the stay-at-home brother would take some cockatoo feathers from their pandanus-leaf wrappings, put them on, and fly up into the sky. This he would do when his brother, far away in his forest garden, could not see him. Then he would throw down all kinds of food and firewood, a bamboo knife, a stone scraper, and a red-coloured pig. (In the other version he would throw down a bamboo knife, leaves for wrapping food, firewood, edible ferns, stones for the earth oven, and finally a large sow.)

All of these things he would tie into bundles (*rogo*) and throw down. Then, coming down from the sky, he would take off his feathers, put them back in the house and sit down again. He would cut up the pig, throw the stomach and intestines into the lake, cook all the rest of the pig with vegetables, and eat. Then he would clean up everything so there were no traces of the cooking. And after that he would sit down by hearth ashes. (In the other version he would pretend to be sick.)

The brother who made gardens knew nothing of all this, so he always brought food from the garden for his brother. But one day, on his way to work, he looked back at the house from a short distance away, and he saw smoke rising. He returned and hid behind a clump of banana trees.

*Note: this text combines two versions.

He watched all that his brother did.

Then he went to fetch the pig stomach and the intestines from the lake where his brother had thrown them. He washed them and cooked them with vegetables from his garden. Having done that he brought this package of food to the house, thinking that his brother would give him some pork.

He approached his brother and told him that he knew about the trips to the sky and all that had been going on. The skygoing brother replied that he had been afraid of what might happen if what he did became known; that was why he kept his conduct hidden from the other's knowledge.

(In the other version: the gardening brother took the pig stomach over to his garden, where his two wives were working, and cooked it and wrapped it up in leaves. Then he called out to his brother, but the place appeared empty. The other brother was sleeping in the house. So he came up and said, "I have collected some mushrooms which I have tied up."

Some water was leaking from the bundle. The other brother unfastened it.

"Ah, brother, what have you done?" he asked in surprise.

"Swallow this," the other said.

"Brother what have you done?" asked the first one again.

So the brother, the one who had gone up to the sky, said, "Well, I see what's happened. No matter, but you and your wives must continue to get firewood, make gardens, look after pigs, and fight. I alone will get these things for eating."

"We will not do it that way! *I* am going up there, I truly am!" the gardening brother countered."

On the following day the gardening brother again said, "I want to go up into the sky!"

"Certainly not!" replied the other.

1ii But when the cultivator brother still insisted, the other finally agreed. He told him, though, that up in the sky he would see a big white pig, first in a row of pigs. This pig he should leave, and instead take one of the other ones. Having heard this, the gardener put on the cockatoo feathers and went up to the sky.

1iii But he did not listen to what he had been told, for he took the big white pig. But just as he did so, it attacked him, bit off his penis and threw him down from the sky. Below, his brother saw something fall, and at first he thought it was a pig. (Second version: He saw something fall, then looked again and saw a bark belt stained with blood, a tooth, and a femur.) Then he knew it was his brother; he knew that the pig had killed him.

11? Amula Ipiri told me this story, and then he told me that something would happen to this land because the white men had come here.

Then the brother tied together his brother's remains, set them aside, put on the cockatoo feathers, and flew up into the sky to stay. Later, something will happen because of this, Amula Ipiri said.

(Omitting the last two paragraphs, the second version concludes:

11i The surviving brother divided the land with his dead brother's *pase* (wife's brother). One of them wanted to put the boundary mark further up, the other further down. With their spears and bows and arrows, they fought, there between the two marks, where a stream goes underground. After they had fought for a while, the brother wounded himself: he shot an arrow straight up in the air, and it fell and hit him where he stood. Then he got a length of bamboo and filled it with his blood. In two *neka* (wells or sinkholes), Madatepe hole and Kwima hole, he poured this blood.

11ii In these places new plants grew: shoots of the oil palm, the *taga* variety of banana, and the pearl shell tree. These things used to grow here, but then they went down to the pool beside the Sugu River, and even there only one sago and one black palm still grow there. The rest all went further south, though one *wapu* tree remains in Wapi.

That is what happened to Sika and Lopala. Sika and Lopala bore Walu and Kurupunaki. Kurupunaki and Walu bore Pari Mata and Talipu. The children of Pari Mata and Talipu used to be here, but they died. Those men bore others, and we are here now. I am here with my son. Not long ago, this child of mine was born, and soon perhaps I will die in my sleep, I don't know.)

Tale 4: Pudi, Pepana, and Their Wives

0,1i There were two brothers, Pudi and Pepana. Pepana often went hunting in the forest. On one of these occasions he bagged two nice, fat possums. He wrapped them up with fresh leaves and tender vines and then slung the bundle over his shoulder. As he went along, though, the vine broke and his bundle rolled away downhill. Down it rolled until it finally struck an old woman, and there it came to rest. The old woman picked up the bundle and felt it. It was heavy, but it was also soft, for the possums were fat, the leaves fresh, and the vines thin. Guessing there might be nice possums inside, she put the package down beside her.

Pepana, who had followed his bundle downhill, saw the old woman and asked her if she had seen his package. She showed him where it lay, and then the two of them made ready to cook the possums. The old woman fetched vegetables from a garden nearby – good sweet potatoes of the *opa, koname,* and *binibi* varieties, good *rani* spinach and the *kusaru* variety of lowland pitpit, as well as some highland pitpit of the *akena* variety. Taking all this food from the garden, the two went to a small house.

There she told Pepana to cook the possums, and he did so: he heated stones, gutted the possums, and did all the rest. While they were sitting inside waiting for the food to cook, the old woman asked him to help her go outside – she had to urinate. Pepana did so. Then they removed the cooked food, ate some, and hung the rest up in netbags along the wall.

Next, the old woman asked the youth to prepare her a sleeping place. He made a comfortable one, with a good covering and a headrest. The two lay down on either side of the hearth.

In the middle of the night Pepana was awakened by what sounded like the laughter and chatter of young women. Looking from where he lay, he saw several young women approach the house and then come inside. Two especially good-looking women sat close to Pepana's sleeping place. They all ate the food the old woman had taken from the netbags and given them. Trembling with fear and anticipation, Pepana dared not move. He kept still and watched.

When daylight broke the girls were no longer there. "Now you must go home," said the old woman, and she gave Pepana two *kaipi* netbags, the kind that women carry in dances, and two nice mats woven of pandanus leaves. As well, she gave him two ceremonial staffs (*ekepai*) with these instructions: "Go along this path and you will come to two small wild plantain trees. Go up them and take aim at them with these staffs, saying, '*ne baya, ni baya;* you there, I here.' Then continue on your way."

Pepana went along the path until he reached the two plantains. As instructed, he took aim at each of them with the staffs – without actually striking them – while repeating the spell. Then he continued on his way. He had not gone far when he heard something behind him. Turning, he saw two good-looking women on the path. "Give us those netbags and those mats," they said. Pepana did so, and the three of them went on together.

1ii   When Pudi saw the two women he asked Pepana for one of them. "We should share them, one for each," he said. But Pepana demurred. "Go find your own," he replied, "there are others. Why do you stay here at home and expect someone else to give you your wives?"

So Pudi went out to the forest as his brother had done. He killed small, red-colored *loke* possums, not the nice *kepa* ones, and he wrapped them with coarse leaves and tough *amape* vines. This made a tight, hard bundle, quite unlike his brother's. As he walked on, his bundle broke and rolled off, just as had happened to his brother. The compact bundle struck the old woman hard and she cried out in surprise, "Ah, what sort of thing is this that hurts me so!"

When Pudi approached she indicated the bundle, and Pudi picked it up. The old woman then gathered some vegetable foods to cook the possums with, but this time she got inferior varieties of sweet potato, greens, plantains, and sugar cane. When they arrived at the house, the old woman asked Pudi to prepare the food. "Oh, I won't cook for an old woman such as you," said Pudi. And when the woman asked to be helped outside to urinate, he refused. Later he made her place to sleep, but it was a poor one.

Again in the middle of the night there was the sound of young women laughing and chattering. Pudi wakened to see the young women gather inside the house and eat the food they had cooked that evening. Two of them sat especially close to where he lay. They were heavy, homely girls, and Pudi was apprehensive. "I won't have them," he thought. "If they follow me, I'll leave them."

Near daybreak the young women disappeared. Then the old woman said to Pudi, "It's time you went back home," and she gave him two heavy staffs, two netbags and two mats. "Take aim at the two wild plantains you will see beside the path," she told him, "and say '*ne baya, ni baya.*'" But when Pudi reached the plantains, he did not simply take aim at them with the staffs, he actually struck them. Continuing on his way, he heard some noise behind him, and when he turned he saw two women with unpleasant, coarse features. They were the ones he had seen that night, except now they had blood on their faces. They asked him for the netbags and mats, and he handed them over.

Back at the brothers' house, Pudi again asked his brother whether he would share his good-looking wives with him. But Pepana refused.

"All right, we will stay this way," Pudi agreed.

1iii,9Ai   One of Pepana's wives became pregnant. When Pepana saw this he climbed a tall *yawi* black-palm tree and made a hole in the trunk near the top. Then he told his two wives, "When you are nearly ready to give birth, I will go to the forest to find game. When I do so, you must stay hidden inside the trunk of this palm tree."

Pudi saw that one of the wives was pregnant and guessed that soon his brother would go hunting. So he went to a place in the forest where he had seen a deep natural well (*neka*), and over it he made a platform of rotten branches, camouflaging it with dead leaves so it looked like the forest floor. Close to this well he had seen a dead tree.

Pudi returned and announced, "I've found a dead tree in the forest. Let's go and get grubs." Pepana agreed, so the two of them went and chopped the tree down. It fell with its branches over the platform concealing the well. Having seen this, Pudi said, "I'll stay at the base of the tree and chop it apart. As for you, go and take grubs from the broken branches, where it will be easy to find them." Pepana agreed, and he walked out along the trunk and then stepped off it. He broke through the rotten platform and fell into the well. His brother quickly gathered dead branches and other debris and threw them into the hole.

Returning home, he looked around for Pepana's good-looking wives and soon found them hiding in the black-palm tree. Having ordered them to come down, he stayed with them.

9Aii   Pepana, meanwhile, felt his way along an underground tunnel at the bottom of the well. On and on he went. Hungry and without food, he began to eat his armbands, his breechcloth, his bark belt, and his own hair. Growing steadily weaker, he searched for a way out. Finally, just about dead, he saw something shining in the distance, small as a star. "I must see what that is," he thought, pushing himself on. It was daylight, for he had reached another opening of the tunnel. But as he climbed out he got himself caught in a possum trap that someone had set there.

An old man was sitting in his house not far away. He thought, "Well, yesterday and the day before yesterday I didn't check that possum trap. Today I must see if I've caught anything." So he went. When he saw that the trap had sprung, he drew closer. Something that looked like a frog was caught there, surrounded by flies. He removed this thing from the trap and looked again. "Eh! What is this?" he wondered.

9Aiii   The old man took this thing to his sugar-cane garden, and there he made a little house of sugar-cane leaves, branches and sticks. Leaving this thing inside, he returned to his own house.

After a month had passed, the old man went back to the garden where he had left this thing. It seemed as though it was becoming human, growing eyes, hands, and legs. So the old man made a larger house in the garden, using *kapipi* tree-fern leaves. Another month passed before he returned again. Now he found a little boy moving around inside the house. As it happens in tales, the boy grew apace. After only one more month, the old man saw that teeth were showing and that the child was beginning to crawl about on hands and knees. So the old one made an even larger house, again of *kapipi* leaves.

He began feeding the boy with ripe *rokoma* bananas, which children enjoy. He peeled these and fed them to the child. From then on, whenever the old man cooked food outside his house for himself and his own son—for he had a grown son of his own—he would put some away for this foundling. Always secretly, he put some aside and conveyed it to the boy. As the boy grew, the old man would leave him with clumps of ripe plantains or cooked taro, no longer actually feeding him by hand.

In time, when the boy had grown to be a youth, his new father made all sorts of ornaments for him: bark belt, breechcloth, armbands, legbands and so on. Now, the old man's true son thought these were for him, but the old man was actually making them for both youths. Ornaments such as a *raguna* head-covering or a bailer shell he made for them both. The foundling, who still lived in his house of tree-fern leaves, grew to be a tall young man with thick hair that he kept well combed.

One day the true son said to himself, "I must find out what my father is doing. In the morning he always goes off somewhere!" He went to the sugar-cane garden and looked inside the small house built there. Inside he saw a tall youth combing his thick dark hair. "What are you doing here?" he asked. "My father might come and kill you!"

But the youth inside replied, "Oh brother, it is so good to see you I could come and eat your feces and all other things of yours, too!" He was overjoyed to see another youth like himself, and he hugged him.

"My father didn't tell me about you," said the old man's son.

"Then say nothing to your father."

"I won't. Stay here," said the son, but when he reached home he said, "Father, I know what you've been doing! I have been to your sugar-cane garden."

So the father had to concede: "Yes, it's true. So now I'll go and fetch the youth here." He did this, and, standing side by side, the two youths were very pleasing to look at. The old man named his own son Ole, and the other, the foundling, he called Ale. The three of them stayed there together.

One night a small gecko lizard came to their hearth and sang, *"Na koda abi, na koda abi"* (my *koda* dance will be now).

"What's that?" asked the old man.

"Na koda abi," repeated the lizard, for it had seen the youths.

"All right, I will let them go tomorrow," agreed the old man. "Gecko, you can go."

Then the old man took the ornaments he had prepared—the armbands, legbands, cassowary plumes, breechcloths—and put them on the two youths. Having done this, he spun twine as one does for a netbag. This twine he made in two pieces. One end of each piece he tied to each youth's wrist; the other ends he held.

The two youths set off that morning. When they arrived at the dance ground everyone exclaimed, "Ole has come, Ale has come! Ole has come, Ale has come!" The two youths stood in the first row of dancers, holding their stone axes.

3Ci   But then an old woman came onto the dance ground. She had wild pandanus palm growing on one side of her body, while streams of water ran down the other. Mushrooms, too, grew on her skin. This old woman grabbed Ale and carried him off. Just at that moment the father felt one of the lengths of twine go slack. He rose and chopped down his casuarina trees, ravaged his gardens, broke his house and cult house apart. Such was his sorrow. Crying "Ale, Ole!" he pulled at his hair, tore at his ear lobes, wrenched off his ornaments, and rubbed earth over his face and skin.

3Cii   Eventually Ole returned home and told his father what had happened. He saw how the old man had destroyed his house and gardens. The two of them then fetched a large pig, killed it, cooked it in an earth oven, and put the pork into a netbag with pieces of salt. Ole shouldered the bag and returned to the dance ground. From there he followed the path he had seen the old woman take.

After going some distance he came upon a little old woman, and he offered her some pork and salt. She accepted, and in return she gave him a small bundle. Further on Ole met another old woman, and she, too, left him with a small bundle after receiving pork and salt. He continued on and met another old woman, and the same thing happened. But this one also told him, "Some people like you have gone on further, but I have not seen them return!" Yet another woman was there on the path, and she asked him "Do you see where the smoke is rising? Your brother is over there." She gave him a bundle. Opening it, he saw the feathered skin of an *ita* hawk. Ole put on this bird skin and flew into a tree. Then the old woman gave him an identical bundle and told him, "When you see your brother, give him this."

Ole flew away to where the smoke was rising from a garden. He sat on a branch and sang softly to Ale, who was felling a tree nearby.

Ale, your father is cutting down his *koda* bananas,
Ale, he cuts down the spirit houses,
Ale, he cuts his *kebelea* bamboo clumps.

Ale heard the singing. He cried out to the old woman, "Hey, I'm thirsty! Show me where I can find some water!"

"Keep on working," the old woman said. "I'll go fetch some water. But you must cut me a bamboo container."

Ale did this, but when he cut it he left no bottom in it. "Go now," he told her, "and I'll stay here and work." The old woman went to a spring nearby and held the bamboo in the water, where it spilled over a rock. Though she waited and waited, the container did not fill.

Meanwhile Ale came and hugged Ole, who gave him a piece of cooked pork. After the two had eaten quickly, Ole unwrapped the other bundle the old woman had given him. It, too, contained a hawk skin. Ale put it on, and the two flew up into a tree.

The old woman finally saw that the bamboo container was not filling because it has no bottom. Furious, she hurried back to the garden and saw the two youths perched in a tree. He long teeth gnashing, she cried out, "O Ale, why didn't I eat you sooner!"

Attacking the tree trunk with her tusks, she toppled it. But as it fell, the two youths flew off to another tree and perched there. Again the old woman cried out, "Ale, why didn't I kill and eat you earlier!" and bit the tree in two. Once again the two flew off. And yet again, and again, this happened. When they were drawing close to the old man's house, the youths cried out, "Father, they want to kill and eat us!"

The old man had prepared soft, well-cooked taro leaves, some sweet potatoes of the soft-textured *moma* variety, and a bundle of ants from an ant hill. Then he guarded the path to the house. When the two youths reached him, both quite exhausted, he told them to go into the house quickly. The big woman was on their heels, saliva dribbling from her mouth. He threw the taro leaves and sweet potatoes into her face. Then he took the ants and threw these at her as well.

11i Finally, taking a woman's ceremonial staff (*ekepai*), he brought it down hard onto her head. She split in two.

11ii From one half of her came Mount Ialibu, and from the other half came Mount Giluwe. The old man became a *mumakarubi* quail. Ole and Ale took their *wiruapu* bows, broke them in two, and stuck them into their anuses. They flew off as *walawe* lorikeets, which have forked tails.

Tale 5: Webi, Pisimi, and Their Wives

0,1i Webi and Pisimi lived together. Webi had a couple of dogs, and he was accustomed to going into the forest and hunting possums. One day when he was in the forest, he came to a garden near Kubiada, and there, below him, he saw an old woman. He rolled his bundle of possums down the hill; it struck her in the back. She picked it up, looked at it, and put it in her netbag. Then she dug some good *momani* sweet potatoes, *ragua* plantains, *kayabo* sugar cane, and *kusaru* greens. Webi joined her and spent the night in her house.

The next morning the old woman gave Webi a ceremonial staff (*ekepai*) and told him a spell to say over it. She told him to take aim at certain wild plantains beside the path and say, *"baya."* Then she gave him many varieties of uncooked foods in netbags; this he was to leave beside the plantains. After he had said *"baya,"* he was to walk on and then turn around.

Webi did this. When he looked around, he saw two good-looking girls standing there who looked shyly at him and followed him. They picked up the netbags and carried them. Webi led them back home.

1ii When they arrived, his brother asked him, "Where did you find those two women?" Again and again he asked, so at last Webi told him what he had done and instructed him to do the same.

But when Pisimi went to the forest he did not kill good possums; he killed small, thin *loke, kapea,* and *wapa* possums. He covered them in leaves, rolled this tight little bundle down the hill, and it struck the old woman hard. It was not a soft bundle like Webi's. She picked up the bundle, looked uphill, and saw Pisimi. Then she got some poor sweet potatoes, tough *kalainya* sugar cane, and tasteless *rogoma* plantains. With these, the two went to the old woman's house to spend the night.

In the morning she gave him a staff and told him what do with it. But when Pisimi came to the plantains, he did not simply take aim at the tree, as he had been told to do; he actually struck it and broke it open. So when he turned around to look, he saw two women, with blood on their faces and bodies, and with scars and scabies on their skins. Women like them we call "Nadame."

Pisimi did not help them carry the netbags of food, for he was angry. Nor did he talk to them. When they reached the house, Pisimi said to Webi, "Brother, we must share the good ones and the bad ones. Let's each take one good one and one bad one." But Webi refused.

Later Pisimi tried to steal one of Webi's wives, but Webi guarded them carefully.

Some time later, the two brothers were making a large forest garden. In it grew a tall *yamo* tree with branches extending toward Melpa land in the north, Mendi land in the west, Wiru land in the east, and in other directions. The two brothers had cut some forked posts for a ladder, so they could climb up the trunk and cut off the branches.

1iii,9Ai   Webi was working by himself up in the tree, cutting its last branches. From his place high up there, he happened to see his brother carrying off one of his wives (Pulua Raguame he had named her) to the other side of the Yaro River, up the slopes of Mt. Ialibu, and then to a place full of pandanus trees. His brother had also cut the vine bridge across the Yaro River after he crossed over. Before leaving, moreover, Pisimi had taken down the ladder, leaving his brother up there with no way to descend the tree.

9Aii   Webi sat down on the branch, which extended over an old garden, afraid that he would fall down. He sat and sat. Becoming hungry, he ate first his armbands, then his cordyline leaves, then his breechcloth, but eventually he became very thin. Presently a wind gathered and blew him down to the garden below, where he lay on top of some greens and ginger planted there.

9Aiii   His other wife had kept watch over him while he sat up in the tree, and now that he had fallen, she quickly found him. She took some *wano* bark, wrapped him inside, and heated him over a fire. Then she stretched out his skin and put him to one side.

When he had recovered, Webi asked her where his other wife had gone. She answered truthfully that she had seen Pisimi carry the woman off in a certain direction, but she did not know where they had gone. But then Webi remembered he had seen where his brother had gone; he had seen them while he was up in the tree. He considered what to do.

He decided that he would buy the help of others to retrieve his wife. So he brought together the things he would need to purchase this aid. He gathered much wealth in shells and money, but everyone refused these things. Then he asked a *pakena* possum if it wanted wealth, and it said it wanted a bushknife. It agreed to help.

"I'll climb the pandanus trees near the house where they keep her," said the possum. "If I can't cut down those pandanus nuts, I'm worthless."

"When they hear you cutting the pandanus nuts," Webi said, "they'll all come outside. Then I'll be able to steal her back!"

Then dusk came to his aid and said, "I'll make it dark!" and rain said, "I'll make it rain!" and the cicada said, "I'll cry out!" And the *pakena* possum said, "I will cut down the pandanus nuts!"

Having all agreed, they set off. When they reached where Pisimi was staying, the possum climbed the pandanus tree, darkness fell, the cicada cried out, and rain fell. Hearing the pandanus leaves rustle, the men rushed out of the house to get the possum. Some came with arrows, some with pieces of firewood, some with wooden tongs. Meanwhile, Webi went inside quickly and grabbed his wife by the wrist and dragged her out. The men could not pursue him in the darkness and the rain.

11i-ii   When he brought the woman back, his *wiruapu* bow exulted, "Uuu!" As for the *pakena* possum, today it still tries to eat our pandanus nuts. Its teeth are the bushknife Webi gave it; it uses them to bite through the nut. The rain and the darkness that Webi engaged are still here now. Today, too, we give the name "Ialibu Raguame" to very attractive women, like Webi's wife.

Tale 6: Asali, Mapuwiali, and Their Wives

0   There were two youths, Asali and Mapuwiali, who stayed together. One of them, Asali, was a hunter; he would go to the forest and find many possums. The other, Mapuwiali, was a gardener; he cultivated taro, sweet potato, and plantain.

1i   One day Asali killed a *koyamu* possum and some cassowaries. He put these in a netbag, slung the bag over his shoulder, and walked on further in search of more game. As he was walking along a low ridge, a low branch caught the bag and pulled it off him. The bag rolled down the mountainside and came to rest beside an old woman who was sitting looking for bush rats. Asali followed it downhill and saw the old woman, who had put the netbag to one side.

"Where's my netbag?" he asked.

"Over there," she pointed to it.

"Carry it, then, old woman," he told her. But she was feeble, so Asali slung the netbag over his shoulder, lifted the old woman, and carried her to her small house in the forest. There he laid a good mat on the floor for her, and gave her some good sugar cane. "Sit and eat this," he told her. Then he fetched some good *kamo* taro to give her.

"Can you cook these possums for us?" he asked.

"I have no cooking stones, how could I?" she replied. So he removed the intestines, singed the fur off, cooked them, and put them into a netbag when they were done. The old woman then gave Asali two small shoulder bags, a bark cloth, and a pandanus-leaf mat.

Night had fallen now, and the old woman told Asali to sleep. But Asali, wondering at it all, only pretended to sleep. After some time he looked over to where he had left the cooked possums for the woman. There he saw a group of young women, laughing gaily. They stood in a row before the old one, and each received some cooked possum meat from her.

"I'll take one of those good women there for my wife," Asali thought. "Or perhaps even two!"

Morning broke, and the old woman said to Asali, "Go along this path and you will see a wild plantain tree growing. With this staff take aim at it, but do not strike it down. Then proceed." So Asali did as he was instructed: he went along the path, came to the plantain tree, took aim at it without actually striking it, and continued along the path. After going a short distance he turned around and looked back: there stood two good-looking young women.

"How did you come here?" he asked. In reply, the two women said, "Let's go to your house." The three went on.

1ii   Mapuwiali came back from the gardens and saw the two young women that the other had brought. "Let's share them," he said.

Asali refused: "Certainly not!"

The two argued. Finally Asali said, "Listen, go along the path I take when I set traps in the forest. There you will be able to find the young women." So Mapuwiali went to the forest and found many possums, just as his brother did. He put them into a netbag; but, dislodged by a branch, the bag rolled down the hill and came to rest near the same old woman.

"You must carry it for me," Mapuwiali instructed.

"I cannot," she protested. But he made her carry the heavy netbag anyway. Then, back at the house, he ordered her to clean the possums and singe their fur off. The old women obeyed. Mapuwiali did not lay down a good pandanus-leaf mat for her; he simply spread some leaves, and he brought her sugar cane and taro of poor quality.

"Now cook the possums," he told her. She did so, and then when it was time to sleep he gave her but a thin bark cloth to cover herself with. The old woman told him to close his eyes and go to sleep. Like Asali, however, Mapuwiali did not. During the night he saw ugly women with blemished skins come to the house.

The next morning the old woman told him to go along the path. She gave him a staff and instructed him to swing it at the wild plantain that grew nearby, but not to actually strike it. When Mapuwiali reached that place, he did as the old woman told him. When he turned back to look, he saw two unattractive young women with scabies.

He took them back home and said to Asali, "Ah, brother, we must share the good and bad women."

"No," said Asali. "Indeed not." They argued.

Finally Mapuwiali agreed: "All right, have it your way. You keep your women and I will stay with mine. But let's the two of us go to the forest."

9Ai   The two went but found no game. But Mapuwiali had a plan: he led the other to a dead tree, which he began to split apart in search of grubs. Prying the trunk apart, Mapuwiali pointed out a large grub and asked Asali to pick it out. He had split the log half apart and wedged it open with a piece of wood. When Asali reached in, Mapu-wiali pulled out the wedge, pinching Asali's hand and holding him fast. Then he hurried off.

9Aiii   Asali could not extricate himself, but presently a *wapa* possum came walking along the log. It gnawed at the wood until Asali could release his hand. The youth hurried back to the house.

1iii   When he arrived, he saw that his two wives were no longer there: Mapuwiali had taken them away, and the two ugly women were there.

11i-ii   But Asali was not going to stay with them. He killed them both, and the two flew away as *mumakarubi* quail. A small red *walawe* lorikeet also flew away—that was Asali.

Tale 7: The Garden Despoiled

0   Ogeasi and Neabua were two brothers. Ogeasi would go hunting small *asakari* birds in the forest, while Neabua would go after possums. They always did it that way. The two brothers had no gardens, but hunted each in his own way, looking for birds or possums. Neabua usually got many possums which he alone cooked and ate; as for Ogeasi, he alone ate the birds he killed and cooked.

1i   One day Neabua came up to a clear place where patches of grass grew. There he saw a *malue* sweet potato leaf growing. He cleared away the grass around it and saw this one sweet potato leaf, a plantain shoot, a cucumber plant, a bean plant, and other crops.

The youth made a garden there, and on his way to hunt he would often go to look at it. Soon many sweet potatoes were growing there.

One day he returned home with three sweet potatoes.

"Where did you find those?" asked Ogeasi.

"An old Imani woman gave them to me," replied Neabua, evasively.

"Oh, if we could eat that woman's vulva, that would be a good thing, too, because she gave you sweet potatoes!" Ogeasi exclaimed. "Some day, brother, I'll follow her. If she gives *me* sweet potatoes, I'll eat her vulva straight away!" Then he added, "We always eat only small bush things, and I'm tired of them."

Neabua shared out the sweet potatoes, and he and his brother ate well. When Neabua found possums he shared them, too, but Ogeasi would always eat his birds by himself.

Each time Neabua went to the garden he would carry back only a few of each crop. And each time his brother would exclaim about the old woman from Imani, whom he thought was giving them the sweet potatoes, corn, beans, and bananas. From then on the two brothers ate vegetables.

1ii   One day Neabua decided to show the garden to Ogeasi. He told the boy, "I'm going to hunt possums now, and you can go to the garden. But be sure to cut only a few of each kind!"

Ogeasi went there. He dug up many sweet potatoes, pulling them out with all the roots and runners. He got other crops as well and filled up a large netbag. Then he went back and cooked all this food in wide earth ovens.

Presently Neabua returned. When he saw all the food, he exclaimed, "Oh, brother, what have you done!"

The next morning Neabua rose early and went to his garden. Everything was dried up. "Oh, this brother of mine! I'll kill him!" he thought.

1iii,9Ai   So one day, when Ogeasi was about to go out bird hunting, Neabua beat him with a casuarina branch, rubbed his skin with stinging nettles, and flailed him with thorny cane. Ogeasi's body swelled. Then Neabua pulled the boy to a river and threw him in.

A heavy rain had fallen, and the river in flood carried the boy a long way downstream before depositing him on its bank. But the water revived him, and he saw that the river had left him beside someone's old vegetable garden. Looking around, he saw many ripe cucumbers. He decided to eat, and after having three of them, he drifted off to sleep.

9Aiii   Soon an old man approached. In a strange dialect he said, "Who has come and cut my cucumbers?" He looked down and saw Ogeasi, woke him up, and asked him what had happened to him. After Ogeasi had recounted his story, the old man was sorry for the boy and carried him home.

The house and garden belonging to that old man were very fine. In the yard grew tall casuarina trees and thick clumps of cordyline and croton shrubs. The old man lay some leaves down and on them placed some cooked bananas for the boy to eat.

For three weeks Ogeasi stayed in that house. He grew quickly and became a fine and handsome youth. The old man kept him hidden from his wives and children, who lived in a separate house.

One day, when the old man had gone to the forest, one of his two sons came and found Ogeasi. "My brother!" he exclaimed, and sat down with him.

Later this son told his father that he had seen the youth, and from that time on they stayed together.

3Ci   Later they heard that a singing was to be held in a distant village, and the two sons wanted to take Ogeasi with them. The old man refused, however, and proceeded to tie Ogeasi's wrists with a vine. He and his sons went off, leaving Ogeasi tied to the house.

Not long after they had left, a very big woman came to the old man's house, broke the vines, and carried Ogeasi off on her shoulder. She carried him a long, long way. When the old man returned and saw the broken vines, he was deeply saddened and covered his face with feces and mud.

3Cii The next morning one son followed the youth's and the old woman's footprints part of the way, so he knew the direction they were headed. Then he planted a stake in the ground and returned.

The next day he and his brother shouldered netbags heavy with food and set out on their search. Everyone they asked said they had not seen the ones whom the two were searching for. But one day they found an old man and a woman, offered them some pork and taro, and questioned them. The man had seen the missing youth and told the two brothers where he was. They went there. Ogeasi was up a tree lopping off its branches while an old woman was burning dry garden debris below. She was the one who had carried the youth off.

The two sons signalled to Ogeasi, and Ogeasi answered with a low whistle.

Ogeasi loosened the stone blade of his axe and threw it into a deep well near the base of the tree. Then he cried to the old woman, "Woman! my axe blade has fallen into a well. Go and get it, for I've no other!"

The woman had to climb a long way down into the hole. Meanwhile the youth descended the tree and hurried off with the two others. The three of them kept walking swiftly for many days.

But the woman had not been long in retrieving the axe blade; she emerged from the well, all bruised and scratched. She saw no one about, but found three pairs of footprints. Guessing what had happened, she set off in pursuit. She travelled more quickly than the youths and gained on them each day. She finally caught sight of them when they had almost reached the old man's house.

When they had climbed the last ridge, the three cried out to their father, warning him that they were coming. The old man palisaded the house and stayed at the gate with his big dog. The three youths ran inside, with the woman right on their heels. The old man barred the entry just in time and threw some ashes in her face.

"Ah! these are just insects biting me, I think nothing of it!" the woman cried out.

Then the old man's dog came and bit her, but she said the same thing. The man shot her with arrows and, unharmed, she made the same retort.

11i   Finally the man pulled up a fence post and brought it down on her head.

11ii   It was at this time that the earth and sky broke apart, for before that they were not separate.

Tale 8: The Stolen Sweet Potatoes

0,1i   Yetape and Toape were two brothers. The one, Yetape, would make gardens, while the other, Toape, would kill possums in the forest. Yetape's gardens contained sugar cane, banana, taro, and other crops. That was the way they did things, Toape hunting and Yetape cultivating.

1ii   One morning Toape lingered in the house, not feeling in the mood to go hunting. Seeing that Yetape was not going to his gardens, Toape went there instead and dug up two *opa* sweet potatoes. He scraped the peel off them with a bamboo knife and then cooked them in hot ashes.

Later Yetape came up to his garden and saw the ashes and potato peels. When he asked Toape why he had done this, Toape said that he had felt hungry, so he had cooked them.

"And those that I dug up yesterday and left for you, why didn't you eat them?" Yetape asked.

"I'm tired of eating yesterday's sweet potatoes," Toape replied.

1iii,9Ai   Then Yetape cut a bunch of good *oda* bananas, some cucumbers, and other foods. He told Toape to eat these things, which he did because he was afraid. Then Yetape brought out a casuarina branch and struck his brother with it again and again. Finally, he struck him with stinging nettles and thorny cane, so hard that the boy bled.

Toape staggered off to a place called Ulumada and fell unconscious amidst some pitpit.

9Aiii   In the morning Toape awoke and found himself lying in a garden among the weeds at its edge. He saw an old man approach, wearing a tattered breechcloth and a string of Job's-tears seeds around his neck. He had scraggly hair, and he carried an ax in his bark belt. The old man saw the flies on the boy's wounds and asked what had happened.

Toape replied, "I stole two pieces of sweet potato, and then...." Thus he told his story.

When he had finished the old man said, "It is well; I am looking for men. I stay alone here, so I am glad you have come." He put the boy in a small house near his own, made a fire, and offered him food. But Toape was not hungry.

"Truly, I shall die," he moaned.

The old man came back later, built up the fire, heated some water and washed the boy's skin. Again he offered some food, and again Toape declined.

When the old man came back the next day he found Toape sitting by the fire, somewhat recovered. Then the old man boiled some wild greens, so the steam would soothe the boy's skin. This helped, and the boy improved. The old man cut some ripe *oda* bananas, and Toape ate two from the bunch.

Four days later the old man came back. He found Toape sitting by the fire, looking quite well. He had finished the bunch of bananas. So the old man fetched yams, taro, pitpit, beans, plantains, and sugar cane; he carried all this food, along with Toape himself, to his house. There he took down a gourd full of tree oil and rubbed some oil on the boy's skin; he gave him a good breechcloth and bark belt; and he fitted him with armbands, bead necklaces, and a fine bailer shell. The boy was now handsome indeed. The man called him Pelepai (foundling).

9Aii   One day the old man led Pelepai off to pollard trees in a new garden. The youth climbed up one of them, and far in the distance he saw his brother in his garden, having very much the appearance of a poor-man with dirt in his hair. Toape, or Pelepai, whistled to him, climbed down the tree, and told the old man what he had seen.

9Aiii   The old man instructed Toape to fetch his brother. He cut a clump of ripe *oda* bananas and gave half of it to Toape, instructing him to offer it to Yetape and to bring him there.

When Toape arrived, Yetape was nowhere to be seen. So Toape waited, dozing.

Soon his brother approached, carrying a bamboo water container. When he saw his brother sitting here, so changed, he drew back. But Toape told him to come forth. The two embraced, and Yetape quickly got his things together and went off with Toape. On the way Yetape shot a *sikita* bird and offered it to his brother; but Toape told him to take it with him, which he did. Then Yetape shot a *masa* (owl) and carried it, too. Soon the two came up to the man's house.

He was inside, cooking a large amount of food for the youths. Toape entered first and called Yetape to come in, for he was lingering back.

The old man wiped the mucus from Yetape's nose and sat him down, and asked him about himself. Yetape gave one of the birds he had killed to the old man, who was much pleased. He in turn took out the food he had been cooking and shared it with the two youths.

Then he spoke at length to Yetape, going over the events he had heard from Toape. He told him that someone other than his brother might not have gone to bring back a brother who treated him so. He told him that he had beaten a good person and reprimanded him. But, that said, he got some tree oil and rubbed it on the youth's skin. Yetape now looked quite handsome, and both were pleased.

Some time later, the three went to a garden, again to pollard some trees. Each youth climbed up to the top of a tall tree, while the old man worked below.

Toape's axe blade came loose and fell into a deep hole in the earth below, and the same thing happened to Yetape's blade. The old man climbed down into the hole to retrieve them. Yetape's was easy to get because it was near the top, but Toape's went very far down and the old man could not reach it quickly. Meanwhile the two youths had come down from their trees and waited.

3Ci Suddenly, there appeared an old woman with red skin and teeth as long as a pig's tusks. She grasped both youths by the arm and hurried them off.

3Cii,11i When the old man emerged at first he could not see the boys anywhere. Then he saw them at some distance and immediately gave chase. He pursued them for a long long way. He followed them to Koima and from there to Nana. There he caught up with the three. Seizing the paddle-shaped staff which the old woman had dropped, he hit her on the head with it, splitting her in two.

11ii From one side of her Mount Giluwe stood up and from the other side came Mount Ialibu. The old man became Kita Yalaepaloa, a wild man who lives now on Kita Mountain. He is one of those who eat men, leaving behind only their hair, headdress and bark belt.

Tale 9: An Old Man and His Tree

0,1i There were two brothers, Pawa and Ropa. They stayed and made gardens. One day, seeing the fine weather, Pawa announced, "I'm going to the forest to find game. If you go out to the garden and carry back some food, we'll cook it all together."

So Pawa set off to the forest and killed some small possums. He went on, across Yopene Stream to Munire and to Kawakure. From there he descended to a grassy area near Walawalikara. This place had a reddish colour. In the field he saw a circular fence topped with dry *kati* leaves. Proceeding, he crossed over a small stream and entered the grass field. There were footprints on the ground. Approaching the fence, he saw an entrance barred with dry wild pan-

danus leaves, which would rustle if someone attempted to pass
through. But Pawa moved them very gently aside and went inside.

There he saw a tall *modasa* tree with many nuts on its branches
and with a shield on the trunk to keep the possums from climbing it.
Pawa looked around. Having now come quietly through the pandanus-leaf barrier, he climbed up the trunk, picked some nuts and
found them tasty. He ate a few, put some others in his netbag, descended, and left the place. He returned home with his possums and
nuts.

1ii   When he reached the house he told his brother that he had
found these good *modasa* nuts. Ropa then wanted to go and fetch
some, too, but Pawa warned him: "No, there's a high fence, which
must have been built by strong men." But Ropa insisted, and finally
Pawa gave in. "Go carefully," he said, "and keep yourself hidden as
you move."

"Are there many nuts?" asked Ropa.

"Very many."

Ropa took a large netbag and, following his brother's directions,
went to the tree and climbed it. He began to pick the nuts, stuffing
them in his bag. When the bag was full, he tied it up and threw it to
the ground. Then he picked even more nuts and stuffed them inside
his bark belt. Finally he started to climb down.

1iii,3Ai   While he was up there, the old man who owned that tree,
Modasa Kuya, an old-time man (*abasanya ali*) was some distance
away. Feeling his testicles itching, he began to scratch them. He
wondered why they itched. "Hm! are they killing a pig of mine?" he
wondered, but the testicles continued to itch. "Is someone carrying
off a daughter of mine?" he asked next, but still they continued to
itch. "Has someone stolen some of my bananas?" but they itched yet.
All the things in his garden he asked about, but still his testicles continued to itch. Then he asked, "Has someone taken away my *modasa*
nuts?" His testicles stopped itching, and he knew that was it.

Ropa, meanwhile, had sat down at the base of the tree and begun
to eat some of the nuts he had stuffed inside his belt. He had decided
he would eat just a few before setting off for home. But once this old
man had received his answer, he came quickly. Seeing this youth, he
cried out, "Hey, hey! I own this tree!" And quickly he ran to the
opening in the fence and secured it.

"Well, very good!" he said. "Now I know who's been taking my
nuts." And, drawing out a cassowary-bone dagger, he skewered the
boy's wrists, tied them together, threw the boy into his netbag, and
went to his house.

At the head of the Yopene stream, in Kuyanapuri, stood this old
man's house and his *ribu* cult house. He took his captive to the *ribu*
house and tied him there. Inside this house was a stout *rugi* pole, cut

from a *pora* tree trunk and covered from top to bottom with the bones of people the old man had eaten: finger bones, leg bones, femurs, ribs.

This old man had several sons. To them he said, "Give some food to this pig of mine, which I've just brought home, lest it become thin."

Pawa meanwhile was still waiting for his brother to return, wondering what had become of him. Having given him up for dead, he sat in mourning.

The old man said to his sons, "Look after this pig well! I'm going to fetch some plantains and cooking leaves over in Kumiali ground. Stay here."

When he had gone, Ropa heard the children outside laugh and say, "Oh, let's eat this pig's ears, let's cut off a bit of meat!" The old man had told them to look in the house occasionally while they played at their games. They were playing at string figures. They made one design after another until they came to the figure for dawn. This one they could not do, though they tried and tried. Finally one of them said, "Let's ask father's pig. Maybe he knows!"

They did so and Ropa replied, "I know these figures, both the one for dawn and the one for the Yaro River bridge. I could show them to you, but your father has tied me up."

So one of the sons took his father's axe and cut the rope binding his hands. "Good, now I'll show you," said Ropa. "To make dawn you must first close your eyes." To show them, he shut his eyes, but not so tightly that he could not see, and then made the string figure. When he finished, he told the boys to shut their eyes and try it. As soon as they had shut their eyes, Ropa picked up the stone axe and killed them all. Then he ran along the path toward home. From Nayatade he went on across Yopene stream.

The old man, however, had put one of his sons up on the roof of the *ribu* house. This one called out, "Father, we're being killed!" The father had already left Kumiali and returned as far as Yapiri when he heard the boy's call. He immediately dropped his load of cooking leaves and plantains and hurried in pursuit. As he went, he cried out, "Oh, why didn't I eat him sooner!" He quickly gained ground.

3Aii Ropa reached Mokodamapu, a place with many wild pigs. Breathing hard, he ran through the field, scattering the beasts. The old man had now nearly caught him. After a final dash, Ropa came upon a huge wild pig, the size of a cassowary. "Come and crawl inside my anus," said the pig. Ropa did this; he hid in its belly. When the old man approached, the pig attacked him with its sharp tusks. But the old man just laughed: "You're scratching my scabies, you're tickling me!" The pig continued to bite.

Finally the old man retreated, but many other pigs gathered and attacked him. They killed him outside a small garden there.

Then the wild pig said to the boy in his belly, "Now in that old man's house, only an old woman and children are left. We'll kill them. But first I will take you back to your house."

The wild pig ran up to Wakiare Hill and on to Kuwi, where the brothers had their house. Pawa was sitting outside with the mud of mourning on his face. When he saw this wild pig approach, its long tusks turning its mouth into a grin, he was afraid. "Will it kill me? Has that old man turned into a pig and come?" he wondered.

The wild pig approached. Pawa moved toward the base of a near-by tree, thinking he would climb it if necessary. But then the pig ejected his brother from its anus. Ropa picked himself up and stood beside the house. He told his brother what had happened since he had left him. Pawa looked at the pig. Though not a man, it knew how to fight like one, and looked almost human.

Pawa asked, "What kind of *kaberekale* compensation shall we give it now?"

Ropa replied, "We have three large pigs, each a big one, a real Puramenalasu like this one here. But since these are pigs like itself, it may not want them." Indeed, the wild pig said it would not take pigs as compensation! The brothers offered shells, but these too the pig refused. The brothers offered all sorts of things, but they were refused. They complained, "We're just youths, what more can we give you!"

Now the gardens that these brothers made were very large, and the pig said, "Show me what grows in your forest garden!"

The youths dug a quantity of sweet potatoes and heaped them for the pig, which replied, "Yes, I'll eat that, but since the sweet potatoes are in the garden you must show me the garden itself." And it added, "I alone did not kill this old man; all the other wild pigs helped me. You must make a boundary in your garden. Some of it you must give us, and the remainder you can have for yourself."

This is the reason for the difficulties men have with wild pigs that attack their gardens: the brothers gave the pigs claim to them.

Then the pig said, "Now you've shown me the gardens, but there's something else I want: two bundles to put on either side of my neck, which will be a telltale (*lakata*) for me." Those brothers offered many bundles, but the pig did not want them; and they did not know what kind of bundle would do. Finally they took a small bundle their father had hidden underneath the roof, a small round object, and said, "This thing, a fight talisman (*yadaparame*) is what my father used in warring. Take it." The pig did.

11i-11ii   Today, wild pigs come to our gardens, but however careful we are they always run off before we catch them. That is because of this telltale the youths gave. And nowadays as well, pigs attack us with their tusks: they are following what they did when they attacked and killed that old man, for their teeth still have that old man's blood on them.

Because the two brothers gave the pig claim to their gardens as compensation, wild pigs invade our gardens. Those youths showed that pig all the land from the Yaro River to Yopene Stream. Wild pigs escape us because they have this telltale, a talisman, which warns them of our approach. This is the story I heard from my mother, Kekoinyu.

Tale 10: The Broken Arrow

0   There were two brothers, named Yali and Boso. Yali had a wife; Boso did not. They made gardens from the Yaro River to Keresa Mountain, and from Kuare to Kolapi. Many wild pigs used to come to raid the two brothers' gardens. Again and again the two brothers fashioned bamboo-tipped arrows, shot the pigs, and cooked them. But invariably the largest pigs got away, unharmed by their flimsy arrows.

Yali remarked on this: "The shafts of our arrows are too weak. If we had the *kapo* variety of sword grass (*kabe*), it would be different!" Yali then decided to go searching for *kapo kabe*.

1i   So he searched and searched around Mount Keresa. And finally at Yasale, where a *sawia* tree grew, he found a clump of this *kapo kabe*; but there was only one long stem of grass suitable for a shaft. The rest were either rotten or too short.

He took this one stem back. "Good enough!" he thought to himself happily. And he put it inside the house above the hearth. When it was dry, he straightened it and fitted it with a bamboo tip. Now, when he took the arrow to shoot the pigs, the beasts fell and died straight away. Soon he had killed all the wild pigs around there. None were left, or at least none came to their gardens.

One day Yali said, "I'm going now to a southern village where I've heard they are going to kill their pigs." To his brother and his wife he said, "Shoot pigs only with ordinary arrows. This one arrow of mine made of *kapo kabe* you must not use. It's the only one there is."

He took some twine, covered this one arrow up in layers of wrapping, and then tied it beneath the ridge pole of the house. That done, he put on his ornaments and went down south of Keresa Mountain. Before he left, however, he planted a banana shoot and told the other two, "As long as the leaves have not grown out, I'll be going down there. When the leaves are coming out, I'll have turned back and will be carrying pork home."

After crossing Keresa, he spent the night at Labogo. The next day he passed through Paya and slept at Batire. And the third day he crossed Kanara and slept in the forest near Erave. Finally he reached the place where they were killing their pigs.

1 ii   While he was there, his brother and wife went on hunting wild pigs. Some they managed to kill, but the bigger pigs they could not kill with their flimsy arrows, the ones made of the *modo* variety of sword grass. These shafts would always break.

By now the leaves of the banana plant were beginning to grow out.

One day they saw a huge sow, as large as a water tank, rooting in the gardens. Both Boso and Yali's wife watched it with fear as it ate up their sweet potatoes and sugar cane. Their weak arrows did not harm it. They thought, "If we killed this one wild pig, perhaps the others would not come. Why not use the arrow of *kapo* sword grass? Yali will surely not be angry if we use it just this once." So they took down the bundle, unwrapped the arrow, and went after the pig.

The arrow struck the pig and felled it. But when the pig fell, it rolled over on the shaft and broke it. The arrow had killed the pig, though, and the two cooked the carcass, and, as proof of its size for Yali, they kept the head, jaw, and backbone.

The banana plant had grown out completely, and presently Yali returned. On his way, he had noticed that there were many wild pigs around. Remembering his arrow, he decided to go out and hunt. So when he reached his house, he dropped his bag of pork and went inside to fetch the arrow. He saw the wrappings scattered around. Angrily he asked his wife and his brother what had happened to his arrow.

Boso replied, "There was a large sow, which must have given birth to all the other pigs. We tried to kill it, but the arrows made of *modo* grass were not strong enough. So finally I shot the pig with your arrow, but the arrow broke when the pig fell on it."

1 iii   Yali heard his brother out, but said nothing. Greatly annoyed, he went outside and rubbed feces and ashes on his face.

"Are you doing this because of the arrow of *kapo* grass?" Boso asked, seeing his brother in mourning.

"Yes. Why did you have to take it?"

"All right!" said Boso decisively. He tethered their pig, Pura-menalasu, killed it, singed it and cooked it; then he unwrapped a large block of salt and broke it into pieces, which he made into packages. Next he borrowed a good netbag from his brother's wife and put all the salt bundles into it. Then he fetched his bow and arrow, his ochre-coloured cassowary feathers, and his shoulder bag. He shared out the pork: he divided the cooked meat into two halves and gave one side to his brother and brother's wife along with half of the innards and head. The rest, half the meat and half the stomach and intestines, he wrapped and put into his bag with the salt.

Then he announced, "Stay here. I am off to find the source of the *kapo* grass."

On and on he went, leaving the path his brother had taken earlier and going further on, heading toward the downriver part of the Erave River. He went on, and further on, sleeping in the forest and eating taro or sweet potato with pork and salt. Finally he came to a wide river, the Erave. There an old man lived.

"Who are you?" asked the old man.

"I'm going to find *kapo* sword grass," said Boso.

"I have some in the house. Take it and then return," said the old one.

"No, I am really going to where it comes from, its "base" (*re*)."

"Oh," said the old man, "Well, some men like yourself have gone on further, but I've not seen any of them come back!"

Boso took some salt and pork from his netbag and gave it to the old man. In return the old man gave him a bundle. Then Boso continued down to the bank of the river.

There was no bridge across it, but there was a tall *yawi* (black palm) tree standing there, which looked as though people had walked on its trunk. The old man had told Boso that when he reached this tree he should repeat a spell, *"Era yawi pata pata"* (Erave palm lie down, lie down). After Boso had said these words, the palm bent down, just as did another palm growing on the far bank. He walked over from the one palm to the other, and when he stood on the far side he said, *"Era yawi reka reka"* (. . . stand up, stand up), and the two trees straightened.

Boso continued on, until he saw another old man, who asked, "Who are you?"

"I'm searching for the origin of *kapo kabe*."

"Take some of mine," offered the old man.

"No, I'm really looking for where it comes from." Then the old man said, "I have seen men like yourself going further, but not returning. Better spend the night here first." So Boso passed the night with the old man, who gave him a bundle of banana leaves. In return Boso gave pork and salt. In the morning he went on until he came near a place where many dead trees stood. It was a garden.

Approaching, he saw many tall sugar canes and bananas tied to stakes, but no one was about. Continuing on past the garden, he came to a large men's house. He went and sat on the sitting log and waited. Looking up, he observed that the sides and roof were made of pearl shells, while the rafters were made of bushknives. Thinking about this, he went to hide beneath a clump of *irayamu* grass.

3Ai   Presently a big old man arrived. Boso hid, crouched over, weak with fear. He watched the old man approach with a load of firewood such as several men might carry. When he dropped his load, the earth shook.

As Boso looked on, the old man entered the porch and smoked awhile. When he finished he picked up his stone axe and began to split the firewood. As he chopped, a sliver flew off and landed in the clump of grass where Boso was hiding. The old man mumbled to himself, "Well, it wasn't close by that I found this firewood, so I might as well retrieve this piece." When he walked over, he discovered Boso.

"Who are you, boy?" he asked.

"I've come looking for *kapo* sword grass," replied the youth.

"Well, this is where it comes from, right here!" was the reply. "Come on out!"

Boso sat down again on the sitting log and the two ate. Then they lay down to sleep. But Boso was afraid of the old man. So when the old man told him, "Go sleep in that empty room," the youth replied that he did not usually sleep in his own room but in the company of other men.

"There are no strangers about," said the old man, "and you'll be safe by yourself." But Boso insisted on their sleeping in the same room. So the old man agreed, "I'll sleep by the door here, you sleep over there."

3Aii   Boso lay down and secretly opened the first bundle he had been given. In it were two fireflies that shone like little stars. He put one over each closed eyelid and went into a sound sleep.

In the middle of the night the old man rose quietly and picked up a ceremonial staff (*ekepayo*), intending to kill the youth. But he saw the boy's eyes still shining. "Why don't you go to sleep?" he said to the youth. "No one's going to kill you!" But Boso heard nothing, for though his eyes were shining as if he were awake, he was sound asleep.

3Ai   Daylight broke. The old man decided to load him down with valuables—with shell valuables such as bailer, nassa, cowrie and *pokai*— as well as with bushknives and axes. He hoped that the youth would be so fatigued with the load by the time he reached the Erave River that he would be easy to kill. So after they ate he told Boso, "I'll give you the rootstock (*re*) of *kapo kabe,* so you can plant it, and also some dry shafts so you can shoot game." Along with the grass he gave the shells, axes, and bushknives.

"Goodbye, now that you're going," said the old man. So Boso departed carrying the gifts in his netbag along with the one still unopened bundle. On and on he went, retracing his steps. Eventually he reached the river and was about to say the spell, *"Era yawi pata pata,"* when a great darkness came with rain, wind, and cloud. The earth trembled as well.

Boso looked around. He heard voices crying out from different sides, "He's going off! He's escaping! Come downriver! Come upriver!"

3Aii   The youth sat down, much afraid. He put his burden aside and opened the second bundle he had been given. It contained the blood-red juice of a cooked pandanus fruit. He took this red liquid and rubbed it all over his sword-grass stalks, bark belt, breechcloth, cordylines, and other apparel and possessions, leaving all of it strewn around. Then he took refuge in a small cave by the river bank.

Then came many old men, all sounding a war cry, *"Uuuu!"* They hurried up, sniffing the air around them. When they saw the things Boso had left, which looked so bloody, they suspected that one of them had already killed and eaten him. They argued angrily among themselves. Then they all went away. The old man who had given Boso the valuables muttered, "Why didn't I come sooner!" looking around him.

Boso then emerged briefly from his hole and called out to the ghosts: *"Su ya, yaa ya lopada!"* (Things of earth and sky fall down!) Then he quickly returned to his hiding place. When the other old men heard this call, they returned, killed that old man, and ate him.

When they had gone, Boso collected his bark belt, breechcloth, cordyline leaves, and other things; he shouldered his bag containing the sword grass and the valuables; and he spoke the command, *"Era yawi pata pata."* The two *yawi* trees bent down to join. After he crossed over he said, *"Era yawi reka reka,"* and the two trees stood as before.

On Boso went, sleeping once at Batire and once at Labogo, then crossing Mount Keresa. When he reached home he went directly to his brother Yali and said, "Brother, is this what you were looking for?" He gave him the rootstock as well as the dry shafts of *kapo* grass. And he said, "Now what do you say!"

11i   Next he gave out the bailer shells, of which he had carried many, but the bailer-shell "base" (*re*—meaning, here, a very large shell) he gave to Yali's wife. After sharing out the *poi* (or *pokai*) shells, he gave the *poi*-shell base to Yali. As for the *rogo* (cowrie strings), having shared them out as well, he kept its base for himself.

11ii   Now we see a bird called *aroka,* which has a white breast. That is Yali's wife wearing the bailer shell. Boso became a *padeto* bird, which has two white wing-patches: that is him wearing his *rogo* shells. As for Yali, who is wearing his *poi;* he became an *aroaki* bird.*

---

*These are all small unidentified birds. The *aroaki* inhabits the forest and casuarina tops, the other two inhabit village area and gardens.

CHAPTER 2

Of Improper Brothers and Sisters

Tale 11: Riawa and Tyame

0 Riawa and Tyame, a brother and a sister, stayed together and cultivated food gardens. Riawa had married two wives. One day the siblings heard that some Wiru people were intending to hold a *yasa* dance. Having decided to attend, they decorated themselves with fine ornaments, Riawa helping his sister adorn herself. Then they set out.

2i When they arrived at the ceremonial ground, Tyame joined the front ranks of the male dancers. Riawa also participated, though not beside his sister, who marched with other men. More and more people gathered for the dancing. Then, unexpectedly, Tyame's skirt fell off. She tied it back on, but it fell off a second time. Riawa now felt very ashamed.

2ii Angry with her, he struck her a blow with his axe. She fell down there in front of everyone, but then picked herself up and ran off. Her brother looked around, waited for her, but she did not return. She had gone off in the direction of Kalane, to the north.

2iii It was a snake that had carried her off. Having given her up for lost, Riawa set off for home. "Go and take her," he sighed.

2iv After a whole year had passed, Riawa still felt remorse for what he had done. And this is the beginning of a rather long story. One day he went to Rakiare, where he had a taro patch, and uprooted some taro. Next he cut a clump of bananas and peeled them, piling the prepared ones to one side. Leaves for cooking he got next, and some firewood as well, for he was intending to kill his pig named Puramenalasu. Having done this, he made an announcement to his two wives. "I am departing," he told them.

After killing his pig and singeing it, he butchered it and cooked the cuts of meat. In the cooked stomach he stuffed some fat and salt.

Then he put on his ornaments – plumes, a bailer shell, a fine "bone" pearlshell, and the rest. Telling his wives to stay home and eat the pork he could not take with him, he shouldered his bag and set off. You see, he had put all the flesh, fat, taro and bananas in this one net-bag. It made a very heavy load, but – as happens in tales – he bore this heavy load easily. He also took his bow and his axe.

A long way he walked, across the bridge over the Yaro River at Katipa, then on to Podoma, to Epe, and Kadai, to Yekia, Aliyago, and Rokopini. Here he met an old woman by the path. He gave her some pork and salt. She told him, "Your sister has gone beyond. I saw her pass by here." And she gave him a small bundle. Riawa went on and eventually he met another old woman. This one also said, "Your sister has gone on further." He gave her the same gift of pork and salts and received a bundle in return. Next he arrived at Poloko. There he heard the same news: "Your sister has gone beyond." On and on he went, to Kilipini and to Bolora. There he met another old woman, who warned him, "None of the ones who went further than this have I ever seen return!" They exchanged their gifts, and Riawa continued his journey. On to Taguru, to Ekomeka, another old woman, and yet another with the same message. On he went.

At Mele Riawa met another old woman who told him, "Your sister is in Pure, where you see smoke rising on the mountainside." And she too gave him a bundle. In it was wrapped a ceremonial staff (*ekepai*). Riawa went on. After crossing the Poru River, he met a red-skinned woman who said, "Listen, men live around here, but beyond they do not. What do you want to go on for? Anyway it's almost dark."

Her husband, an old man Riawa knew to be a cross-cousin, said, "Oh, you must stay here overnight! Tomorrow I'll show you the way to your sister."

But Riawa asked, "Is it far?"

"Not so far," said the cross-cousin, "but you should go tomorrow morning."

"I shall go now," said Riawa.

Then the old wife said, "Take this staff from its bundle, go close to the mountain called Pulumakana and say '*Pulumakana kepea kepea*' (open open). Then swing the staff down. Do not strike the rock, just aim at it and say this spell. It will split apart."

Having heard this, Riawa left the two old people. The old man had pointed out how to reach this mountain, and he had said, "Your sister's place is down there. But listen, men come only this far. Beyond, there are none."

Using the staff, Riawa crossed through Pulumakana. On the other side he saw a thicket of red-leafed stinging nettles barring his way. Aiming at them with the staff, he recited the spell. They parted and he walked through.

After going on for a while he arrived at a house. It was a fine place, shaded by casuarinas, good *koda* plantains, tall hoop pines, and thick bamboo clumps. He approached the long house and looked inside. The floor was strewn with sugar-cane peelings. Riawa entered. There he saw his sister sitting to one side.

With the woman were her sons, numerous as sword-grass leaves. They were not human children, but snakes. Two small black ones, seeing him enter, immediately cried out, *"Awa, awa!"* (Uncle, uncle!) Riawa sat down crosslegged on the floor, opposite his sister. The two little snakes came to him and curled up on his thighs. They would not leave him. He fed them pieces of pork.

Tyame, however, did not move or speak. She just sat there. Riawa took off his netbag and put it down beside him. Tyame relented; she got up and the two of them hugged.

3Ai   Then she spoke, "Listen, my husband will be arriving soon. Do you see all his sons? And beware. When he comes, you'll be afraid of him!"

From a great distance, as far away as Kagua is from here, came a *buuu* sound. Upon hearing it, Tyame said, "Did you hear that? He's coming!" The sound became louder, and soon Riawa saw a huge snake. It was thick as a wild pandanus tree, and its skin shone with many colours. When it had come close, it said, "Something smells good to eat!" But the two small snakes cried out, "Uncle, uncle! Uncle, uncle! Our uncle's come to stay!" The large snake said nothing. But it curled up, raised its head and pressed its mouth to Riawa's face.

Riawa showed the snake all the food he had brought, and the two of them cooked it, all the taro, bananas, and pork. Then they lay down to sleep. The big snake slept outside the house in a large, hollow *waria* tree. This was the snake which, a year earlier, had carried Tyame from the dance ground.

That night Tyame told her brother, "Tomorrow we are going to get some *padi* and *rani* greens from the garden." The next morning, accordingly, they set out. One of the small snakes curled up in its uncle's netbag, still calling "Uncle uncle," though neither the big snake nor Tyame saw it do this.

The brother, his sister, and her snake husband went a considerable distance over rough ground. Soon they came to a bare face of rock on the far side of a wide pool. This seemed to bar their path, but the snake husband rested its tail on this rock and the two others were able to cross the water on its back. As they walked to the edge of the bluff on the other side, Riawa questioned his sister. "Is this what you often do?" he asked. She did not answer. Riawa wondered, "What am I going to do? Maybe the two of them are planning to kill me." They continued on.

Soon they reached another rocky outcrop with a deep chasm where the ground dropped off precipitously – a place called Tiki-lapiame Kana. But this too was no obstacle. With its head at the top of the rock, the snake extended its tail to the bottom. "You two climb down my back," it said.

At the bottom Riawa saw a garden planted with sugar cane, banana, taro, manioc, and yam. After gathering some *kuni, rani,* ripe bananas, and sugar cane, they split some firewood and prepared to cook these foods.

Riawa asked his sister, "Are we going to spend the night here?"

"No, we'll return today," said Tyame.

Feeling hot from the work in the garden, Riawa went down to a pool below the garden and threw some water over himself. He kept his netbag beside him. When he returned to the garden he saw that his sister and his snake brother-in-law had already departed. Looking upward, he saw the two of them at the top of the cliff.

They were crying out a spell, "*Su ya, yaa ya!*" (Earth there! sky there!) They were calling to ghosts. "We've prepared food for you!" they cried to the ghosts. Here's a man, which is cassowary and possum for you. Come and eat him!" The two said that, and then they disappeared from view.

3Aii   Riawa wondered how he would ever escape before nightfall, with the cliff and the lake in his way. But then the small snake crawled out of his netbag and called out "Uncle!" It said, "The two of them want to kill you. So now you must listen to me and do as I say. Go inside that pile of garden debris and make a small shelter with bark and leaves. You'll hide there when you've finished it." It was now nearly dusk. When the house was finished, Riawa put some food inside. Then he covered it with more debris from the brush pile. The snake put its uncle inside the house. Then it went over to the cliff, crawled into a small hole it had seen there, and closed the entrance with a flat stone.

All sorts of men were coming, some with teeth on their anus. But, finding no one around, they could only cry out, "Why did we not come sooner?" The two of them, Riawa and his snake nephew, threw out pieces of bark belt and food, which these attackers ate.

These ghosts continued to eat the things that the two threw to them, and this went on well into the night.

"Uncle," said the snake, "dawn is approaching. I fear that they will kill us now. Take those bundles and unwrap them."

Riawa opened the first bundle and in it he found a small bird, a *kiliwapili*. He released it and immediately some of the ghosts departed. (Hearing its song, the ghosts thought it was dawn.) In another bundle he found a *gai* cicada which, when released, made more of the ghosts leave. In a third bundle was another bird, a *lealea*, and in a fourth a *bolota* bird.

When all the ghosts had left, the little snake said, "Uncle, they still want to kill us, so we must go now. Follow me carefully." And now the little snake did just as the large one had done. Riawa climbed up to the top of the cliff on its back. In this way did the little snake help its mother's brother. When they reached the pond, the two crossed as before, Riawa walking along the snake's back. Soon they came to Tyame's house.

When she saw them, this woman did not greet them. She did not say something like, "You've come!" She did not say, "You've come in spite of them, and now you must take something of value with you when you go." No, she said nothing. So Riawa said to the snake, "They are both angry with me. I think I must leave now. I will spend the night with the cross-cousin I met on the path on the way here." So Riawa departed, taking with him his nephew, the little snake.

He came back to the mountain called Pulumakana, unwrapped the staff, took aim, and said the spell, "Open open." When the rock opened before him, he passed through. He had already crossed the patch of nettles growing on the other side. Soon he came to the old man's house, where he spent the night. The next morning he continued his return voyage.

4i   When he was nearing his home, the snake said, "Your two wives might want to kill me. Lest they try to do so, you must not take me to your house. Put me in your garden."

Riawa agreed. After a short while they reached Mugura, where Riawa had a nice forest garden. The man made a house in a brush pile (*kubura*) in the garden. He made it with walls of strong *kole* wood and slabs of stone, and on top he piled up debris. In this place he left the snake.

10Ai   Riawa said nothing at all about this to his two wives. He only told them, "They wanted to kill me there, but I was resolute and was able to return."

4ii, 10Aii   One day Riawa told the women, "I'm going to a ceremony in a southern village. Wait for me here. But be sure not to go to my garden in Mugura, where there is a brush heap with small burrows in it." Planting a banana-plant cutting, he told them, "So long as the leaves have not grown, I'll be far away. When they start to grow out, I'll be on my way back." Having said this, he departed.

4iii, 10Aiii   Some time later, while Riawa was still absent, one of his wives went to that garden in Mugura. She looked in the brush heap and saw burrows such as rats make. So she set a trap with her netbag. In the brush she saw many insects, too, and she managed to gather these as well as to trap rats. While sitting beside the pile, cleaning the rats she had trapped, she caught sight of the snake, moving slowly underneath the brush. She saw its head, now as broad as the trunk of a wild pandanus tree.

"Why did you break the house which my uncle made for me?" asked the snake. "Do you want me to move in with you?"

"Oh no, I didn't mean to," said the wife. "I'll build it up again." But the snake would not allow this. It followed her back to the house.

This woman had brought some dry tinder to start a fire. The snake coiled itself on the other side of the hearth while the woman kindled a fire. She cooked the insects and ate them one by one. As she was putting the last one into her mouth, the snake asked her, "What are you doing?"

4iv,10Aiv "I have eaten these insects and am just finishing the last one," she replied. "Slowly, I want to see how you eat an insect," said the snake. And when the woman opened her mouth, the snake forced its way in. It went all the way down into her stomach, where it curled up.

Her stomach expanded and was wide around. The woman was now very afraid, and she deliberated for a long time. She could think

Plate 1. Looking across the Iaro River valley to Mount Ialibu (right) and, beyond, Mount Giluwe.

of nothing to do. She was unable to move; she could not fetch firewood or food. Grass and weeds grew tall outside her house during her sickness. The co-wife helped her with firewood and with food, but the undergrowth grew up.

Eventually Riawa returned from the ceremony. When the co-wife told him what had happened, he just said, "I see," and began to cook the pork he had brought with him. When it was cooked he cut it up and gave out pieces to the people who lived nearby. Then he took a thick piece of fat and a chunk of salt. He spoke to the snake in his wife's stomach, "Come out and eat!" He held the fat close to the woman's mouth, where the snake could smell it. First the snake's head emerged. Then the rest of it gradually came out. The snake curled up on the floor of the house. Riawa gave it a large piece of pork to eat.

11i   While the snake ate, Riawa hacked at it with his axe, once, twice, many times.

11ii   From one part of its body Mount Murray stood, from another piece Mount Ialibu, from a third piece Mount Giluwe. You see, Riawa's sister had given birth to that snake, so it came back with Riawa. But then it went into his wife's stomach. When Riawa heard about this, he was angry because he thought that the snake would kill his wife. So he cut the snake into pieces, and the pieces became the mountains. And that is the end of my story.

Tale 12: Sister and Wife

0,2i Limu and his sister lived together, working in their food gardens. Since the young woman was of marriageable age, once in a while men would come with valuables and offer to take her in marriage. When they came with their shells and pigs, Limu would say to his sister, "Now that men are coming, go to the garden and fetch some sweet potatoes and *padi* greens." She would do so. But later, while Limu and the men were discussing the bridewealth, she would return without her skirt. This made Limu deeply ashamed. He would go to her quickly, hoping others had not seen her, and tell her to put the skirt back on.

Again and again this would happen. Men from many parts had heard that the young woman was ready to marry, and they came to make bridewealth offers. But the sister would always appear naked. Sometimes Limu himself had to go and knot the skirt around her.

One day some men from Erave came with shells. Limu, thinking that his sister's skirt was perhaps poorly made or falling apart, had himself made a new, strong one for her. When the men approached with their shells, he once again told his sister to fetch some food from the garden while he shared some bananas and sugar cane with the guests. Presently he looked up and saw his sister returning from the garden. Once again she was naked. Limu took the skirt he had made and tied it on her tightly.

When the food was cooked, the siblings and the suitors ate their meal and talked. In the afternoon, when the men were about to return to their home, the sister was again without her skirt. Those men had agreed to give shells and pigs for her, but when they saw this, they gathered up their valuables and departed, as had all the others before them.

2ii   Limu, both ashamed and angry, struck his sister on the head and went into the house to sit by the fire.

2iii   The woman did not join him there. She went to one side of the house and then away. He did not bother to find out where she might have gone. He did not care, for he had many clansmen there, as many as there are here in Karapere, and he had his dogs, too. So he would stay without her.

2iv   But one day sometime later he sat and thought about her. "Ah, this sister of mine, she has gone off someplace and is lost. I must find her," he said to himself. So he took his dogs and set off. First he went to the forest at Apirawalu and hunted possums. From there he went to Karanda, over to Mount Kata, then to the forest at Alamu. In a dense part of that forest he came across a clearing where the daylight penetrated to the forest floor. Trees were lying toppled in different directions, and visible between them were the leaves of food crops. Many sorts of crops grew there in luxuriance – bananas, sugar cane, and taro of the good *binale* variety. Limu tied his dogs and approached quietly to the edge of the garden.

5i   In the middle he saw a young, good looking woman with long hair down to her shoulders, wearing a white skirt. She was busy mounding the soil and planting sweet potato runners. Limu, somewhat fearful, hesitated to go further. Deciding to return home, he took a step backwards. But as he did so, he stepped on a dry branch underfoot. It cracked. "Hey!" the woman called out. "Who's there? Are you someone from a village (*ada ali*) or from the forest (*ra ali*)?" Limu, recognizing his sister's voice, replied, "I am someone from a village."

When she heard his voice, the young woman knew it to be her brother's. But she said only, "All right, come forth if you are really a man of the village." Limu did so, and the two wept because of the sympathy (*yara*) they had for one another.

Then the sister told him, "I have everything I want here except for one thing that I hunger for. Do you still go to the forest with your dogs?"

"Yes, I came hunting with them," replied Limu, and he showed her the bag of possums he had left by the edge of the garden. In an earth oven the siblings cooked the meat, with *kuni* greens of the good *palasu* kind and with *binale* taro.

10Bi   Then the sister said, "I grow many good foods in the gardens, but I do not eat possums or pork. You must continue to kill and cook these for me." So Limu went to kill more possums for her in the forest around the garden, telling her to keep them to cook later.

5ii   "Return now," she said, "but first I will give you something to take with you." And she handed him a couple of large pigs, two net-bags full of pearl shells, a bushknife, and an axe.

4ii,10Bii   When Limu was about to depart, the woman gave him some advice. "All these things I have given you. In return you must return with more pork for me. Do not bring me fat, however, only the lean meat. Moreover, when you come here, do not do so along the main paths; but take the path I took when I fled from your house after you struck me. Near the edge of your house stands a tall *waria* tree with a mounded base; there you will see my footprints still. Now I am giving you this payment (*pe*). Use these things to marry. Take two wives. One must be from Ialibu land, and one from Erave. Do not take a Palea (Wiru) wife." Limu assented to all this and then departed for home.

4i,5iii,   First he married a Ialibu woman. Later he was about to marry an
10Biii   Erave wife, but a Palea woman came to stay in his house. She stayed with him even though he offered no payment for her. Limu wondered why she had come. Her presence worried him, for he remembered what his sister had said.

His clan brothers were concerned as well. "Why do you not marry that Erave woman, as your sister told you to do? Even though this woman has come, you must take an Erave wife as well." Limu tried to send this woman off, but she stayed.

On the occasions when people were killing pigs and distributing their meat, he would give much pork to his Ialibu wife, but to this Palea woman, who had come on her own, he gave only a few poor pieces. Then he would set off in secret and give lean meat to his sister. The pieces of fat he always gave to his two wives, the one from Ialibu and the one from Palea land. When he returned from his visits to his sister, Limu would always come back with pigs and shells she had given him.

The Palea wife wondered why she was always given pork fat. Now one day Limu went to where they were killing pigs down in Batire, leaving his two wives to stay at home. While he was away his Palea wife, still desirous of understanding why she received no good meat, went over to Limu's brothers' house.

"When Limu comes and gives you pork, does he give you flesh as well, and meat on the bone?" she inquired.

"No," they replied, "he gives us only fat. See, we are getting *rani* greens ready to cook the fat he will give us when he returns." She heard this, thought for a while, and then went around to the other entrance of the men's house. She asked the other men there, and received the same response. Limu had told her he had to give all the good meat to these clansmen, but now these men told her they received the same as she did, just the fat.

She heard what they said, returned to the house, and then set off along the little-used path that Limu took from the mounded base of the *waria* tree.

On and on she went. To one side of the path she saw an *opo* tree, whose strong wood is used for making digging sticks. Cutting a short length of it, she made a pointed dagger which she hid in her netbag.

Presently she arrived at a forest garden in which grew abundant plantains and sugar cane. In it she saw a long-haired young woman. "Are you Limu's sister?" she asked.

"Yes," replied the other.

"Limu comes here to you, does he?"

The sister heard her accent and thought, "Ah, this is a Palea woman he has married!" and she was troubled. But she asked only, "Why have you come? Do you want to take shells and pigs home?"

4iii,10Biv   "No, I have not come for that," said the Palea woman, looking gravely at her. The two sat. After a short silence, the Palea woman said, "I will pick the lice from your hair, lest your long hair be spoiled." She sat behind the sister, as one does to look for nits. Drawing her *opo* stake from her netbag, she stabbed the other woman in the back, into the kidney, then rose and quickly departed. The sister crawled to the porch of her house, where she lay on her side and murmured, "Only when I have seen my brother shall I die."

Limu returned from the pig kill carrying pork. He saw that his Ialibu wife had brought piles of vegetables to be cooked with the pork, but that the Palea woman was just sitting looking preoccupied. She had not brought food. Limu was troubled. Perceiving his worry, the Ialibu wife whispered to him, "She has been off someplace and has returned just now." Limu thought for a while and told the Ialibu woman to take care of everything: she could cook all the pork and share it out as she wished. "I am sick," he said, "and want to lie down inside the house."

But while the two women were busy preparing the earth oven, he stole out of the house and went quickly along the path that led from the *waria* tree, taking with him some lean meat on the bone.

Presently he came to his sister's house. As he drew close, he noticed flies buzzing around him. Then he saw his sister's body covered with flies. Peering into her half-closed eyes, he saw she was still alive.

"What happened?" he asked her.

"That Palea woman has killed me, the woman I told you not to marry," she replied. "I offered her pigs and shells, the way I did to you. But she didn't want any, and she killed me. Did you wish I should die, that you broke your word and married her?" She said no more.

Limu was grieved. He carried his sister to a place in the forest where rats make their burrows. In that soft earth he dug a deep hole with a piece of *opo* wood. He placed her in the pit, threw dead leaves and twigs on top, and then covered her with earth. That done, he walked slowly back home and lay down inside his house. All this time, the two wives continued to cook the pork. He told them they could give the meat away, for he was still sick. But he sat up, mourning for his sister, his eyes filled with the tears.

Then one day he decided to put an end to his mourning and killed a pig. He cooked it and gave out the meat, but ate none himself. After that he lived normally, working in the garden and doing other business.

4iv,5iv But he had not forgotten. One day he took out a stone scraper and prepared bamboo-tipped arrows. He took his axe to the sharpening stone in Yopene Stream and honed down the blade's edge. Then he told his two wives, "Since I didn't eat any of that pig, I'm hungry to eat meat. Let's go and kill some rats in the forest."

The Ialibu woman replied, "You know I'm no good at catching rats." The Palea woman, however, agreed to go.

So the two went. Limu led her toward that place where he had buried his sister, and there the woman exclaimed, "Ah, there are rats here; see the burrows!"

He told her to dig for them, and he went and fetched the *opo* stick he had left, saying, "Look, other women have come here to dig for rats. Use this!" She found many rats, digging deeper and deeper.

Then Limu said, "I'll go and stand with my bow and arrow at the ready, lest our enemies surprise us here. Dig quickly and we shall go back." He stood back while she dug down through the loose earth.

Finally she thrust her hand into a rat burrow and suddenly jerked it back.

"Dig on," Limu told her. She uncovered part of the sister's body and recoiled, crying out, "Oh no!"

Limu said, "All right, why did you kill her?" The woman did not answer. "You came to eat, now go ahead and do so," he said, indicating the body. He fitted a *kane* arrow to his bowstring and took aim.

So the woman began to eat, and she ate and ate. Presently her stomach could distend no more; she had eaten all she could. Then Limu shot and killed her.

11i-ii He took his *wiruapu* bow and broke it in two, stuck the pieces into his rear, and flew off as a *walawe* lorikeet.

His Ialibu wife waited for a long time for the two to return. When they did not, she got many pigs and shells and put them inside the house. Then she burned the house down, and she was consumed as well. She became a *mumakarubi* quail. She had thought, "There's no one to stay with now," so she set fire to herself and all their possessions. The grass grew over the burnt house site, and in such places we sometimes now see these *mumakarubi* quail.

The brother had made *ali kalia* compensation for the death of his sister by killing the Palea woman. We still observe this custom.

Tale 13: The Eel-Child I

0,2i A brother and sister stayed by themselves looking after their pigs and gardens. One day the young woman was wading in the Sugu River when an eel came and swam into her vagina, after which she returned to the house. The woman then fell ill, and thereafter she repeatedly refused marriage offers from men. Eventually she gave birth to an eel, and from then on she went every day to the Sugu River to breastfeed it, her son. She did not work in the garden any longer. And because of this her brother, who was aware of what she had done, became angry.

2ii So he thought of a plan. He told his sister that he was going visiting and that she should look after his pigs during his absence. But instead of leaving, he went down to the river and struck a tree with a stick to call the eel, just as he had seen his sister do earlier. When the eel emerged, crying for the breast, he swung his axe and killed it. Then he carried it back to the house and cooked it.

His sister was about to leave her garden for the river when she saw smoke rising from their house. Curious, she went to look. The youth said, "Oh, sister, I was going to go visiting, but as I was walking along I saw a snake that a dog had just killed, and I'm cooking it." "Fine," replied the sister, "let's eat it. Take it out of the earth oven, if it's cooked."

The youth opened the oven pit and then exclaimed, "Look, I went and caught an eel in the river!"

The sister was horrified and cried out, "Ah, your sister's son — and you killed him!"

"But you didn't tell me," the brother replied. The sister wept and wept.

2iii Only the brother ate, for the young woman would not touch the food. At dawn she left the house and journeyed a long way to where the eel, her husband, lived. She told him what had happened to his son, and afterwards she stayed with him. She made gardens while he

went off to the forest to hunt possums and cassowaries. After a
while she gave birth to a second son.

2iv,10Bi The brother soon grew tired of working in the gardens and
looking after the pigs by himself, so he went and followed the path
his sister had taken. After walking a long distance, he arrived where
she was living.

"Why have you come?" she asked him, giving him some cooked
sweet potatoes and some *padi* and *rani* greens. Then she told him to
stay at the garden head and await his brother-in-law's arrival.

Presently there was a loud *buuu* sound; the woman's husband
was coming. The brother was much afraid when he saw the great eel
emerge from the forest, its face painted, wearing a *subi* leaf on its
forehead, and carrying weapons. But the brother did not flee. The
eel came and wound itself around him in coils and told him, "You
killed my first son, but I will not make much of that. The two of us
are brothers-in-law!" Then the three of them ate a large meal.

10Bii Then the second son of the eel said, "Father, I want to go with
my mother's brother!"

The father eel replied, "No, my first son died there; you cannot
go." But the son insisted, and finally the father eel gave in. But it
warned its brother-in-law: "If something happens to this son of
mine, you will hear from me!" The youth and his nephew departed.

The two returned to the brother's house. The brother showed
the eel a hole in the tree to sleep in, and he told it he would always
give it food after rapping on the trunk. And so he did; the youth gave
good food to his sister's son: ripe bananas, sugar cane, and big
chunks of pork.

10Biii Then one day the youth told his nephew, the eel, that he wanted
to journey to a place where they were killing pigs. After pointing out
a few sweet potatoes and bananas that the eel could eat during his
absence, he left.

Now while he was away, a man came looking for possums. He
peered into the hole in the tree. The eel came out and said, "You're
not my mother's brother!"

The stranger hurried back to his village and told his brothers,
"There's a snake there whose mother's brother has run off!" They
came back and began to cut the tree down. The eel protested, "My
mother's brother put me here. You mustn't kill me! Look, here is the
food he has left for me. I'm the child of this woman!" But the men
did not listen; they killed, cooked, and ate the eel.

When the youth returned he heard the news. He rubbed his face
and chest with ashes and mud, and asked these men, "Who was it
that did this?" They replied, "You did not warn us. We thought it was
game, so we ate it."

After three weeks had gone by he decided to go to his sister's husband's place. So he journeyed there and told him what had happened. The eel only replied, "Yes, I hear what you say." The two spent the night together.

10Biv   The next morning the eel dug up a large taro. It told the man, "Though this taro is very heavy, you must carry it back to your house." So the brother put the taro on his shoulder. The eel was in there: it had hollowed out the taro and had curled up inside.

The brother walked slowly, for the burden was heavy. When he had almost arrived, the eel emerged and tightened itself around his neck, but the brother kept his word and continued to walk on toward his house.

11i   Nearby was a man chopping firewood. He looked up and saw the youth approaching, carrying a large taro and an eel that had wrapped itself around his neck. So, quickly sharpening his axe, he cut that taro open in the middle.

11ii   The eel broke apart, and the largest piece was carried down the Erave River. Only the smaller part, the head, remained. That is why we have no large eels here.

Tale 14: The Eel-Child II

0,2i   There were a brother and sister. Only the brother worked in the gardens; the girl just sat around in the house. One day the youth said to her, "Now you must really do some work in the gardens! I'm the one who always does it. Come, I will show you the taro, bananas, and sugar cane there."

But the girl replied, "No, I don't want to go and work in the gardens. You go."

"Well enough," he replied.

2ii   One day the brother decided to watch her, to find out what she did all day. He saw her take the netbag she was making down to a pool and sit on a stone by the water's edge. He watched. Something roiled the surface at the middle of the pool and approached her. He saw an eel come out and suck from her breasts.

"Ah, that is what she does when I am hard at work in the gardens," he thought. Having understood this, he decided to deceive her. So the next day he told her, "I'm tired. You really must go and dig some sweet potatoes in the garden. They should be ready now. Bring some taro, bananas, and greens as well." He told her where these things were in the garden. "I will stay in the house," he said, "and we will eat later."

But instead of staying there he went down to the pool, taking with him two small *karubi* gourds which he put on his chest to imitate nipples. Sitting on the stone by the water's edge and holding a cassowary-bone dagger, he called out to the eel the way his sister did: *ssss*. When the eel came out of the water to suck at the breast, he thrust the dagger into its ear and killed it. Then he carried it back home and cooked it.

The sister, meanwhile, was sitting in the garden. Feeling a painful pressure in her breasts, she stopped digging up potatoes and hurried back to the house with the few she had gotten. Arriving there, she saw that her brother was cooking something in an earth oven. She wondered what it might be.

After a while, he opened the oven and began to uncover the food beneath the layer of leaves. A good odor filled the air. Some of the eel's skin was stuck to the fern leaves the eel was cooked in, but the sister did not see it. "Eat the fern leaves first, and then we'll eat the rest," the brother said.

But she did not eat; she saw her eel and began to cry; it was the son to whom she had given birth that her brother had killed and cooked.

2iii   Seeing her distress, the brother said, "Listen, sister, this is not something to breastfeed; it's something to be eaten." But she said nothing; she wept and wept.

"Sister," said the brother finally, "you don't want to listen to me. So I will leave you be." Having said that, he killed a pig, cooked it, and divided it into two, entrails as well as meat. He gave one side to his sister and kept the other for himself. While he was doing this, the young woman continued to weep.

He was about to leave when his sister finally said, "Ah, brother, I didn't mean this. Come and eat this pork with me."

But the other replied, "No, you didn't want to listen to me. Now I am leaving you."

He went along a path that he had not taken before. On and on he went, southward to the land close to Sumale (Mount Murray). The men who lived there saw him coming alone, killed him, and prepared to eat him.

Now after a while the sister thought, "Well, I will follow him anyway." So she set off. After going a long way she met a woman who said, "You there, what are you doing here?"

"Oh, this is what happened," the sister began. And then she told her story.

The old woman told her, "You mustn't go down there. They will kill you, just as they have probably killed your brother. Go back. I will go down there and see what they have done to your brother." So the old woman went there alone and said to those men, "Listen, all the rest of this man you have killed you can eat. But the liver you must give to me!" The men agreed to this.

9Bi   She took this liver and put it in a bamboo container. This she gave to the sister, telling her, "Go to where you see a *sawia* tree. At the base of it bury your brother's liver. Then return home. After several months you will begin to see some lightning in the sky. Do not do anything, but when you see it glowing repeatedly, return to the tree."

Having agreed to this, the sister set off, buried the liver under a *sawia* tree and continued on her way home.

9Bii She stayed there a while. Eventually she saw a single glow of lightning in the sky. But she followed the old woman's instructions and waited. When she finally saw many glows in the sky, she knew: "I must go now."

So she went to the place where she had buried the liver. There, surrounding the *sawia* tree in the middle of the forest, was a large garden with many bananas and sugar cane. Warily she approached it and walked along the garden fence. Inside she saw a man standing on a branched post tying up tall sugar cane. Afraid to enter, she continued to walk along the edge. But then she stepped on a dry branch, which broke with a crack.

"Who's that?" the man called out.

2iv She approached. And when she drew close, she saw that in fact there were two men. One was a grown man, the other a young boy. Looking closely at them, she saw that they both resembled her brother. This made her happy. The three of them stayed there, living off that garden.

Some time later a famine approached. The two men said, "It will soon be a difficult time, and we must make a new garden. You, sister, cook some food for us, and we will feast with other men who will come to help us with the work."

So the sister began to harvest different kinds of food from the garden while the other two went off to fetch the helpers. She dug sweet potatoes and taro, and she cut bananas, all new ones not yet fully matured. Then she peeled them. But since there was not much, she went over to the base of the *sawia* tree, where *mulu* taro were growing profusely. She had planted only one taro, but now there were many. So she dug them out.

11i But as she dug, blood welled up. She took them anyway and peeled them, though blood continued to flow from the taro. She cooked these taro along with the other foods.

After a while the two men returned. They complained of feeling ill: "Oh, my liver is hurting me!" They hurried to the base of the *sawia* tree, and there they expired.

11ii The two died because she had dug up their livers, which had grown up as taro from the liver planted there. If she had not done this, we would be able to take the livers of dead people, put them in bamboos, and plant them; and they would grow up again. But now we die for good, never to come up again.

Tale 15: Brother, Sister, and Ghosts

0   Peleme and his sister Koipiame stayed and looked after many pigs and gardens. One day Peleme told his sister he was taking his dogs to the forest to find game. In the forest he took off his head-covering and his ornaments, then hid them in some leaves at the base of a wild pandanus tree. Then he went on in search of game.

Presently a *loke* possum came down the tree. It saw the ornaments and put them on.

2i   Koipiame was working in the garden when she saw someone she thought was her brother coming. She wondered why he was not coming with his dogs. When he had drawn close, he threw some clumps of earth at her. She was perplexed: was this something a brother should do? Ashamed, she lowered her eyes and began to weep.

The possum went away, put the ornaments back in the dry pandanus leaves, and climbed up the tree to sleep in the house it had made there.

2ii   Peleme soon returned to this place, having bagged many possums. He put on his ornaments and returned to the house. There he found his sister, sitting outside. She had brought back neither food nor firewood; and she just sat there and wept.

"What's wrong?" he asked. But she did not reply. Instead she turned away from him and continued to weep. Peleme then gathered some cooking leaves and firewood, and he cooked the possums he had brought. His sister refused to eat a share, so he alone ate. Meanwhile she continued to weep.

2i   The next morning, Peleme went into the forest again. He left his ornaments in the same place as before, and once again the *loke* possum came down, put them on, went to the garden, then threw things at the sister; as before, it left, replaced the ornaments, and climbed back into its house of leaves and moss. Later Peleme came back, put his things on again, and returned home.

2ii   He found his sister at the house. She was weeping as before and still had not touched any of the possums he had brought her the day before. Again he asked her why she was weeping, but she did not answer.

2iii   Finally Peleme said, "Stay and weep, then. I am leaving. We will divide our things." Then he went to fetch firewood and cooking leaves, and he killed and cooked a pig. Having done this, he divided the pork between them, one side along with half of the belly for each. Thus did they divide everything between them: pork, salt, pearl shells, bailer shells, and so forth. Then the brother left. Five pigs he took with him, and five he left for his sister. On and on he went, to Paya and then beyond. Eventually in the forest he met a tall young man, who asked, "Who are you?" Peleme answered him and told him what had happened. "Good enough," said this youth. He took half of Peleme's burden, and the two went along.

3Ai   After a while the youth spoke again: "We are going to a bad place now. You must do as I tell you."

Presently they came to a house, and there the young man then warned Peleme about his father, a man who kills. So the two took some pig stomach, belly fat and salt, and hung these beside the path the old man would come along. The youth made Peleme sit in the back of the house, fearing what his father might do. They sat down to wait.

Presently the old man came home. He had found the pork and salt, and he wanted to know where it had come from. His son explained. Immediately the old man began to look around inside the house, but he found no one. So he piled the pork and salt in a corner of the house. Peleme continued to hide.

The old man made another search of the house when his son had gone to sleep; but, not being able to find Peleme, he finally went to sleep himself. The next morning the old man left by the same path on which he had come. When he had gone, the youth prepared some bananas, sugar cane, sweet potato, and taro for Peleme. But, still afraid of what his father might do, he kept Peleme indoors.

3Aii   One day, though, the old man only pretended to leave. Instead he hid and watched the house. He saw his son cook the food and take it to Peleme. Now he understood. He waited until his son left to fetch some firewood and food, and then went inside and found Peleme. He bit him in the kidneys and killed him. Then he left.

Later the youth came back and saw Peleme lying there dead. He wept with anger. When his father returned, the youth announced, "Now that you have done this bad thing, I will leave."

"Why are you going?" asked the father.

"Because you have killed this friend of mine, whom I brought and kept here."

The father replied, "Oh, that was something to be eaten that you had there, so why do you complain so?" But the son did not listen. He went away, taking the path by which Peleme had come.

After a long walk he came to a house. There he saw a young woman. She had a good house, full gardens, and many pigs. It was

Koipiame. He stayed there with her, but she was afraid of him. Once she said, "I would most like to see my brother's face."

"There is no way he can come," was all the youth said in return. So the two stayed on.

9Bi   One day this young man said, "I am going out to check my possum traps. You go to the gardens, fetch some food, and bring the pigs in." She went and did all this quickly, the way things happen in tales. Then she waited. Before leaving, the youth had told her, "If, while you are waiting for the food to cook, you remember your brother's face, you must turn from the east and face the west."

So now she was alone; she sat and waited while the food cooked. She stayed and sat. Presently she began to think of her brother's face. She sat facing the west, as she was told to do, and there she saw repeated glows of lightning. She thought, "I am thinking of my brother and now I see this. Does that mean he is coming?" The youth who left her still did not return, so she continued to look toward the west.

9Bii   Presently she saw someone coming. It was her brother Peleme. She noticed how his thick hair was covered with a *raguna* hat and white *mara* leaves. He was wearing a good bark belt, and he looked very handsome. The sister rose and, with a cry of compassion, hugged him around his legs. Now she understood that the other youth had not gone to check his possum traps at all, but had gone instead to fetch Peleme; that was why he was so long in coming. She understood that the lightning was glowing because her brother was coming back.

The two siblings sat down and waited. Soon the other youth arrived. "You see him here as a ghost," he said to Koipiame. "I told you I was going to look for possums, but actually I went to fetch your brother. You were crying so much for him that I went to bring him back to you."

2iv   The three of them stayed together. The brother, Peleme, looked after his gardens and pigs, while Koipiame and the other youth, now her husband, looked after theirs.

One day Koipiame said, "Now that you have brought this dead one back, we must go and find a wife for him."

"No," said her husband. "We will not find him a wife; we can help him with garden work." But Koipiame put the same question again, to her brother this time. He replied, "It is true, I do not want a wife. If the two of you help me with my pigs and gardens, I will be content to do without." So they lived like that.

One day, then, Koipiame's husband went to look for possums in the forest while the brother and sister stayed home. Then he left to visit a pig kill. He went on and on for a long distance, and on the path he met a young woman. "Who are you?" she asked. He told her, and she replied, "I have not seen people such as yourself come back from where you are going. Don't go."

"No, I will go on," he replied.

But the woman insisted, "Really, I have said enough."

So he turned back and headed home. He walked on and on, slept for a while that night, and then continued on. During the night he saw a firefly come close, so he caught it, put it on his forehead, and walked on by its light. On and on he went, thinking he was about to arrive, but always finding himself not yet there. Finally he reached the house. Those two had been waiting for him a long time. They had cooked food for him, been obliged to consume it themselves, cooked more food for him, ate it, and so on. They had just finished cooking another pig when he arrived.

11i   The woman, Koipiame, said nothing. She did not look at him. Peleme saw that she was angry. So he said, "Oh, sister, once before you were angry with me like this. You sat and sulked, so I left. Now once again you are angry, and I think I must leave."

11ii   After Peleme said this, the two brothers-in-law went away: as *walawe* lorikeets. She became an *ita* hawk.

Tale 16: Brother, Sister, and Foes

0   A brother and a sister lived alone, for their father and mother were both dead. They tended their pigs, which were many, and made large gardens around their house.

One day the brother announced, "I am going to the forest." He got his bow and arrow, his stone axe, called his dog, and went along a path to a place where he had found a possum's sleeping spot. A *loke* possum was sleeping there, and he killed it with an arrow. Then, having cut some leaves and tied the possum up, he continued along.

Presently his dog barked into a well in the limestone. Thinking that there must be a possum in the hole, the brother took off his bark cloth and left his stone axe and everything at the edge. Then he climbed down into the hole.

2i   While he was down there the *loke* possum that he had bound untied itself and stood up. Then it put on the bark belt, the ear and nose ornaments, the shoulder bag – all the things that the man wore. It then went along the path to where the sister was working in the garden, and it looked at her from the edge of the garden.

The possum deceived her. As a young man might do, it took some nuts from a tree, entered the garden, hid behind some undergrowth, and threw one of the nuts at her, aiming at her breasts.

The woman looked up but did not see anything, so she resumed her work. Then the possum threw another nut at her breasts, and this time she looked up quickly and saw someone she thought was her brother.

"Can it be my brother throwing these things at me?" she wondered. "Does he want to marry me?" She began to weep. Sobbing, she fled the garden with the few sweet potatoes she had dug.

Then the possum returned to the hole in the earth which the brother had entered. It put the bow down, took off the bark belt, took off the ear and nose rings, the netbag, all these things, and put them in a pile as before. Then it wrapped itself up in the leaves and tied the rope around the leaves, finishing just before the brother came out of the hole. The brother looked around; there was his possum as before. Having put on his things, he went and shot some birds and one more possum. Carrying some of this game on one shoulder and some on the other, he returned home. When he reached the house he found his sister weeping.

2ii   "Brother, do you want to marry me? Is that why you came and threw tree nuts at my breasts!" exclaimed the sister.

"Eh, sister, I did no such thing!" the youth replied.

"Yes, brother, it was you. Since our father and mother died, you have been looking after us, and now you want to marry me!"

But the brother protested, "Sister, it wasn't I."

The woman continued to weep. Her brother said, "Sister, don't cry so much. I'm sorry for you." Soon everyone was talking about the brother, saying things like "Does he want to marry his sister? Is it because he wants to have her that he throws things at her breasts?"

2iii   Finally the brother said, "Sister, you are right; I will go to my enemy's place. Stay home, I'll go alone." Meanwhile the girl made plans to visit one of her relatives.

The brother cooked his possums in the morning. He ate until his stomach hurt and put the rest in a netbag which he hung in his house. Then he tethered his pigs, killed them with a club, and distributed the meat. He gave the head and backbone to his sister and gave a live pig to another relative.

"All right, stay here," he told the girl, and he took his axe, his bow and arrow, his cassowary feathers, and other possessions. He put a few pieces of pork into his netbag and set off for his enemy's place.

After walking for a long time, he came to a good spot to spend the night. He decided to prepare a shelter, so he took off his netbag and put it down. He was about to begin when his sister approached. She was still weeping.

2iv   "A dove is crying," thought the brother at first, but then he caught sight of her. "What's this! My sister!" he muttered.

He rebuked her, "You made me ashamed back there, so now I'm going to my enemy's place. But here you are following me!"

He was angry and thought of killing her. So when night came he went to strike her with his axe. But when he looked down at her and saw she was still crying, he relented.

"Do you know what you are doing?" he exclaimed, for he was going to the place of their enemies.

The next day he went on, and the girl followed in his footsteps. He saw this and said, "All right, let's go on." And on they went, eating the food that they had cooked and brought. The brother, still angry, walked on ahead while his sister followed a short distance behind. They went up a mountain, the girl still weeping and carrying her netbag of pork. "They'll kill both of us, but let's go on," the brother murmured.

So he led and the woman followed. At one point, when they were descending a ridge, the girl saw something move in the bush. "Hey, there's a small *sawari* possum," she said to herself. It made a rustling noise in the dead leaves. The girl went slowly, caught it, and put it into her netbag. She showed it to her brother.

"It is just a small one," she said. "Its mother ran away in the forest and I carried it here."

They were about to start off again when the little possum cried out "*Ama!* Mother!"

The brother heard the voice and asked, "What's that talking?"

They took the possum out of the bag.

"Oh!" the youth said, "it was that *sawari* possum that said 'Mother.' Well, I don't know about this, but let's look after it. Keep it." The brother felt ashamed; his brow was burning. "Let's go on!" he said.

As they continued on down the mountain, the possum spoke to the girl: "Tell my father to strip the bark of that *warapi* tree over there." So the girl told her brother; he cut the bark and gave it to his sister, who put it in her netbag. While they walked on, the possum sat in the netbag, stripping and rolling the bark into rope. It kept on doing so until many coils of rope lay in the bag.

Once again, as they were going on, the possum said, "I need some more *warapi*." So the youth cut some more bark and put it in the net-bag, and the possum kept on making rope.

Then the little possum said, "Now we are getting close to the village. Down there is where they wash." It pointed out the enemy's village. "There's the men's house over by that palm tree, the coco-nut.* And over there, near the men's house, is where your elder sister lives," it said. (The siblings' elder sister had married into this village.)

They saw that this elder sister had come down to the stream to

---

*Not indigenous to the Kewa area. The Motu word was used.

wash. So the possum took a piece of bark and wrote on it with a pencil – I don't know how, but it did this – and floated the bark down the stream to where the older woman was washing. When the elder sister picked it up and saw the name of her younger sister, she began to weep.

"Let's go down to your sister," the possum said, and they advanced to the edge of the stream.

There the younger sister said to the elder, "We heard that the big-man of this place married you, our elder sister; that is how you came to stay here. Then our father and mother died. We never came to see you after you married this big-man."

"But," the elder sister asked, "since your enemies are here, and they will kill you, why did you come?"

"Well," replied the younger sister, "let's see whether they kill us or not. The leader of this place will say."

The elder sister agreed, "I don't know whether he will say 'let's kill them' or not. But come, we shall soon find out. Go this way, take the path by the coconut tree, which leads through the forest to my house."

Then the woman went on the path directly home while the girl and the brother took the path through the forest. They met and sat down inside the house.

"My husband is in the men's house. He will come soon, so let's wait," the elder sister said. And it was not long before they heard the husband of the first-born daughter come up.

"Hey!' he said, "Who's this here? My brother- and sister-in-law!"

The girl told him the story of how the people of her village heard the story about her brother throwing things at her breasts, and the brother spoke of how he had left home and how his sister had followed. After he heard all this, the husband said that other men there would do whatever he said. If he said, "Fight," they would fight; if he said, "Wait," they would wait. But he did not say which he would tell them. After sitting down for a while, he returned to the men's house.

3Ai   Then the elder sister said, "Your brother-in-law is a man of bad thoughts. He might urge his clansmen to kill the two of you. I will go to the wall of the men's house and listen to what he says. Wait for me here." So she left for the men's house to overhear what the men were planning.

The husband had gone inside. It was now night, and the men were sleeping. "Wake up!" he told them. "If you all wake up, it would be good!"

Then, while the men built up fires in the hearths, he spoke: "A wild pig came here and a female wild pig followed it, and the two are sleeping. I think we should kill them and cook them in earth ovens! Will you do this? I have been uneasy ever since they came." He went on to say, "Tomorrow, when the birds awake, you must surround the house and kill the brother and sister!" The others agreed. "We'll kill them!" they said. They did not sleep because of the excitement.

His wife had listened through the walls. When she heard this she returned and told her brother and sister, "This man is bad; he intends to kill the two of you. He has urged the others to do it."

"Very well," the brother said with resignation, "it was I who chose to come here, so let them kill me."

Knowing for sure that her husband was going to kill her brother and sister, the woman felt saddened. She got some food for them. She killed a small pig and unwrapped a block of salt to eat with the pork. The brother discussed with the elder sister how they happened to come here. His younger sister wept, saying, "Brother, now they'll come and kill you."

3Aii   Then the possum said, "Why do you do all this crying? It's all right, let them come." It said to the sister, "Give me the rope which I made before. Keep everything else, but give me the rope."

So the young woman got the rope from the netbag and gave it to the possum. Then the possum asked the two, "Have you eaten enough food?" And when they said they had, it told them to go to sleep. It would wake them when the men were about to come, it said. Then the possum crawled into its netbag.

Eventually the two siblings went to sleep. While they were sleeping, the possum rose and went to the coconut tree. It took along the netbag belonging to the young woman whom it called mother, and it began to build a house at the top of the tree. When it was done it fetched the salt, the pork, and other foods, and it carried them to this tree house. Then it came back to watch over the brother and sister while they slept. The two woke up startled, but they saw it was only the possum.

"You can sleep, for I am holding something against my belly. If they come, we shall see what happens," said the possum.

After some time had passed, the possum woke them. "Now at the men's house they are getting everything ready." Over there the men were indeed preparing for the fight: they talked excitedly while they readied their bows, arrows, shields, and spears.

The elder sister spoke to her siblings: "I was married to this man when they were not yet fighting; I do not have pig or shells to give you, and I did not ask you to come. Why then did you come?" she asked miserably. Then the brother replied, "My sister spread bad talk about me, and all the men were angry, so I decided to leave. She followed."

The three sat there together. Then the married woman announced, "If they come to kill you, they will come to kill me as well." Now the possum spoke: "They have gotten their spears and bows and arrows, and they are coming. Let's go."

The older sister got up and embraced her sister and her brother, and the three of them wept. "Where will you go and what will you do?" asked the elder sister.

"We do not know," said the younger. "We'll listen to the possum; it will tell us which way to go. Let's just say goodbye."

"If you see your brother-in-law, shake hands with him and go quickly," said the other woman, but the possum said they could not wait. They did not leave through the door; they crept through a hole in the wall that the possum had made during the night.

"Don't go too slowly or they will catch up with you and kill you," the elder sister called out.

The possum led the two to the coconut tree and carried them up, first its "mother" and then its "father." From the tree top they could see their elder sister sitting and weeping outside her house. Then the possum said, "I think this coconut tree should be taller, very tall," for it was a small tree, really, not very high. The tree lengthened. From this new height, the possum pointed out the men outside their men's house; they had taken up their spears, shields, and bows and arrows, and they were waiting for the morning light to grow. Then the possum spoke again to the coconut tree: it wished for it to grow even taller. And the tree grew higher and higher. "Go up," the possum had said, and the tree did. Then the possum said, "No, that's too much, go down a little," and the tree top came down a little.

Now it was fully dawn, and they looked down at the elder sister's house. The possum pointed out how the men were now surrounding the house. They were chopping it down, throwing half to one side, half to the other. They took the whole house apart, looking for the brother and sister. But though they looked long and hard, they could not find them. The men could not figure out how this happened, since the husband had secured the door from the outside some time before.

The possum told the coconut tree to grow up, and it grew up, up, up into the clouds. They looked down and saw the men far below. Then the possum pointed out its mother and father's village, far away in the distance. The possum told the tree to bend in the middle and to rest its top in that village. So the tree began to lean in that direction. It bent down and down until its topmost branches nearly touched the earth outside the brother and sister's house. The possum said to the tree, "Leave off one of your branches," and the branch broke and touched the house.

The villagers there exclaimed, "Look! Something's there at that house!"

"Yes," cried another, "it's a coconut tree!"

"Those two went to our enemy's village," said a third. "Have they been killed and come back, or what? How did this happen?"

But the brother and sister said, "Wait, we will tell you." The possum told the coconut branch, "Go back to your tree!" and the branch went and joined the trunk. Then the possum said, "Straighten!" and the tree stood as it was before, in the enemy village. It had disappeared from sight.

Then the brother and sister told their story. Having told it all, they asked the possum, "Since you saved us from our enemies, what do you want as a reward? Will you take pearl shells, will you take salt?" But the possum did not reply.

11i   That same morning the brother took his axe, spear, and netbag and went to the forest, telling his sister to look after their possum. In the forest he saw another *sawari* possum and shot it. He returned to the village, cooked it in an earth oven, and offered the meat to his sister and to the possum. But the possum would not take any; it did not eat—it was angry and wept.

11ii   Then the possum told the brother, "I can stay with you no longer. I helped you, and then you went and shot one of my clan, my brother! During the day, therefore, you will not see my face, only at night. I shall go deep into the forest, and while the sun is up you will not be able to see me. I will walk around only at night, when you are not in the forest."

That is all. Here we eat *sawari* possums, but some people living far away from us do not; they have put a taboo on them.

Tale 17: The Siblings and the Wildman I

0   Once there were a brother and a sister who lived by themselves. There were no other people about, since a wildman (*alomogiali*) had killed them all.

2ii   One day the brother decided to visit a pig kill in another village. Having told his sister to stay in the house he departed. So the girl waited at home while her brother walked to a village in the north. One night, while he was away, a wildman came up to the siblings' house, sat down inside, and said to the girl, "Roll me a smoke!"

She was frightened, so she rolled up one cigarette and then another. Each time the wildman threw it down his throat and swallowed it.

2iii   When he had finished he said, "The sun is about to rise, and I must go. You will come with me!"

So the woman went to put on her good skirt while the wildman waited, sitting where the brother used to sleep. After she changed into her good skirt, the sister took a cooking bamboo and filled it with ashes from the hearth. Then she followed the wildman along the path, all the while leaving a trail of ashes.

Presently the two of them came up to a place where a bird was perching. The bird called, "Pull up that *kope* plant there!"

After the wildman uprooted the *kope* plant, the two descended into a hole in the ground which opened up underneath them. After passing through some gardens, they soon came to a house. This was where the wildman lived with his several daughters. The two stayed there, and eventually the girl became pregnant.

2iv   After attending the pig kill in the northern village, the brother returned home carrying much pork. When he arrived he saw how the house had been eaten by beetles and how weeds had grown up in the yard around it. He wondered, "Ah, what's become of that girl!" He walked around looking for footprints.

"Aha! There're ashes spilled over there!" he noticed. So he put down his pork and followed them a little way. Seeing that they would lead him a long way, he planted a stick in the earth to mark the spot and returned home to sleep.

The next morning he put his pork in a netbag, put in some native salt as well, and followed the footprints. Soon he came to a high cliff.

"What's this!" he exclaimed. But when he approached he heard a bird cry, "Pull up the *kope* plant there!" So he pulled it up and followed the pathway leading down into the earth. It was not long before he came to gardens and a house. Hearing someone talking, he retreated to a bushy spot in a garden area. There he sat down, looked around, and saw his sister nearby mounding the soil for sweet potatoes.

She had put her newborn son on the ground close to where she was working. After a while she picked up the baby and put him in the shade quite close to the brother, of whose presence she was unaware. When she had left, the brother came and pinched the child in the belly, and it cried. Then the woman saw her brother. She wept, and then she asked why he had come to this place.

The two went back to the wildman's house, though the brother did not enter. Seeing that her husband was out, the sister asked one of the wildman's daughters where he was. The girl said she did not know, but he had probably gone off to kill and eat men somewhere. Then the sister said she would cook some food, and she asked the daughters to fetch some banana leaves to wrap it in. All refused to go except the youngest.

The brother meanwhile had gone to hide in the stand of banana trees outside the house. When this youngest daughter came up to cut the leaves, he grabbed her by the wrist. She was frightened, for she had never seen him before, and she ran back to the house crying.

"Why didn't you bring the leaves?" the sister asked. Weeping, the girl replied that she had seen a strange man in the trees and that she wanted to marry him.

3Ai   The brother entered the house, and soon afterward the wildman returned.

"Oh, I want to kill that man!" the wildman announced.

3Aii   But his daughter protested, "No, I want to go with him!"

"All right," said the wildman, "since that girl wants to go to your house, she will be your wife; and I won't kill you." Then he added, "Since I brought your sister here for nothing, I will give you payment." So he gave his daughter bamboo containers full of pig-water and of shell-water—when poured from the bamboo this water would turn into pigs or pearl shells.

10Bi   "Now I've given payment for your sister," he told the brother, as his daughter loaded the bamboos of pig-water and shell-water into her netbag. Then it was the brother's turn to speak. "Let's go and get some things. Come." So the brother, the wildman, and the wildman's daughter went to the brother's house on top of the ground. There the wildman took back some of the pig-water and some of the shell-water and returned to his underworld home.

10Bii   Later the daughter took the remaining pig-water and shell-water and poured it on the floor of a new house that her husband had made for her. Suddenly there were many pigs and shells everywhere. The woman warned her husband, "You must not come inside this house. Even when I am in the garden, you shall have to stay outside. You'll need nothing here. All you need to do is get firewood. Otherwise, stay inside your own house."

10Biii   But one day the youth grew tired of sitting down in his house, tired of weaving arm bands. So he went and looked inside his wife's house, and he saw all the pigs and shells. "Hey, what a lot!" he thought. Then he carefully closed up the doorway and returned to his house.

But when his wife came back from the garden, she saw this, for the door posts had visibly been moved. "Aha! someone has opened the door," she thought.

She questioned her husband: "Why did you open the door?" All he answered was, "I was hungry." The wife decided to excuse him this time.

10Bii   "Now that you have seen everything, you must not open it again. I don't want to see you doing this again," she reprimanded.

10Biii   But once more her husband opened the door to look at all the pigs and shells.

10Biv,11i The woman found out. "What's this!" she exclaimed. "Now I will leave you and stay with my father." She left, taking with her all the shell-water and the pig-water and leaving only a few shells and pigs behind.

11ii   That is why men, we who live on top of the ground, have pigs and shells, but only a few. She left a few small pigs behind when she carried hers away. Some of the pigs live in the villages, and the others in the forest.

Tale 18: The Siblings and the Wildman II

0,2ii A brother and sister lived by themselves. They had a good house and good gardens, and they looked after a big pig named Puriminalasa. One day the brother announced he was going to a southern village to carry back some tree oil. So he put on his ornaments and left. Meanwhile this sister stayed with Puriminalasa and worked in the gardens.

2iii   One day she heard a noise, *duuii!* coming from various directions in turn. She was frightened. Soon she saw an old man approaching, a person with long hair and long, tusk-like teeth. He was a wildman (*kiliapu*), and the noise she had heard came from the stick he carried. He walked heavily, being a very big man.

"Why are you afraid?" he asked. "I have come because of you." Fretting, the sister went to fetch food from her gardens, for the old man had told her, "Tomorrow I'll take you to my place." The woman wept.

Early the next morning she took her walking stick and put dark *ulupapu* colouring on the base, so that she could leave marks in the earth as she walked. The two departed, slept the night in the forest, and arrived the following day.

This wildman's habit was to hunt cassowaries and wild pigs every day and carry them back with great pieces of dry *walu* firewood. The wildman and the sister, along with a daughter the wildman had, lived together and made gardens.

2iv   When the brother returned from the south, he found his house deserted with grass growing tall around it. He sat down and pondered. "Did someone kill her or carry her off?" he wondered. But then, looking down on the ground, he saw the marks that his sister had made with her walking stick and, having followed them a little way, decided to pursue her the next morning. He returned home, dug some sweet potatoes from the garden, ate, and slept.

The next morning he harvested some yams, taro, and sweet potatoes, planning to kill and cook the pig, Puriminalasa. But Puriminalasa said, "You don't have to kill me; just put a stake in the ground and I'll die. And you don't have to butcher me; just indicate cuts with a stick and I'll break apart." So the brother put a stake in the ground and Puriminalasa died. Then he singed its bristles off. Next he indicated the cuts he wanted with a stick, and the pig fell apart in those pieces. Some of the food he ate, and the rest he put away for his sister. He stuffed the pork along with his pearl shells into a netbag.

Then, shouldering his bag, he set off following the marks his sister had left. It was during the morning of the next day, when he was sitting beside the path eating, that he heard a whistling noise and saw two beautiful young women. One he recognized as his sister, and the other was the old wildman's daughter. The brother exclaimed, "I have come!" and the two women embraced him.

"*Na bani!* My brother!" said the one.

"*Na ani!* My husband!" said the other.

The three of them went to the wildman's house. The pork that the brother had brought for himself he gave to the old man's daughter to carry, while the pork he had brought for his sister he himself carried. The daughter carried his pearl shells as well, for he had put them in the same bag with his pork.

3Ai When they were approaching the house, the two women warned the brother about the old man: "If he brings a cassowary to the house, cook it immediately; if he brings firewood, you must split it quickly. When you sleep, get a couple of Job's-tears seeds and put them over your eyelids. That way, he'll think you are awake and won't try to kill you. And always hold onto your axe, even while you sleep or when you take food from the oven."

The brother hid in a woman's house nearby. Presently he heard a loud noise coming from the forest, but he was not afraid. The wildman approached and quickly smelled the presence of the stranger. "Something has come to sit outside my house!" he exclaimed.

3Aii The brother stepped out of the house. Immediately the two women came to stand on either side. "*Na ani!*" "*Na bani!*" they cried out.

"He can stay, then," the old man said, "but not in this woman's house. He shall stay with me in the big house."

He gave his pork to the wildman, who ate it all. Then the wildman said, "I have some cassowaries I've killed. Go split some firewood!" The brother did this quickly. Then the wildman told the youth to cook the cassowary, which he began to do by heating the cooking stones over a hot fire.

Suddenly the old man grasped the brother and threw him onto the fire, intending to cook him. But the brother jumped out and threw the wildman on the fire in the same way. Then the old man leapt out and again tried to cook the brother. Again and again they did this. Finally the old man stopped.

"Now you are both my brother-in-law and my son-in-law (*na pase suba kene*)," he said.

The next day the two men went to the forest with their bows and arrows. They came across a cassowary, and the youth shot it. "Son-in-law, you didn't do that. I killed it!" said the old man.

The youth carried the cassowary under one arm, and they walked on. After a while they came across a wild pig, and again the youth shot it dead. This one the old man carried. "Get some cooking leaves," the old man ordered, and the youth did so. They carried back some dry *walu* firewood with which to cook the cassowary and wild pig. Then they ate and, later, slept.

They did this kind of thing often.

3Ai   But the brother did not really sleep, for he was afraid of being killed. Repeatedly the old man would get up in the night intending to kill the youth. But, mistaking the white Job's-tears seeds for the whites of the youth's eyes, he would assume that the youth was awake. "Ah, son-in-law, you never sleep!" he would say.

3Aii   One day the youth's wife had a plan. "You and my father shall go to the garden surrounded by the stone fence, the one where there are plantains growing. Take this stone scraper along, and throw it into the deep well there. Then tell your father-in-law that a wild pig made the noise."

Later that day the brother and the wildman went to that garden deep in the forest. Plantains grew there, along with many varieties of greens. The old man said to the youth, "This good garden is mine. Go and cut some greens and plantains." But the youth, following his wife's instructions, complained that he was still tired from the last night's hunt. When he was not being watched, he threw the stone into the well, and then he called out that a wild pig or cassowary was there. When the old man went down into the hole, a flood of water welled up and engulfed him.

11i-ii   The youth hurried away back to the house. There he broke an arrow into three sections. He thrust one into his wife's anus, one into his sister's, and one into his own. The three of them flew away as *puluma* pigeons.

Tale 19: The Escape from the Otherworld

0   There were a brother and a sister, Kawaro and Yokane, whose story I shall now tell. They lived with their old mother and looked after their pig, Puramenalasu.

One day the sister was working in the gardens when a little gecko lizard came to her and said, "*Na koda abi!* My singing is now!" She told her brother about it, and he went to the forest at Walu to gather vines for making armbands and bark for a belt. He made a

Plate 2. A young man with his improvised headdress.

belt and armbands for both of them. Then he brought out his stone
axe, some tree oil, and some red body paint. The two of them
decorated themselves and practised *koda* dancing. That done, they
set out for the dance place at Tibi. Others had already gathered there
when, at about noon, Kawaro and his sister arrived.

The two of them danced on the first row, and many looked
approvingly at them. Since Yokane, though a woman, was wearing
male ornaments, the people there thought that they were two

brothers. These onlookers were pleased with the pair's appearance, and the young women there tied pieces of string around their wrists, saying, "He's mine! He's mine, that boy!"

2ii   As the dancing continued, all the young women tried to join that pair. All sought a place right next to the two dancers, so they could hold their axe handles. They argued among themselves. Around four o'clock, when the sun was getting low, Kawaro decided to join some *tome* courtship singing with the girls near Pawabi. He told his sister to go back home, where their mother would be cooking some food for them. Then he left.

2iii   Yokane was about to leave for home when an old man came onto the dance-ground and carried her off.

2iv   When Kawaro reached home much later he did not see his sister. "Mother," he asked, "where's my sister?" "I don't know," she replied. The young man began to worry; he felt an ache in his forehead. His mother asked him what had happened, but he said he did not know. To find out, he returned to Tibi and asked the people there if they had seen his sister. They replied that they had seen an old man lead her away. Kawaro returned and informed his mother. "We must do something," he said. So he killed their pig, Puramenalasu, cut some *gusede* plantains and some taro, and cooked these with the pig. Then he fetched a good-sized block of salt, broke it apart, and put the pieces into his netbag. Having done all this, he set off along the path the old man had taken.

When he came to Laboko, he met an old woman. He gave her some pork and salt, and she gave him a bundle in return. In Koia he met another old woman, who told him, "Your sister has gone on further." The two made the same exchange. Down in Tepe an old man gave him two bundles in return for salt and pork, just as the old women in Laboko and Koia had done.

From the heights of Tepe he looked down and saw a wide body of water called Dika Kumi. The water there was as wide as the distance between Sumale (Mount Murray) and Ialibu. Kawaro walked to its edge. There he met an old woman who taught him some spells and gave him bundles, while he in turn gave her salt and pork. She told him, "Climb to the top of that tall *yawi* palm and say 'Era yawi pata pata' (Erave *yawi,* lie down, lie down). That's how the old man crossed over."

Kawaro did so. And after he had uttered this spell he saw another palm tree, standing on the far side of the water, bend to meet his and form a bridge. By this means he was able to cross to the other side and continue his journey.

On he went. Presently he saw in the distance a good place where many casuarinas and bamboos were growing. It was a reddish place; the bananas, casuarinas, and bamboos all had that reddish tint. Even the grasses, the house itself, the pitpit, yams, all these were reddish, too.

Kawaro was about to draw closer when someone, a man standing on a low hill close by, called out to him: "Many men such as yourself have I seen come this way, but none have I seen come back!" Kawaro paused to tell him why he had come. "If you want to find your sister," said the other, "she's down there, where you see the smoke rising." Then he gave Kawaro two large dark bundles and some spells, in return for some salt and pork. Having listened to the spells, Kawaro went on.

He approached the house and saw his sister sitting in the porch. She was surprised: "What are you up to? Why have you come, brother? This is surely a bad place, and it's a bad man who lives here." But she held him closely and wept. He in turn took out the cooked pig's stomach and gave half to his sister, along with salt, taro, and bananas.

Then the woman said, "Listen, you must not sit out here. You and I must hollow out a place to hide in the houseposts. My husband will be coming back!" So the two made a hollow in the centre post and then in the rafters as well. Then the woman told her brother to crawl into the hole and go to the furthest rafter if necessary. "When my husband comes, I'll sit with my back against this post; I'll be able to slip you food behind my back. I will not eat the pork you have brought for me; my husband will devour it all!"

Kawaro agreed, but first he opened up the big black bundle that the man up on the hill had just given him. Inside was a tree-fern stalk that had been fashioned into the likeness of a man, with a face, hair, legs and arms. Kawaru took it and put it in the corner of the house where the sweet potatoes were stored. Then he took off his ornaments and put them on this wooden figure. When that was done, his sister told him he must now hide inside the post. She put him inside and then draped bark cloth over her head and back, concealing what was behind her.

Soon they heard a great *guuuu* noise and felt heat. "Brother, my husband is coming now," the sister said. "Before, I asked you why you had come, and now you'll see why!" Kawaro sat, afraid.

3Ai "Oh, good odours, good odours here!" said the old man as he approached. He walked into the porch, carrying a load of human limbs, men's arms and legs—he had already eaten the rest of the bodies—which he dropped there. Then he questioned the girl, "Yokane! Who has come? There's a new smell!" And, having said that, he began to bite and tear apart all the timbers of the house. Kawaro looked on.

Yokane wept, for she was much afraid. The old man said, "Hey, you cry too much. Have you seen all this pork I have brought?" "Yes," replied the young woman, "but I am weeping because of the way you are tearing the house apart and because I fear that you'll kill me too."

3Aii   "But before you did not weep like this. I wonder why," said the old one, and he approached her, opening wide his jaws. But then Yokane took a large piece of pork and some salt and threw them into his open mouth. He crunched it and said, "Oh, it's very good! But where did you get this pork?" She replied that her brother had come and that he had brought it.

"I will not kill him; he can sleep here," said he. He then ate more of the pork and then some of the flesh from the human limbs he had brought.

When he had finished, the old man went to sleep in the back of the house. The sister's place to sleep was in the front, and across from her Kawaro and Yokane put down a mat. On top of this they lay the tree-fern stalk. Then Kawaro climbed into the hollow post and lay in one of the rafters underneath the eaves. He took with him the bundles he had been given, stowing them in the corners of the house.

3Ai   Meanwhile the old man was sleeping soundly. But in the middle of the night he awoke. He had digested the meat he had eaten earlier, and he felt hungry for more. So he rose quietly and bit into the sleeping figure, thinking it was Kawaro.

3Aii   "But this is not flesh!" he thought. "It's more like a piece of wood!" Suspecting he had been deceived, he searched through the walls, the sitting log, the posts, the rafters; but all this time Kawaro was hidden in the corner. When it was five o'clock, not yet dawn, Kawaro opened one of the bundles and a *kiliwapili* bird flew out; he opened another and a *nole* cicada came out and signaled dawn by crying *kepea! kepea!* He opened another bundle and an *aluba* bird flew out, crying *gai!* In another was a *bolota* bird, which cried *roloroloro!* Believing it now to be daybreak, the old man thought, "Ah, soon men will be awake and about." So he stopped tearing apart the house and went off in search of men to eat.

Now Yokane called her brother, "He has gone now and will not be back soon. Come down!" Kawaro came out of the rafter and into the room. "Let's go now quickly," he said. "Get your things!" While Yokane prepared to go, he opened up a pair of other bundles, and they held two large dogs, named Kili and Wamili. He covered them up again.

Kawaro led the way, holding his sharp axe at the ready; his sister followed. When they reached the black palm on the hither side of the water, they climbed it with loops of vine. Then Kawaro repeated the spell, *"Era yawi pata pata,"* and the tree bent over to meet the other palm growing on the yonder shore. They crossed over and then standing on the far shore, he spoke the other spell, *"Era yawi kepea kepea,"* (Erave *yawi* spread apart). The two trees separated. Then Kawaro cut down the palm on that side.

3Ai They went on, but soon they heard the old man pursuing them, calling out, "Oh, why did I leave them! Why didn't I eat them sooner!" Kawaro heard this and worried. Opening a pair of bundles, he saw a pair of cassowaries with long sharp claws. He let them loose, for that old man had crossed the water and was gaining on them. The cassowaries attacked him, digging their claws into his side. "That's nothing; just biting insects!" said the old man, and he kept gaining on the siblings.

When the old man had chased them as far as Kola, after crossing Kema mountain, Kawaro released the two dogs, Kili and Wamili, which ran and snapped at the old man's testicles. Kawaro cried to the dogs "Kili Wamili attack and kill!" but still the old man felt no pain. Both dogs and cassowaries bit and clawed him without result, and the two siblings continued to flee.

3Aii,11i When they reached Tibi, Yokane said to Kawaro, "We must do something! Do you see this wild taro? The old one has dreamed on this. If you cut it he will die. Do so quickly with your axe!" The dogs and cassowaries had attacked the old man to no avail; but as soon as the youth cut the taro, that old man died from these very wounds, first breathing heavily and then expiring.

11ii Now, if that old man had lived on, his red-tinged house would still be there. But Yokane had heard him say, "I go and eat men, and I have dreamed of this large-leafed wild taro." So they killed him, and now this man no longer lives there. I am closing my story now. That woman and man stayed as bush fowl, the *pale* and *ealo* birds. The old man lives no longer. The cassowaries today live in the forest, and they attack men just as they did the old man. As for the dogs, they behave the way Kili and Wamili did; they snap at men, bark, and are generally of bad temper. Not only our own dogs but those of the Europeans bite men the way Kili and Wamili did.

CHAPTER 3

Of Jealous Spouses and Siblings

Tale 20: The Cannibal Wife

0,4i   Down in Batire lived Kapolu Yetu and his sister. Yetu had been looking for a wife, and he found one at Kilimi. He married a woman from there, one with reddish-coloured skin, and he brought her back to Batire. Eventually she gave birth to a son.

4ii   All this time Yetu kept his sister hidden in the gardens, so his wife would not know of her existence. The husband and wife stayed and worked together in their gardens; the sister lived apart.

One day the wife heard news that her clan was preparing to kill their pigs in Kilimi, her home, and she told this to her husband. He said in reply, "I will go there and help my brother-in-law. I'll leave right now. Prepare some food to take, and then come with the boy."

"Good, we'll come tomorrow," she answered, and Yetu left.

When he was in the middle of the forest, halfway between Batire and Kilimi, he shot an *aluba* bird, wrapped it up in leaves, put it in his netbag, and continued on. Upon arriving he learned that the people there were going to kill the pigs the following day. Now they were bringing their pigs into the village. Yetu met his father-in-law, who asked, "Haven't your wife and child come with you?" Yetu told him they were coming later.

4iii   Back at Yetu's home in Batire, his wife had discovered his sister. Until then, the wife never knew of the sister's existence, although the sister knew about the wife and about her garden, red like her skin. The sister was afraid of this place and avoided it carefully, hiding in the forest. If she went to dig sweet potatoes or cut sugar cane, she did so only when the wife was away, to avoid notice. But on the day when the wife was to leave for the pig kill with her son, she caught sight of the sister in the garden.

"Don't be afraid of me; I'm your brother's wife," she reassured her. "Your brother gives me the work of the garden and pigs, while you are one who hides in the forest. Why should *you* fear *me?*"

The wife urged the sister to come with her to her parents' place. So the two of them put on ornaments and walked through the forest toward Kilimi. When they reached the high point on the slopes of Mount Keresa, they looked down to the village.

There, on the dance ground, the village men were tethering men and women to stakes, intending to kill them along with their pigs.

3Bi   The wife led the sister down to her village. When Yetu's father-in-law saw his daughter and the woman with her, he exclaimed, "Ah, my daughter has brought a new pig! I'll kill it with the others." And he tied the woman by her ankle to a pig stake.

3Bii   But another of his daughters, his youngest said, "Oh father, you always kill pigs such as this. For once you must let me kill one. Father, let *me* kill it!" But her father refused. The girl pleaded, but the father would not hear of it.

Yetu, sitting in the porch of the men's house, was surprised to see his sister there. Now men were starting to club the men, women, and pigs they had tied to stakes. Again the youngest daughter asked, "Oh, father, give me the club. *I* want to kill this pig!" The father finally consented to give her the club, and he told her to kill the woman, Yetu's sister. After instructing the girl to strike her squarely, he left to singe the hair off a pig he had just killed.

There was so much smoke blowing about the ceremonial ground that no one could see very well. When this girl saw her father hard at work, she drew close to Yetu's sister, raised her club, and brought it down hard on her tether. The rope broke. Then she said, "Look, there's your brother at the men's house. He is already mourning for you. Go over quickly while they can't see through the smoke." The sister did so.

"How did you come here?" the brother asked her. "That youngest sister of your wife's told me to come here," she said. "But what do we do now?" Neither knew.

Then Yetu remembered the *aluba* bird he had killed. He unwrapped it and took some feathers from one wing. These he put along the back of his sister's arms; then he took some breast down and feathers from the back and put them on her. "Fly up to the top of this house," he told her. So she flew up through the open front of the house, up to the roof. Then the brother called to her again: "Now fly up to a branch of that casuarina tree," and she did that, too. She cried out like an *aluba* bird, *ki gai gai*. Then the brother plucked the bird's other wing, and attached feathers to his own body in the same way. He flew up to his sister, and both began to call out again like *aluba* birds. They flew back to their home in Batire.

"What'll we do now?" asked the sister again. "Your wife will return."

"Just wait, we will do something," Yetu said. So they waited for the wife's return.

4iv   Later the woman returned, carrying their son and a heavy load of pork. She reproached her husband: "Now why did you leave so early, and leave me to carry all this meat?" The two of them, Yetu and his wife, heated cooking stones and began to prepare the pork for the earth oven. While she was not looking, Yetu quickly dug a hole, and in the bottom he placed two sharp stakes. Then he covered it over and concealed it with plantain leaves.

"Let's cook the pork now," he called to his wife. "The oven's ready." When she came over with the pork, he told her to sit with her son on the plantain leaves. The two sat there, fell into the hole, were speared by the stakes, and died.

11i-ii   Then the brother called to his sister, "Come!" The two of them flew into the trees crying *ki gai go*. They were *aluba* birds. Today, when we try to kill these birds, they fly away quickly. They are wary because that woman tried to kill them and they had to flee.

Tale 21: The Jealous Sister

0   Pepana had two wives. One wife gave birth to a son named Karea and a daughter named Lano; the other bore a daughter, Kokonyu. Karea lived in Epei, on the far side of Yaro River, while the two young women lived at Kaluake, on this side. Karea used to go hunting in the forest, and he would always kill many possums, which he would leave for his two sisters at their house at Kaluake. He used to kill big *pasolo, koyamo,* and *rumana* possums.

4i*   One day the two sisters came back from the gardens and saw that only a little *kapea* possum had been left for them. "We won't eat that," remarked Kokonyu, for the *kapea* is a small, inferior possum. But Lano said, "Let's eat it anyway," and they did. On another occasion when they returned home, again there was just a small *kapea* possum. On a third occasion, the same thing happened. As for *pasolo, koyamo,* and *rumana* possums, they no longer found them.

One day Karea told the two that he was going to a ceremony in a southern village and that they were to stay home. He told them to watch the banana cutting he had just planted; when the new leaves were growing out, he would be on his way home.

*The implicit meaning of this paragraph is that the brother is keeping the better possums for his new wife. Hence the identification of this paragraph as function 4i (see appendix 2).

4iii   So the two sisters stayed. Lano now decided, "I must go over and
have a look at Karea's place. I want to know why he is giving us those
small *kapea* possums." Kokonyu tried to dissuade her: "No, don't
go." But Lano insisted: "Really, I'm going." And she went.

She crossed the vine bridge over the Yaro River. On the far side
she saw her brother had made a high fence topped with dry *kati*
leaves, the kind that rustle when someone moves them. But she
made an opening in the fence and went on to Epei. From there she
looked down to Yokapini. She saw abundant gardens with good
kayabo sugar cane planted in them. There too, she saw a young
woman with long tresses; she was working in a sweet potato garden.
Lano went over to the edge of the garden, hid, and watched the
young woman. Then she approached.

Scratching her head, Lano said, "Come here and pick lice from
my hair."

But the other replied, "It's nearly dark. I must dig some sweet
potatoes."

"No. Come here first and then go and dig them," insisted Lano,
and the other woman consented to search for lice in Lano's hair.
When she had finished, Lano said that now she would look for lice in
the other woman's hair. But as she sat behind her, Lano took out a
sharp *kipame,* a cassowary dagger, and thrust it into the woman's
ear. Then she returned to Kaluake.

Kokonyu said nothing at first; she did not even ask what her half-
sister had seen. But Lano told her anyway: their brother had taken
a wife, and that was why they had received inferior possums. The
large ones he was keeping for the wife. "And I killed her," she added.

Kokonyu asked her why she had done that. But Lano took of-
fence and did not reply.

The next time they looked at the banana planting, they saw that
the leaves were growing out. And it was not long before Karea
returned bearing legs and backs of pork. Some of this meat he left
with his two sisters before continuing on his way home. When he
reached Konoka he saw some footprints which he recognized as
Lano's, and after crossing the Yaro River bridge, he took note of the
broken fence. When he reached Yokapini, he found his wife. She
was barely alive and could only say, "Lano has done this to me,"
before dying.

Karea carried her body across the river, turned from the path
that led back to Kaluake, and walked through the forest at Ribupalu.
After climbing a low hill, he buried her where the ground was soft.
After smoothing the earth above her, he made some small holes like
those that rats make. Then he returned to Epei.

4iv   Later, on a sunny day, he made an unannounced visit to Kaluake.

"It's a good day," he said, "let's go up to Ribupalu to fetch some pandanus leaves and hunt rats."

Kokonyu, who guessed his intentions, said, "I don't want to go." But Lano said, "Yes, let's go." She had no thought about what she had done.

"Then the two of you go," agreed Kokonyu. "I will stay here."

With Karea in the lead, holding his bow and arrow, the brother and sister went in search of *repoto* rats. They ascended the low hill and came to the place where there were small holes in the earth, the ones that Karea had made. "Rat burrows," said Karea, and he asked Lano to dig. She began to do so, and down and down she dug. Presently she unearthed a human ankle. In horror she withdrew her hand, and just at that moment Karea shot her in the side with a bamboo-tipped arrow. Lano died. Karea covered her with earth and set off for Kaluake.

Now before leaving home, Lano had said to her sister, "He may kill me now. If you see a *kapea* possum approach you in the garden, you will know that he has killed me." So when Kokonyu saw one such possum come toward her, look at her for a long moment, and then retreat into the forest—when she saw this, she knew what had happened. Picking up her sharp digging stick, she killed herself with it.

Not long afterwards, Karea came to the garden and found her lying on the earth with the stick in her side. He buried her, too. Then he cut some dry firewood and carried it to the two sisters' house.

11i-ii   But those two women (i.e., their ghosts) came and waited for him, each on one side of the path, each with a big walking stick. As he passed by, they struck him down and killed him. Today women ghosts kill men just as these two women killed their brother.

Tale 22: The Sky Wife

0   A brother and sister lived together. One day, when the brother was walking through the forest, he came to a *kaipa* tree in fruit. Many birds had gathered to eat its red seeds, among them a *wiliedo* parrot. The youth shot the bird and left it in a garden hut he had made the day before.

4i   While he was doing this, some girls were coming down toward him. The youth heard them come through the forest, singing and laughing: "Aaa haa, aai oh." He took his bow and arrow and hid. Who could they be? he wondered. No one lived in those parts except for the two siblings, whose parents had died along with others.

Concealed by clumps of tree-fern, he peered at the girls. They were climbing up a vine rope which reached into the sky. But by the time he drew near them, they had all climbed up. The end of the rope dangled in front of him.

Looking up, he saw a good-looking girl. When, curious, she descended to look at him, he seized her hand. The other girls, higher up, saw him grab this one's hand, and they fled higher up the rope. The youth held to her.

"I want to go back, let go!" she cried out, and she struck him with brambles and thorny cane. But he did not let her go, and finally she let herself be led along the path. While they were going, he told her about the birds he had shot, ones that had the colour of red ochre. Talking of such things, he took her back to a forest garden. There he showed her the garden hut he had built of dry banana and sugarcane leaves. And he pointed out the birds he had left inside it.

10Ai   He left the girl there and went back to the other house.

4ii,10Aii   He lied to his sister: "I shot no birds," for she thought he had been out hunting all that time. Then, announcing he was going to visit a pig kill in another village, he told her not to go near the forest garden where he had built the hut. Reassured she would not, he departed.

When he reached the place where they were going to kill the pigs, he found the villagers were still constructing the *neada* longhouses. So he returned home, going directly to the garden hut and leaving the sister by herself. He stayed a week with his woman from the sky, and then he returned to where they were going to kill pigs. This time the villagers gave him a definite date for the ceremony, a few days hence. Returning home once more, he again went directly to the garden hut and his wife, without seeing his sister. He prepared his ornaments.

When he stopped by to see his sister on his way to the pig kill, she looked at his decorations and asked where he had found the red face paint. The brother did not tell her it was from a sky woman; he said instead that he had found some ochre in the garden, dried it above the fire, and mixed it with water. Then he said he was leaving to watch the pig killers distribute their pearl shells.

4iii,   The sister decided that while he was away she would investigate
10Aiii   the garden he had forbidden to her. So when her brother was well on his way, she went to the garden. There she saw some smoke rising from a garden hut. She approached, looked inside, and saw a woman with fine red ochre all over her body. The sister admired the paint and asked for some. Hearing the request, the woman gave the paint to the sister. Indeed, she gave all the paint she had on her body. The sister took it back to her house and rubbed it over her skin and skirt.

When her brother returned, the sister, not wanting to show herself, quickly put some sweet potatoes outside the door, telling the brother that they were for him. But the brother caught a glimpse of some ochre underneath her fingernails. He said nothing, but he suspected trouble and guessed that his sister had gotten the paint from his wife.

Hastening to the garden, he found the girl there. She was dying. He picked up his stone axe. "Do not die too quickly," he told her. "I must first kill my sister!"

4iv, 10Aiv   Standing outside the door of the siblings' house, he called to his sister inside, "I'm going once more to look at the pig kill. Come, we'll both go." When she stepped outside, he hit her with his axe and killed her.

Then he returned to his wife's hut, cut a sprig of the red cordyline bush and threw it to her, saying, "My sister is dead; now you too can die!"

11i-ii   Because the sister stole the ochre from that woman, others no longer come down from the sky.

Tale 23: The Sister, the Sky Wife, and the Snake

0,4i   After their father and mother had both died, a brother and sister lived alone. The two of them cultivated large gardens. Often they would work all day in the garden before returning home. One day the brother cut a shoot from a *koda* banana plant and planted it near the house. The following day, when he was alone in the garden, a heavy rain fell, accompanied by loud thunder. Afterwards the sun came out again, and it was then that the brother saw four young women come down from the sky.

The man went back to tell his sister, "Four young women are coming, and I shall marry the first." The other three he sent back. This woman's skin and hair were red, coloured by the paint made of red earth. She told him, "You cannot take me to your house if you want to marry me; I forbid it. You must build me a house near your garden."

The youth agreed to build her a house in the garden. He misled his sister: "I'm sending all four women back. Go back home and put some food on the fire. I'll join you there." So the sister went back and cooked. While she was doing so, the man built a house for his woman from the sky. That done, he split some firewood, lit a fire, and put down a mat for her. Then, returning to the house he shared with his sister, he announced, "The four women have gone." Later he told her never to go to that garden, the one where he had built the house.

Later the youth went to the garden house and said to the woman who had come from the sky, "They are killing pigs up north, and I intend to have a look."

"Good, I have much paint and many ornaments for you," she replied. The youth took these things and put them on.

10Ai   Then he went back to his sister.

4ii,10Aii   When she saw him, she asked where he had gotten the paint. He replied, "Some time ago, when I was working in the garden, I found some red earth. I put it in the house, and just now I mixed it with water to make paint. But now I am going to visit a pig kill. When the leaf of this *koda* banana points in that direction I am going still, if it points in this direction I am returning. And I forbid you to go to the new garden; if you go there you shall surely sicken or die." Having said that, he departed.

4iii,10Aiii Nevertheless, the sister went to the garden, hid, and looked. She saw a house and, inside it, the glow of a fire. Approaching, she caught sight of the red-skinned woman. "Who are you?" she asked.

"Oh, I am your brother's wife!" replied the other woman.

The sister admired the woman's red paint and asked her if she could have some. The wife agreed to give her some.

Then the sister rose, went out to the garden, and began to clear away some brush in search for rats. She killed a couple of rats and gathered some crickets. Then, when she was pulling up a clump of sword grass, she saw a large snake underneath. Frightened, she covered it up and ran off, calling out to her brother's wife that she was going home. But that woman had died; her husband had left her, and she had lost her paint.

Hurrying home, the sister sensed that she was being followed. She turned around and saw it was the snake, a large python. "Where are you going?" she asked.

"You broke my house apart. Now I'll go sleep in your house," the snake replied.

After arriving home, the woman built up the fire while the snake moved to a corner. She began to cook the rats and crickets she had gathered. Seeing her do this, the snake said, "Don't cook the food like that; you must give it to me raw." But the sister disagreed: "No, wait and we will eat it cooked."

When the food was done the woman tried to eat a bit of it when the snake was not looking. But the snake saw her and said, "Hey! Are you eating?"

"No," replied the other, "I am just chewing a bit of sweet potato which lodged between my teeth this morning."

"You are lying," said the snake.

The woman divided the food between the two of them. Then she said, "Someone is outside, go and look." While the snake was outside, she took a few crickets from the pile and ate them. Just then the snake returned and said, "You've eaten something! Open your mouth and show me!"

4iv,10Aiv   When the woman did so, the snake put its head into her mouth and went down to the woman's stomach. The whole snake disappeared into her stomach.

Her stomach was so swollen she could not stand up. "Now who will give me firewood and food?" she wondered. Then she told one of her pigs: "Listen, my brother is gone and I am sick. I have neither food nor firewood." So the pig went and fetched some firewood, split it, stacked it, and made a fire. The woman said, "That is good, but something is missing."

"What?" asked the pig. "Tell me." "Water," she replied, pointing to her bamboo container. So the pig took the bamboo, filled it, and brought it to her. "But I cannot lift it to pour," she complained. So the pig stood back and tipped the bamboo into the woman's mouth. Then the pig left.

Through a crack in the wall, the woman looked at the banana leaf. It showed that her brother was coming back. And indeed he soon arrived carrying a load of pork. When he reached the house, he noticed how tall the grass had grown around it. Inside he saw his sister with her big stomach. He asked what had happened and she told him. He went immediately to the garden hut where he had left his wife. It, too, was surrounded by tall grass. There he saw his wife, dead. He returned, intending to kill his sister; but, feeling sorry for her, he did not.

Then he began to cook some pig fat. The snake smelled it and stuck its head out of the woman's mouth. Gradually the brother enticed the snake out, using the piece of pork, retreating slowly into a corner as the snake came further and further out. Finally the tail of the snake whipped out. It struck the woman in the head, killing her.

The youth then picked up his axe and began to sharpen the blade on a stone. The snake said, "If you're going to give me pork, give it quickly!"

"Just wait," replied the man, giving it a small piece. While the snake ate, the brother took a thick stick and put it between them. The snake asked, "Why did you do that?"

The man replied, "I want to make a bamboo knife to cut the pork. It's to cut on." To prove it, he fashioned a bamboo knife while the snake looked at him with its wide-open eyes.

11i   Then finally the brother held out a larger portion of pork. As the snake slid its head over the stick to take the meat, the man brought his axe down hard, chopping off the snake's head. Severed in two, the snake writhed around and broke the house apart. The youth cut it again and again, and finally it died.

11ii   Then he distributed the pieces of python. Some he gave to

Sumale (Mount Murray), some to Kilua (Mount Giluwe), some to
Yalipu (Mount Ialibu), and some to a mountain near Magarima
whose name I have forgotten. Only the head and the tail remained in
the siblings' house. These became the small snakes we see near the
settlement. The big snakes, the pythons that live on the tops of
mountains, are the ones that the brother threw there.

Tale 24: Abuwapale and the Broken Promise

0   I shall tell a tale about getting pearl shells. In Kilimi many Kuri men
were making *neada* longhouses in preparation for killing pigs. They
made several: a long one reaching from Lemako Stream to Mupalu
Stream, another in Takera, a third in Kiraperana, and others elsewhere. A poor-man, a man without shells and pigs, lived in Kilimi.
He did not tend pigs; he just stayed there. He slept in the long men's
house at Kaluake, and often he found himself sitting at a cold hearth.
When leaving or returning to the house, he would skirt the ceremonial ground, thus keeping a distance from the important men
who were preparing for their pig kill. All the other Kuri clansmen
were constructing *neada;* he alone was not.

One day as he lay in the men's house, he reflected, "I do not have
brothers to give me piglets to care for, so how can I help them kill
their pigs?" He pondered this, sitting there, thinking short thoughts
and long ones too. Then he decided to go to the forest; he carried
with him a little dry wood to start a fire, a fire-starting stick, a bamboo pipe with some tobacco, and his bow and bird arrows. While the
others were busy at work on the ceremonial ground, he went to his
small garden and cut a stalk of *lobanya* sugar cane and dug up a few
small sweet potatoes. Then he followed the path through to Ko-
mapu, Mukatupi, Kogare, Pakorewala and Keresawala, either shooting game or climbing after them.

5i   In the afternoon he stopped and put his netbag of sweet potatoes
down beside him, and he looked over to one side where a tall *karape*
beech tree grew. Its base was clear of undergrowth, and on the earth
he could see freshly cut new leaf buds which looked as though they
had been sliced off with a knife or razor. "How did that happen?" he
wondered. He decided to spend the night there at the base of the
tree. This *karape* tree was a very tall one, growing among many other
smaller *karape* trees; yet only at the base of the tall one had he seen
the new shoots and leaves.

So he made a small house there, using stout vines such as *ra'alipu*
and *porapu* to lash it together. He put in the posts, cut black-palm

bark for the roof, and gathered some scented leaves of the *kapipi* tree-fern for the walls. When he finished his house, it looked more like grasses and forest than a house, and it had a good odour.

Feeling sleepy, he lay down. Soon he heard the sound of women laughing. It was coming from the top of the tree. He looked up, and although it was now dusk, he could see them. They were laughing, picking the new leafs, and dropping a few of them to the ground. From the top of the tree a very long root of a *kaipa* plant dangled down, and using this as a rope, the young women were descending, laughing all the while.

Seeing this, the poor-man stealthily approached the base of the tree and watched them. The last one to come down was a good-looking young woman. The poor-man caught her and bound her wrists with some of the vines he had taken. The other women quickly disappeared. The one he held now brought the man mist, rain, and wind, and she made him feel as if sky and earth were turning over. But the poor-man held her fast. She gave him brambles and thorny cane to hold, but still he held her fast.

He looked at her; she was indeed attractive. She told him then that he had indeed been strong to hold her so, and that if he wanted her to follow him, he must turn off the main paths and go through the forest. "And you must make me a house of *karape* wood, and of stout *ra'alipu* and *porapu* vines," she said.

10Bi   Following her instructions, the poor-man led her through the forest, leaving Mt. Keresa and descending through Takera and then to Kepelea, where the Kuri clan originated. Here there were many grasses, bananas, casuarinas and pines growing in a fine, shady spot. There in the forest he built a house using wild pandanus leaves for thatch, not the usual kunai grass. Then he put *kapipi* tree-fern leaves around the sides for walls. This was not a house he would sleep in, but when it was time to eat, he would come quietly and bring her food.

5ii   "Now that you have been strong enough to hold me, you must listen well to what I say. First, why did you bring me here?" the woman asked him. He answered, "I am a poor-man. All the others have pigs, but I do not."

Then the woman replied, "That can be changed, but on one condition. We will not sleep together in this house. I am not your wife, to bear sons and daughters for you. If you follow my directions, you will find the things you are looking for." "Good," he replied.

At Kaluake all the men were building *neada* longhouses for the pig kill, but at Takera there were a few men who were not. He went there and then on to Kiraperana. There he sat down and looked back to Kepelea, the place where he had left that young woman in her house. During the night he saw the sky glow with lightning. "Aha!" he thought. "What's this? I haven't seen that before."

After staying away for six weeks, the poor-man decided to go back to Kepelea. He came to the hut he had made, and he untied the vines he had used to secure the door. Inside he saw many pearl shells lying about, and the young woman was sitting in their midst. He contemplated this sight happily.

Then she said, "You must go now and build a section of the long-house on some unused space in the ceremonial ground. Make a long one, as if you were going to kill very many pigs." And then she added, "Carry these netbags full of shells and hang them from one end of your *neada* to the other." Onto these fine "bone" pearl shells *(rekere kuli)* she had daubed good paint and tied handsome bands.

"But what shall I do without pig quarters and sides to give?" the poor-man asked. "I cannot just kill shells the way pigs are to be killed." But the woman replied, "Just go and do as I have said."

As happens in tales, things moved quickly. He went back to Takera, found space for his *neada,* and built a very long one. Other men muttered, "That man has nothing, and now he intends to kill many pigs. What a business!" Thus they insulted him. They told him, "You're no Pulaparia Koma (i.e., you are not a wealthy man)!" But he went on working, and when his *neada* was completed, he laid in firewood, stones, and other things for cooking.

This done, the poor-man announced to the others, "Now that you have displayed your shells at Mupalu Stream, I'll do the same at Lemako Stream. We'll make a boundary between us, at Kiraperana." So he made a platform across Lemako Stream and put his shells there in rows. Now everyone saw his wealth. The other men there were not without shells, but they did not have as many. Some of his shells he used to buy the other men's biggest pigs. He gave one netbag of shells to one man, a second netbag to another, and so on. He gave shells to men at Popalu, Kilimi, Kaluake, Kiraperana, and other places.

When he had given out all the shells, the woman told him, "Now, you must go and put in the pig stakes." So he did this. And he made a line of them from Kiraperana to Lemako Stream, and to each stake he tied a pig.

5ii,10Bii   One day the woman said to him, "It would not be wise if the others knew of my existence and of how I, Abuwapale, have been the source of your wealth. Of these shells that you have received from me, some you must share with your brothers. Give to all, and leave no one out, not even a pig or a dog. Give them pigs, too. They may have some, but give them more." He did so. And then he asked her, "But what about cleaning the pig entrails? That's women's work. Who will do it for me?" "That's yours to do," she replied.

The other Kuri men wondered where he had found so many shells; he had been such a poor-man not long before, and now he was giving shells to everyone, old people and young children included—maybe some two thousand people.

5iii,10Biii But he did not give to one person, a little-man named Baki, because this person used to say to him, "Oh, I have nothing and cannot help you." Now he in turn wanted to say the same thing to Baki. "To this one person, Baki, I shall give nothing!" he told the others when he gave them their pigs and shells. He had become a big-man indeed.

They killed their pigs and shared out the pork. When they finished, they went to give an *aliyari* war compensation to the men of Bakili clan. They took some two hundred netbags of shells. Many held the "bone" pearl shells that this poor-man had given his Kuri brothers. When others asked where he had gotten these fine valuables, he gave no reply.

10Biv Baki, the only one who had not received any, pondered this. One day the Kuri people went down to Karada to attend a singing. Karada's own pig kill was drawing near, so those men wanted to distribute pieces of sugar cane to their Kuri guests. Now this man, who had received all the wealth from Abuwapale, did not leave for Karada immediately. Instead he went out to the forest and cut some strong vines and timbers. With these he secured the door of Abuwapale's house. Having done that, he made pointed stakes of bamboo and put them on the path near the house. Only then did he join the others.

But Baki had watched his departure, and he began to wonder if there was not someone else. So after setting off with the others to Karada, he slipped away, turned back, and went up to Kepelea. He found the house, broke all the stakes, and threw them aside. Then he took his axe and chopped the door apart. He found the woman within.

"Are you Abuwapale?" he asked her. "Your man shared out shells to all the others, but to me he gave none, and so I have come here to ask you for some. Your man is now rich from your help."

The woman replied, "I get the shells. He became wealthy because I gave them to him. If you want some, too, I'll give you some." So she gave him two large netbags full of shells. Baki put them to one side. Then he raised his stone axe and struck her on the head.

This woman who gave forth shells was the daughter of Kunala Yekili. After Baki killed her, he went away.

When the other man returned, he soon saw what had happened.

First he saw the protective stakes scattered about, then the door broken in, and lastly the woman lying there with eyes already growing dim. She looked at him with reproach. In grief, he tore his ear lobes and sliced his fingers.

Then she spoke her last words (her *kadipi*): "You were told to give shells to everyone, to every man and every woman and child; but you did not give any to this one man, so he came to kill me. Now I am about to die. Once before, you were a poor-man, and I helped you; you became a man of wealth. Now I shall die. You must not put my body close to here. Make my burial platform near the base of the black palm there, where you first saw me. Cut timbers of the *kole* tree and make a fence around it. I will not return to give you shells or pigs. Now, take me to this place in Asada and leave me there. What has happened was your doing."

5iv He did what she had said, and then he returned and killed Baki. All the Kuri men, to whom he told everything, agreed that he should do this.

11i Baki had killed the daughter of Kunala Yekili, the woman who gave out pearl shells and pigs. "Kill him and throw him into a well," they said.

11ii If Baki had not killed this woman, we would have many shells, for these shells came from her, but the other poor-man overlooked Baki, and Baki took his revenge. Now we have only a few shells, and they come from far way.

Tale 25: Giminyawe and the Jealous Brother

0 A man lived with his two sons, Pulapiapa and Mele. He was intending to find a wife for the younger, Pulapiapa, but this one did not want to marry any of the women there. Rather, he would sit on top of a hill at Yapalapia, scraping vines and working them into armbands while enjoying the surrounding view.

5i One day while he was doing this, he looked down toward Kuare and saw glows of lightning. He came to a decision. Now, Pulapiapa also had a sister, and he told her, "I will kill a pig now." He did so, and his sister prepared vegetables to cook with it. After he had cooked and cut up the pork, he asked his sister for her fine netbag spun with possum fur, and put the pork in it. First, though, he gave one side and the head of the pig to his sister. He also stuffed some salt into the bag.

Below Yapalapia, which is near the source of the Kuare River, there was a dry *sawia* tree. He hollowed it out, and into the cavity he put the netbag of pork and salt, along with cooked bananas, taro, and greens. Then he, too, went inside, covered the opening with tree resin, and told his sister to chop the tree down. She did so, and it splashed into the Kuare River.

The river carried the tree down to where it goes underground. Here the water backed up into a pool, and in it the trunk swirled around and around until it came to rest at the bank. Sensing this, Pulapiapa removed the resin and came outside. He looked up at the cliff above the river and saw a ladder rising up it.

He gathered his things and, after washing himself, carried his netbags to the base of the cliff. He soon reached the base of the ladder, a scaffolding of forked sticks and crosspieces that had been placed against the rock and were now blackened with use. He climbed up to the top.

There he saw a *robake* cult house surrounded by tall *irawapu* grass. Other houses were nearby. He approached the cult house and sat down outside. To one side he saw a tall *yubi* tree and some *kapipi* tree-ferns growing around a dwelling. Here the lightning was glowing. He went to investigate.

A woman was there, and seeing him approach, she asked, "Are you cooked or raw?" "I am raw," Pulapiapa replied. He opened his netbag and offered her some pork kidney and salt.

"I do not know about that," she said. Pulapiapa replied, "This is what we eat. Take some and try it." She did so.

3Ci "It's good," she said. And then she added, "My name is Giminyawe. My mother is a bad old woman. But over there you will see a good pandanus-leaf mat I have just made. Take it. If my mother asks you if you have one, say you already do. If she asks you for a bamboo water-container, say you have one. If she asks you for a bark cloth or for food from the gardens, say you have these things already."

Then she took out some barely started netbags, and he took some unfinished *ropa* armbands. These they put between them in two rows. In the middle Pulapiapa put the pork he had brought.

3Cii Soon the old woman arrived. She looked at the young man and said, "Sit down here on this mat," but he replied, "I have my own here." Then she asked him if he had a digging stick, and he told her he had one. He was able to produce everything she asked for. So they stayed.

One night the old woman said, "You have remained here a long time. Tonight, you must go by moonlight and hunt possums." So he went hunting and got two live *kepa* possums, but when he gave them to the two others each said, "I don't eat that." So he released the animals.

Later the old woman said again, "You have stayed a long time. Do you want to take my daughter?" "Yes," Pulapiapa replied. They gathered netbags and mats together in readiness for departure.

When this woman (Giminyawe) stood up, he heard a *kalala* sound, like things clinking together. "What's this?" he wondered.

When they were about to leave, she instructed him. "Now we are going. When we arrive you must put me in your sugar-cane garden, not near the village dance ground." So he took her to his garden at Uremapu and installed her in a house he built for her there, with flowering shrubs and tall grasses planted around it. Then he returned to his house and to his clansmen.

Everyone there was surprised to see him. They told him that they had thought him dead, that they had therefore compensated his relatives for his death, and that they had given away much wealth. But they wept to see him, many of the women still wearing their long mourning skirts and their strings of white seeds, Job's-tears.

5ii   Pulapiapa returned to Giminyawe and told her that his brothers had spent much wealth to be able to lift their mourning. "That's nothing," she reassured him and asked him to wait up at the hill at Ure. He did so. Soon he heard the same clinking sound he had heard earlier, and then he heard it again. He returned to the house and saw many pigs and shells. With them he compensated his fathers and brothers.

Later he told the woman that the villagers were about to hold a pig kill, and she instructed him to go ahead: she would offer her help. So he went to the ceremonial ground and planted a forked *walu*-wood post to hang up his bags of pearl shells, announcing that there would be many. When the men were about to show their shells, he brought forth three large netbags full of shells. Everyone saw this and complimented him.

5iii   Many men were wondering why Mele, Pulapiapa's elder brother, had not done as well. Mele's wife was particularly angry, so Mele asked his mother's brother to spy on the younger brother to find out what he was doing.

This man, Ake, went to the house at Uremapu. He saw the many *yubi* and *kapipi* trees planted round about, and he saw the lightning glowing. He looked inside the house and found the woman sitting there. He walked in and killed her, cutting her through the liver.

When Pulapiapa next looked in that direction, he failed to see the lightning glows. He hastened there. Giminyawe lay there nearly dead, her eyes half closed, her head nodding. She told him that his mother's brother had killed her.

5iv,11i   Pulapiapa understood. He returned and killed his brother, cutting out his liver and throwing it down at Magua Hill. Then he took some red *kalia* cordylines and gave them to his wife, who thereupon died.

11ii   Pulapiapa turned into a *kaipa kolake,* a plant with leaves that droop just as Pulapiapa's head drooped, in sorrow.

Tale 26: Giminyawe and the Broken Promise

0   There were several brothers, and among them were Keapu, Rame, and Lopa. Keapu and Rame wanted to find a wife for Lopa, but he did not want any of the women. All Lopa's brothers sought to marry him off, but with no success. So they decided to see if he would marry a woman named Giminyawe.

5i   Lopa heard of these plans and agreed. He put the pearl shells they had prepared for him into a netbag and set off. After walking some distance, he came to a fork in the path, where a couple of men waited. One of them, a man with reddish skin, announced to the other, "This is my cross cousin. He is coming from far away." This man showed him the way. Lopa went on, and presently he saw that the path stopped at a tall black palm. He climbed this tree, and when he reached its top, he saw on its leaves the footprints of men who had walked through there. He followed them.

He reached a ceremonial ground with many fine trees surrounding it: casuarinas, bamboos, and pines. Here, too, was the red-skinned man he had seen earlier, engaged in peeling cane to work into armbands.

This man asked, "Why have you come? There was another path over there."

"I heard of you, and I have come," Lopa replied. He took some casuarina branches, laid them down on the porch of the men's house, and arranged his pearl shells on top. Having done all this, the men there brought all the unmarried women and asked him if he liked this one or that, but each time Lopa said, "I don't like her."

It was now nearly dark, but there were glows of sheet lightning in the distance. As Lopa sat inside the men's house, he could see the lightning through the doorway, and by its light, he saw a young woman sitting behind some casuarina trees. His thoughts went to her.

The next morning they asked Lopa again about the women in their village, but still he refused. He told them he wanted to marry only Giminyawe. Then they called out to her, saying that this youth wanted to go with her and asking her to come forth.

She came out. Lopa looked at her and was pleased. They killed three pigs and cooked them. When that was done, they asked the two to stand together and close their eyes. But first they told him, "Her house must not be like our own; it must be different. You must plant bamboos, casuarinas, colourful shrubs and *kapipi* tree-ferns. Make the house look good. After you have made such a house, install her in it. But do not make this house just anywhere. Build it close to a natural well (*neka*)."

Lopa thought, "Where I live there is a deep well, and nearby

grow bamboos that I can take shoots from. I will find some tree-ferns
and casuarinas to plant there too."

10Bi   Lopa did all this. First he cleared around the edge of the well.
Then he built the woman's house over it. Next he built his own
house to one side. Nearby he planted colourful shrubs, casuarinas,
and bamboos. The two of them lived there.

5ii, 10Bii   One day Lopa heard that his brothers were cooking food in
preparation for a pig kill. The woman said, "Go and see if they are
ready." So he went to look, returned, and told her that the men were
indeed ready. She replied "Good." Then, taking some of her hair, she
threw it down into the well. A large-tusked pig came up. Many other
pigs came, and then finally one thin sow with clouded eyes.

"This last pig," she said to him, "you must tie to a rope and fasten
the other end to your own leg." Then she threw more of her hair
into the *neka,* and many "bone" pearl shells came up. This was the
path of shells. Then he loaded the shells in a netbag and prepared to
leave. The woman instructed him, "When you give out these shells
and pigs, do not spare a single person, pig, or even a dog."

5iii, 10Biii   Lopa did this, giving out shells and then legs or other cuts of
pork. Finally one man, a poor-man named Kakapu, was left. Lopa
told him, "Wait, I'll kill this last pig of mine and give you its ribs and
head." Kakapu replied that it did not matter what inferior pieces he
was given; he would take what was offered him, for he was poor.

10Biv   Kakapu, however, did not wait for this gift. Instead he set off
along the path Lopa had come on. He reached the house beside the
well, and there he hid and looked on from a concealed place. He saw
the woman, Giminyawe, with fine shells draped on her shoulders
around her neck and over her breasts. The bird-of-paradise plumes
of her headdress waved back and forth, and her skin glistened. She
was doing a *koda* dance and beating a drum. Kakapu looked on.
swallowing his saliva.

While looking on he was holding a branch, which suddenly
broke with a snap. The woman looked over and saw what seemed to
be a little ghost (*remosi*). She threw her drum onto the roof of the
house and went inside quickly. Kakapu followed her in. "Why have
you come?" she asked. He did not answer, so she cut off some of her
hair and threw it down into the hole. A pig came up.

"I don't want this pig," Kakapu said. So she threw down another
lock of hair and a good "bone" shell came up, but neither was he
pleased with this. "It's you I want; for you have I come," he said. But
the woman again asked, "Do you want salt, or tree oil, or . . ." when
the poor-man thrust his hand into her mouth and cut off her tongue.
She died.

5iv,11i When Lopa returned and saw what Kakapu had done, he killed him.

11ii And now we make *ali kalia* revenge killings in this same way. Lopa became a *kapipi*, a tree-fern.

Tale 27: The Provident Wife

0 There were a brother and a sister. One day the brother announced that he was going toward Mendi to attend a pig kill, and he planted an *oda* banana near the house. As long as the new banana leaves pointed up, he said, he would be away; when they unfolded and pointed downward he would be returning. Then, entrusting the pig Purimenalasa to his sister, he left.

3Bi The sister asked Purimenalasa to bring food and firewood, so the pig left for the garden. She followed it along. While they were there, they saw smoke rising from the thatch of their house, and, returning hastily, they found a little poor-man (*ribualisi*) sitting inside. He had spittle drooling from his mouth, unkempt hair, and dry wrinkled skin. He announced, "I will marry you."

The woman thought, "Why should I marry you, stinker (*agapu-kupi*)?" But instead she said, "Come back when my brother returns."

When the brother returned with the pork and salt he had acquired, his sister told him what had happened. The two were about to cook some of the pork when the old man approached. Then the two men put down their pearl shells. The brother said he would like to give Purimenalasa pig, the whole pig, but that he would only give him half. So he told the pig that he was going to kill it, and the pig replied that it was all right: they had looked after it well, and now that the sister was about to marry they could kill it. So the brother killed and cooked the pig. Then he gave the poor-man half: one side, together with half the head and half the stomach, and half of the intestines as well.

As the sister was about to go off with the old man, her brother gave her four small bundles; he put them in her netbag and told her not to lose these things. So the couple – sister and poor-man – departed, the man leading. After going some distance down the path, he told her to sit down and wait while he fetched his mother and his sister. So she waited for him to return. When he did so, she saw he was eating a cooked human forearm, which she recognized to be her brother's by the armband still attached. He was returning with his sister and his mother, two red-skinned women with long tusk-like teeth.

9Ai   The three of them threw the young woman in the river, which carried her away downstream.

9Aiii   The river brought her to a garden and a house. The house was abandoned but was not yet overgrown, and it had good things growing around it – sugar cane and ripe bananas. This young woman no longer wore her grass apron, for the river had torn it off. So she opened the bundles her brother had given her. These were a bundle containing saliva, a bundle containing a fire-starting stick, one containing an axe, and finally a wrapped-up breechcloth. The woman took the axe and cut herself a belt of bark. Then she cut some cordyline leaves and put these on with the breechcloth. After this she went off to make a garden. She stayed there working in the garden, watching over her many pigs, pearl shells and bamboos full of tree oil

5i   One day, as she was making a garden, two dogs came to her. "Ah," she thought, "there must be a man who owns these dogs, and he must be close to here." So she told the dogs that she lived alone and that if some man approached her, that would be all right with her. Presently she heard a rustling in the brush at the garden edge. She called out, "If you are a ghost, stay out; but if you are a man with warm skin, come forward!"

A man came forth. He was carrying several possums he had killed. "Let's cook and eat these possums," he said. The woman replied, "Yes, let's, *ame* ("brother" – male speaking). This is my house, so let's eat." While her visitor was sitting down, she got up to take some firewood from the rack over the fire. When she leaned over and her breechcloth gaped, the man looked up and saw she had no penis but a vagina instead. "How's this so?" he asked.

9Aiii   The man fetched some *ura* reeds which he had planted nearby, and he told her to strip the leaves and dry them. Then he gave her some twine, unravelled from his netbag, and told her to make a grass skirt quickly. This she did, and the two slept, and she became his wife. She bore him a daughter.

10Bi   The man looked at her things and he saw some twenty pigs and some forty pearl shells, together with axes and bushknives. At this time the man was building a *yaeada* longhouse for a forthcoming pig kill ceremony, and he was planning to occupy its *wasa* (end compartment occupied by important men). Everyone else thought this strange, for as far as they knew he had no pigs to speak of. But when it came time to kill the pigs, he planted a long row of stakes and put up a high forked post (to hang his bags of pearl shells on). Everyone speculated about this.

5ii,10Bii   On the appointed day he came with his wife and daughter to the dance ground, parading and chanting. The wife told him that he must not kill a large white sow of hers, since they needed it to increase their herd. She asked him to put that pig underneath her house, which he did. Then she left, telling her daughter she was going to clean some pig intestines in a stream nearby.

5iii,10Biii   But now this man did not have enough pork to repay those who had given him pearl shells, so he killed the white sow and gave the intestines to his daughter to wash. When she took these down to the stream, her mother saw them and guessed that they were from her sow.

10Biv   She dropped what she was doing and ran back to the house. She killed her husband. Then she took a side of pork from where her husband had hung them, cut a side of flesh and bone from her husband's body, and carried these two things into the forest. She went far away with her side of pork and side of man, but where she went nobody knew.

Tale 28: The Skin Changer

0   A man named Naya lived with his wife. The couple were without children. Both were no longer young and felt their bodies tire easily. Yet the wife became pregnant. And in time she went to the birth hut to bear the child, a little girl. Intending to cut off the umbilical cord, she called out for a bamboo knife. But this newborn girl announced, "I'll go and get one!" The child went to her father and said, "Give my mother and me our things." Then she left, her uncut umbilical cord dragging along the ground and her skin, still unwashed from birth, the colour of red coals.

5i   She did not go back to her mother but on along a different path to Yaparapawi, dragging the netbags after her. Eventually she came to Koali, where a young man named Laimasi had brought together a few other men to help him clear a new garden. Then the girl, with her cord still dangling and with bloodied skin, went to the garden edge, where Laimasi had left his shoulder bag, axe, bow and arrows, and pandanus mat while he worked. She took these things and went away.

When the men were finished working, the helpers left for their homes. Laimasi came to look for his things, but they were no longer there. He searched, and presently he found them nearby. As he stooped to pick them up, he heard a thin voice saying, "Ah, good for you! I moved them lest someone steal them."

"What's this? Laimasi wondered. He quickly snatched his possessions up and ran back to tell his brothers. "Something almost killed me, but I ran away and came!" he told them. Then those men, of

Kubarepa clan, returned with him. They saw the little girl with the blood on her, looking as if she had been born just the day before. Some men took clumps of earth and threw them at her, some took sticks and struck her. They all laughed at her.

8i But the little girl did not mind, and she followed Laimasi home. After the others had departed she told him, "You must keep me in the forest where you go to trap possums." So he took her off and put her in the forest between Walu and Puti, an uninhabited tract of land. She told him, "Do not come to see me often. Why would you want to come, anyway?"

5ii After Laimasi had left her, she cleared a garden for herself— quickly, as these things happen in tales. She put up many houses, stores of all kinds, a wide road, cows and pigs, some metal-roofed houses as well. Once, when Laimasi came to see her there, she told him, "If ever you have a small request, or if you are in need of something, come tell me."

So one day when his father had died and he needed a pig to kill, he went back to her. He saw all the things she had there and thought, "This looks like a place where white men live!" The little girl said, "Good, I am glad you have come. I told you to do so when you were in need." And she gave him a large pig. Later, when Laimasi wanted to kill pigs and repay debts, he went back to her, and she gave him fine "bone" pearl shells and large pigs to take back.

Some time later, men were constructing *neada* longhouses, intending to kill pigs. Laimasi, knowing he could count on the girl, made his own *neada* section and collected firewood and cooking leaves. His clansmen muttered, "Why is he doing all this? He has nothing!" But when they were cooking food to open the ceremonies, one moment it seemed that Laimasi would have but a single sweet potato or plantain, and then, the next moment, there would be plenty. When he cooked food it would be done quickly, and when he put down but one pig stake it would multiply into a long line. Everyone wondered how he could be so much better off than they.

8ii On another occasion, when they were about to feast again, Laimasi came to the girl, and she gave him all sorts of ornaments to parade with in front of the women. This time she decided to attend the feast. So after Laimasi had left her in her store, she took off her little girl's skin. Now she had the light skin of an attractive young woman, with hair falling to her shoulders. This light-skinned woman then put on a good skirt and hung some nice shells around her neck. Thus prepared, she walked to Kaoli and joined in the parading at Laimasi's side, holding to the handle of his axe. All the others admired the two of them, and they cried out, "Koali Laimasi has come!

Mogo Rali* has come!" Thereafter, whenever people made a pig kill and held a dance, Laimasi found this good-looking young woman beside him.

But always she would slip away before the end of the festivities. First she would ask Laimasi to fetch her some food or water, but when he returned she would be gone. By the time Laimasi reached home and went to her forest dwelling, he would find her there as before, looking like a newborn child, with her still uncut umbilical cord and blood on her skin. Yet, he wondered if she might be deceiving him.

8iii   So one day when they were preparing a feast he told a younger brother to go and hide beside the girl's house. This brother watched the little girl take off her newborn's skin and become Mogo Rali, a beautiful woman with handsome decorations. He saw this deception of hers. After she had departed for the feast, he took that little girl's skin and burnt it. Then he left and told his brother, Laimasi, that the little girl was in fact the same woman that had danced with him. And he suggested, "Do not obey when she sends you to fetch her food. She is your woman."

At the ceremony, the young woman came once again and danced with Laimasi. Later, when she failed to evade him and saw that he would no longer be deceived, she gave in. "All right, then. Let's go," she said.

5ii,10Bi   After she saw that her other skin had been burnt she said, "We will each have our own house. One will be mine and the other yours. If you want to marry someone else, I will help you marry her with pigs, pearl shells, bailer shells, and axes." Later Laimasi did secure a wife with her help, and he stayed with this wife.

10Bii   Earlier the woman had told him, "When your wife's brothers give you the return bridewealth, I will take none of it. But when your wife bears her first child, I will take him." She went on, "That is your house, and this is mine. Do not give me the shells or pigs of the return bridewealth; only the first-born child."

5iii,10Biii   Soon Laimasi's wife gave birth to a son. Laimasi took him from her and gave him to the other woman to look after. She nursed him with breast milk of a different kind. The boy grew quickly.

10Biv   One night, however, Laimasi's wife took a knife and stole up to that house in which the two were sleeping. She went up to them and cut their throats.

5iv,11i   Laimasi was appalled when he discovered this. Saddened and ap-

---

Mogo rali means "trailing umbilical cord." But despite the name, Laimasi does not recognize her.

prehensive, he set fire to his wife's house while she slept. She was consumed by the fire. A *kagi* possum ran out of the house as it burned.

11ii   As for Laimasi, he broke his *wiruapu* bow in two and became a lorikeet. The *ali potawe* or revenge killing custom started this way.

CHAPTER 4

Of Marriages to Ghosts

Tale 29: Raguame's Marriage

0   Raguame lived with her mother, whom she looked after in many ways. The daughter built the house the two lived in, built their pig house, looked after their pigs, cleared the garden, built fences, split firewood and the rest. In the gardens she tied up the sugar cane, wrapped the plantain clumps, and generally did all the man's work, while the mother did the woman's work. The two of them lived in that manner.

6i   One day a man from another place took his dogs to hunt in the forest. He went up Mount Keresa and looked down into a valley. Below him he saw extensive gardens, with sugar cane and *koda* bananas growing. In the middle of the gardens he saw what he took to be a man, standing on a branch support tying sugar cane to stakes.

He thought, "I'll not return home today. I'll go to stay with this man, and tomorrow I'll hunt again and then return home." But when he approached the garden he saw that it was no man but a woman. There he found the mother, who asked him, "Are you a man of the community (*ada ali*) or an outsider (*ra ali*)? There is a path here only for the former."

"I am such a person," he replied. "When I looked down here from the mountain, I thought a man lived here, so I came intending to stay the night." Later Raguame came to the house, and the traveller stayed the night with those two women.

The next morning, the two told him to go, for it was morning. But he replied, "Having just come, I want to stay a while. Let's sit together here a little longer."

To her daughter the mother said, "Child, I think since he has come to be here near you, we should kill a pig and then you can go with him."

So the two of them, daughter and youth, killed a large pig, butchered it and cooked it. Then the two left. Raguame carried the head and backbone of the pig and some cooked taro, while the man carried the two sides. On they went.

6ii   Presently they came to a fork in the path, where a smaller, less used path branched off from the main one. The man told the woman to follow the main path, while he took the one less used.

The woman went on along this path until she came to a wide stream. With her heavy netbags, she knew that there was no way she could cross. "How will I go on?" she wondered, standing there leaning on her *walu* walking stick. She waited, and soon it grew dark.

Pausing there, she noticed that her stick moved, and she looked down. It was resting on a dark river boulder, which was loose. At that moment she looked downriver and saw a young woman, much like herself in age and appearance, who had lit a torch and was coming upstream along the river.

As the young woman stood there, still leaning on her stick, the boulder she was resting on moved again, and she saw underneath it a wonderful house (*egapulimiada*), right there in the stream. She made a quick decision; she put her netbags in the porch of that house, rolled the boulder back into place behind her, and sat down.

6iii   Presently she saw the stone move aside and then back into place. The light of a torch approached. It was the woman whom Raguame had seen coming upstream.

"Who's this?" cried out that woman upon seeing Raguame there. "Are you an outsider or someone from the village?"

"Oh, I am from the village. I was walking along and it grew dark, so when I saw this house I stopped here."

"All right, that's good," said the other. The two left their netbags hanging in the porch and went around to the other end of the house, where there was another entrance. Raguame had noticed that one entrance was closed off with branches of a *kapipi* tree-fern. She took a small piece of the pork she had carried and offered it to the woman, who ate it. When she offered more, the woman declined. "I've eaten enough," she said. The two lay down to sleep.

"Once we go to sleep, if you wake up you must not look at me," said the woman. But Raguame did so. In the dark of night she opened her eyes a little and looked over to where the other one was sleeping. She saw that her skin was very pale, like that of a dead person. She thought, "Ah, this one who sleeps here is someone who has died!" She herself slept no more. She just lay there, drawing her breath slowly and pretending to sleep.

In the morning the woman spoke. "It's now daylight. You should be on your way. Take your netbags and be off."

Raguame took some pork and salt from her bag and gave it to the other woman. She accepted it, and she gave Raguame directions. "As you walk along this path, you will see where people have cut some *pai* trees to make a garden fence. There, too, you will see some *ankoro* plants. Do not go further. Stay there, for you will see I have many brothers living there. If you stay, and if you have to do some sort of woman's work, like making a garden or netting a bag or breechcloth, I shall help you with it."

Raguame heard this and set forth. The other added, "You will see an old sweet-potato garden, overgrown with grass. Make your garden there."

6iv She went along the path, and soon she came to a men's house, where the woman's brothers lived. The young men saw her approach, and remarked that she looked very much like their recently deceased sister, whom they had just laid on a *tapa* platform the other day. Now here was this other woman, coming with pork and salt.

One of the young men came around the house from the porch on the far side. It was the same youth who had visited her earlier. "You see this, boys?" he said. "It's my wife who has come!"

Raguame put down her netbags full of pork, and the men set about recooking the meat. Looking around, she saw the overgrown potato garden that the dead woman had mentioned. She walked through it, beginning to dig up some weeds here and there, while the men busied themselves with the earth oven.

6Ai She slept the night there, and the next morning when she looked at the garden, she saw her work had been finished overnight. The entire garden had been cleared of grass and the earth mounded for sweet potatoes. Later on, the same thing happened when she looked after the pigs or carried food to them; always her husband's ghost-sister helped her in things she started.

"So how is it that my wife has such strength, that she does everything so well, never leaving anything undone?" the husband one day wondered aloud in the company of his brothers. "I think we must now see to this. Let us make a new garden at Raipala."

So the men started a new garden there. When they had cleared it, let the slash dry out and burned it over, Raguame brought cuttings of various crops, sugar cane, plantains, taro, pitpit, and others. But she did not plant the lot just that day. In one section of the garden she planted a few banana cuttings, in another some sweet-potato runners, and so on, only a few here and there.

The next morning when they returned to Raipala, the whole garden had been completely planted. "Ah, that woman works quickly!" the men remarked.

"Yes, I saw what she did down where she came from," recalled the husband. "It was the same there as well."

And so it went. One day some of the young men returned from a pig kill in a different village, and they set about sharing their pork with those who had stayed home. Because many of them had gone,

and because she was the only woman among them, Raguame received many pieces of pork.

That night she sat in her house with her husband. While pretending to close the doorway, she threw some pieces of pork through the
opening to the yard. Her husband watched her, without her knowing it. He saw someone with pale skin come and pick these pieces
up.

"That sister of mine!" he thought. "Aha!" Now he understood:
"That's how she does all that work!"

6Aii   Later he spoke to his brothers of this, and he told them of his
plan. They should first start a garden in another patch of forest. So
they did. And as before, Raguame came with cuttings of various
crops. At the end of the day, having just planted a few of the cuttings, she left the rest in the garden, piled up next to her digging
stick.

After she had left, the husband came and lay down beside the
pile of cuttings and the stick.

That night the moon shone brightly. He saw a young woman
coming, carrying cuttings of plantain, taro, greens; it was the same,
pale-skinned woman. The man looked closely, and he recognized
the face and smile of his sister. Now he understood how his wife was
able to do all this work: his sister had been helping her.

Dropping her netbags full of cuttings, this woman came to pick
up the digging stick the wife had left. But as she reached for it, the
young man grabbed her by the wrist. As he held her, he had the sen-
sation of holding thorny *kalamu* and *mabo* wood, and she made it
feel like a heavy rain fell. But the brother held her fast. "I have you!"
he cried.

Seeing she could not escape, the sister lamented,

Aya ainya ayana kepanali neme madi eparipuri, niri pono ra pa.
Oh brother, the one who your mother-in-law sent from home I
     brought back to you, and now I want to go.

11i-ii   Now, we women marry men the way Raguame did. The deceased sisters of men might still help their wives: but because this
man held his sister captive by her wrist, they do not come to help us.
That is my story.

Tale 30: The Ghostsister I

0   A girl lived with her mother and grew to be a young woman. One day her mother told her, "I am going to the garden. Stay and rub some mud on our pig, Puramenalasu, and put it outside with a tether at its leg." The young woman did this; she tethered the pig and sat down nearby.

6i   Presently a handsome young man came up bearing some possums and birds. He gave these to her and said, "Eat some and put aside the rest for your mother. When your mother comes bringing you food, do not eat it. Just weep and say nothing."

6ii   He departed. Soon the mother came back with some cucumbers and sweet potatoes. She offered her daughter some cucumbers and potatoes, but the young woman declined. The mother offered her sugar cane, but this, too, was refused.

"Ah, why is this?" the mother wondered. "When I offer her food she does not take it, but weeps instead." So she said to her daughter, "You weep so much and do not eat. Your eyes are swollen and red. I think you are pining for some man you want to marry. Are you?" The daughter agreed.

6iii   The next morning the two of them killed their large pig, Puramenalasu, and cooked it in an earth oven with other foods. The mother sent her daughter down to the stream to wash out the pig intestines. When the girl arrived at the water, she realized she had not brought along a knife to cut open the intestines, so she looked around for something that would do. Instead she saw a young woman, who said, "Here, I have a knife, come and take it. When you have finished washing out the pig guts, go back quickly, lest your mother be angry with you. Later, when you have left home and come carrying pork and salt, I shall meet you on this path."

The girl returned to find her mother removing the food from the earth oven. After giving her two sides of pork and two blocks of salt, her mother said, "Now if you want to go, do so. Take whatever path you choose."

The daughter followed the path the other young woman had shown her, though she did not know where it led. Along this path she saw a clear stream. Realizing she was thirsty, she decided to go and drink from it. She took off her netbag and leaned over to drink, but as soon as she did so the water ceased to flow there. She went further upstream and tried again, but the same thing happened. Whenever she wanted to drink, the water would recede. In this way she was led deep into the forest.

It was now growing dark, so she sat down and took one piece of pork kidney and one piece of pork flesh and ate. She was tired, but after eating she got up and kept on walking, following the stream which, receding, showed her a path.

Finally she asked the stream, "Did a man make you or what? If a man did, tell me and we two will go." Now she saw a good-looking young woman in the place of the water, which disappeared altogether. They walked on together. After a while, the daughter asked, "Do you want to eat some pork?"

"No, the meat must be cold, and I don't feel like eating it," the other young woman replied.

The two walked on in the dark through the forest. After a while they came up to a long men's house in which many men were asleep. This young woman led the daughter to the compartment occupied by her brother—for this house was in her own natal village. "This is my brother's room," she said. "Put your netbag down and sleep here. You must know that I am not a village woman. Earlier I died. I was buried and now I am a ghost. After you have married my brother, I will help you. When you make a *raguna* hat or *kibarupa* legbands, I shall help you at this. When you want to make gardens, you can make them in many places, for I will help you. But if someone asks you who has helped you, you must not tell them about me. If you say something, you will have to do all the hard work yourself. Should your husband threaten you, do not say anything. Remain silent."

Having said that, this ghostwoman went back to her place, sleeping in the compartment of a poor-man, a little brother of hers who wasn't good for much more than removing lice from the hair of other men.

6iv   When dawn broke and the first cock crowed, this poor-man looked in his brother's room. He saw a young woman sleeping there and exclaimed, "Who is this young woman here?" Others gathered to look at her: they were all pleased. They clasped her hand and announced that the next morning they would kill and cook a pig. They did so, and after three weeks had passed they gave bridewealth for this young woman.

6Ai   Whenever the wife would start a legband or a head covering, the ghostwoman, her husband's sister, would finish it; likewise with a breechcloth she was netting, or a garden she was preparing. The poor-man noticed this and wondered, "How does such a thing happen? Can she alone be doing all this work, or is someone helping her?"

6Aii   One day the men decided to find out how she could work at netting and gardening so quickly. They devised a plan; the poor-man would go and stay the night in some brush at the edge of the woman's garden to see what happened.

He did this, and he watched the new wife work her garden until sunset, when she left. Then, in the dark, he heard a rustling at the edge of the garden: there was the ghostwoman making sweet-potato mounds where the wife had left off. She worked swiftly and presently came to the place where the poor-man was hiding. He sprang from his hiding place, took out a piece of thick rope, and tied her hands together. Then this woman brought rain and turned herself into thorny vines painful to hold. But the poor-man held her fast. The ghostwoman sang,

> *Ainya yalo wakia kili siri marari ipulu, ainya pono ra pa.*
> *Ainya adasu mapu koma wia pirawa, ainya pono ra pa.*
> Brother, I have come picking the Yaro river's wild *wakia* fruits;
>   let me go.
> Brother, I have been making a large garden; let me go.

The poor-man heard her complaint and understood. "Ah, this woman is my dead sister, who has become a ghost. I must release her. She can stop weeping." He went back and told the others.

When the wife heard about this, she cried out, "I did not ask you to hold this woman. What have you done!" She stayed in the house and would not come out for some time. "I am just a woman here; you do not do well," she complained.

9Bi   Later, she went to where men and women were making a new garden on Keresa mountain. To this new garden she took cuttings to plant. As she was going along she saw a very large snake curled up by the side of the path. She kept on going. When she turned to look back, she saw that its head had come forward. When she looked back a second time, she saw more of it uncurling. So she carried this snake with her to the garden and then put it to one side while she planted the cuttings of food crops. When that was done, she put a short thick stick on the ground and using it as a chopping block she cut the snake into pieces.

In the sections of the garden that the men had divided up among themselves, she put pieces of the snake, one in each section. The tail she put in the garden belonging to her husband's last-born brother, the poor-man, while the head she put in her husband's garden. She planted these in the *kubura* (or "brush heaps") in each of the garden sections—a few cuttings and a piece of the snake. Then she went back.

She told all her husband's brothers, "You must not go to the brush heaps which I have made in this garden."

9Bii   When she went next to look at these piles of garden debris, she saw that there were little tunnels and pathways in them. Later she went again and looked and this time she saw that there was a young woman in each brush heap. Where she put the tail of the snake there was a good young woman and where she had planted the head there was a bad one with a homely face. She returned and told all the men to make bracelets, belts, *kura* skirts, and all things that women wear as ornamentation. After this had been done she brought the young women back to the village.

11i-ii   Before, there was only this one woman here; but after she had cut the snake, there were many. She did this work, she alone, and as a result there are now many women. Had she not done this, there would be no one in these parts.

Tale 31: Ipakeala and His Wife

0   The men at Lopeame, near Asumawi, built a *yaeada* longhouse in preparation for a pig kill and invited some of their trade partners from the south to come and receive pork. A young woman from Wilira went there with her father and mother. At another place, a man named Ipakeala put on his pig's tail pendants, his *raguna* hat, and other ornaments, and set off for the same destination.

When he arrived at the site of the *yaeada* at Lopeame, the people there saw him coming and cried out, "Ipakeala has come! Ipakeala has come!" There was much excitement.

Plate 3. A young woman dances with men.

6i   During the dancing, Ipakeala paraded around the dance ground with other men. Then, following the custom of young women, the Wilira woman broke into his row, gripped the handle of his axe, and marched by his side. With her decorations, she looked fine indeed.

As they and the other dancers marched along, Ipakeala spoke to her, "If you are someone else's wife, you must not hold my axe."

"I am not married; I stay with my parents," replied the woman.

But the young man wanted to be certain. "Do you talk truly or do you lie?" he asked her.

"It's true," she replied.

Ipakeala gave out his pearl shells to the pig killers during the shell distribution. When he had finished, some shells were left, and these he gave to the girl's father and mother. As a promise of marriage he put them in the girl's netbag. She thus became his wife. And when, on the following day, the pigs were killed, Ipakeala gave some of the pork he received from them to the woman's parents and brothers.

6ii   That afternoon the pig kill was over, and Ipakeala told his wife that he was departing to receive pork at another *yaeada*, where pigs were also being killed.

"I will go with you," said the woman, and she followed him some distance behind. But soon she came to a man and a woman on the path throwing stones at each other; the two were quarrelling over pork. Afraid of being struck by one of their stones, she returned to Lopeame. Later she set out again to follow her husband, but she was unable to see where he had walked. So again she returned, and she spent the night with her parents.

The next morning she set out with her parents and others along the path leading home to Wilira. But when they reached the Sugu River, which they had to cross, they saw it was in flood. It would be impossible to cross it. The travellers collected on the north bank of the river and conversed. No one knew how they might cross to the other side.

6iii   Presently a man with a running nose and a tattered breechcloth, a little old poor-man (*ribualisi*), came walking along the top of the river singing to himself, "Olo olo, olo olo." One by one he carried all the men and women across the river with their children, their sacks of pork, and even the live pigs they were leading home.

The young woman that Ipakeala had married was the last to remain on the north bank. When the old man came to carry her across she said, "You old stinker (*agapukupi*), you'll just dump me in the river!" She refused to be carried across. From the other bank, her parents urged her to cross. "You are not heavy. Look at all the heavy people and things he has carried across," they said. "He won't drop you!"

But still she refused to go, and eventually the poor-man walked away downstream on top of the water, singing softly, "Olo olo." Those who had crossed continued on their journey home.

The young woman waited. Close to nightfall she began to worry, so she called out to the poor-man, asking him to return. He did; he came back, sauntering slowly, and said, "Come, I will carry you and your netbag of pork." But, still distrustful, the girl told him to carry the netbag across first and then return for her. The poor-man did so.

Then the woman said, "I'll come and stay at your house tonight. Let us go there."

"No," said the poor-man, "you must go to spend the night with your father and mother."

But the girl insisted. "It is almost dark, I shall go with you."

Then she spread out the fine *ominu* netbag she was carrying, and she asked him to make himself a new breechcloth from it, for the one he was wearing was worn to strings. But the poor-man refused, saying he did not want to ruin her good netbag. Next the woman took a nice piece of pig fat and told the other to oil his skin with it. But again he refused. "I am not some youth, that I should do such a thing," he replied.

She asked next if his house was close by. Hearing that it was, she again suggested that they both go there. And there they went.

8i When they arrived at Turigi, the poor-man's place, she saw much pork hanging from posts. After asking about it, she was told that the meat actually belonged to other people who had left it in his care. That was an untruth; it was all his. He cooked some of this pork and put the rest in the house to smoke overnight.

"This is not my pork; but I'm cooking it so that it does not go bad," he told her.

They spent the night there. The next morning, the poor-man cooked some more meat. "If you are hungry, then eat some of this," he said to the woman. "No one will be angry with you if you do." But the woman said she did not want to eat any. The poor-man continued to consume it, taking the meat with ginger and salt. How odd it was, thought the woman, that this poor-man should live so well.

That evening a cricket came and chirped by the hearth. "That cricket is calling us to go to a *yasa* singing," said the poor-man. "But you must go by yourself. I have to stay here and look after these people's pork. Go to Tagiri, for that is where they will be dancing." So saying, he gave her a *kepa* ceremonial staff, telling her that it was someone else's but that she should not mind and take it anyway. Finally, he warned her not to look at the young men there; she should go, have a look around, and come back quickly.

When she drew close to the Tagiri *yaeada,* she heard people crying out, "Ipakeala has come! Ipakeala has come!"

6iv,8ii   "O, my husband is here!" she thought, and she hurried up to the dance ground. There he was again, just as before, dressed in his fine ornaments. Holding her *kepa,* the woman approached the dancers and took a place by Ipakeala's side. As the two paraded around with the others, she holding with him the handle of his axe, the woman reflected, "Before I married this man, but he left. But where did he go, and where does he come from, I wonder."

An argument between two women stopped the dancing momentarily. Ipakeala went to have a look, while the young woman remained behind. She waited and waited, but he did not return. Disappointed, she eventually made her way back to the poor-man's house at Turigi.

There she found the poor-man, bits of ash and dirt on his dusty skin, tending the smoky fire. He offered her some food but she, sulking, would not have any of it.

"Don't be angry with me, just because you have gone to a different place and seen young men," he said. "I know I'm just an old man and that my place is here."

Later the woman ate a little and then went to sleep.

Several days later a cricket came again and called them to another singing. And again the poor-man said that the woman should go alone, this time to Taguere. He assembled ornaments for her, and she went off.

After walking along the path for a while, she paused to wipe away the oil that she had put on her brow and that was now running into her eyes. Stopping for a moment, she looked back to the house she had just left. There she saw the poor-man take off his skin, the wrinkled skin of an old man, and put on fine ornaments. She recognized him to be none other than Ipakeala himself. Then she saw him leave for Taguere along a different path.

Now she understood that he had deceived her. She was annoyed with him. Why did this man always want to be a *ribuali,* a poor-man, she wondered.

The two arrived at Taguere by different paths. Hearing the people there crying out, "Ipakeala has come! Ipakeala has come!" the woman smiled to herself as she walked onto the dance ground. She joined the dancing as before.

8iii   Presently she told her husband that she was thirsty, and she went off toward a stream as if to drink. But instead of stopping there and drinking, she continued on, left Taguere, and returned swiftly to the poor-man's house back at Turigi. Inside she found a bamboo container in the corner. She shook out the poor-man's old, dried-up skin, his dirty, unkempt hair, and his tattered net apron. Then she threw the lot onto the fire.

Meanwhile Ipakeala was growing suspicious, waiting for his wife to return from the stream. Then, wearily, he walked back to his home. When he drew close, he looked around to see if the woman was anywhere in sight. Seeing that she was not, he reached into his room to get his poor-man's skin, but instead he found his wrist suddenly grasped. It was the woman; she had been waiting for him inside the house.

"You deceived me, but now I've deceived you," she taunted.

Ipakeala replied that he had done this because she had insulted him when he offered to carry her across the river. "Now that you have discovered who I am, I warn you not to mention what you have seen to anyone, including me. Never let me hear you talking about who I was!"

Time passed. The woman bore a son.

One day the woman had an argument with her husband. It was over their son, who had defecated in the house. She turned to her husband and said, "You think you are a great headman, but I know you are just a poor-man. So *you* clean up the feces!"

11i   Ipakeala grew angry, for she had broken her word. "All right," he said, "now you must raise sweet potatoes, tend pigs, and do hard work by yourself." Taking his son, he left the Turigi house and started climbing the mountain ridge.

The woman watched the two go. Then, regretting her harsh words, she called them back. "Where are you going?" she called out.

"O, we are just going to look for some mushrooms," her husband said. "We will be back soon."

11ii   But the two of them never returned. The wife followed the path they had taken, but she found that the father and son had turned into tree-ferns. She returned home and wept. She sang this lament: "Husband, your words I have not heeded, and you have gone, O my husband, the father with his son."

Mourning thus, she turned into a Job's-tears plant.

Tale 32: The Ghosthusband

0   A woman and her daughter lived together and looked after their pigs. One day the mother asked the daughter to put the pigs outside on a tether and to rub some white clay on them while she went off to the garden. "You must put the pigs away from the sun. Put them in the shade of the sword grass," she told her. "Then go to fetch some

dead sword-grass stalks for our fire."

6i   The young girl did as she was told. When she had finished, she went to sit in the sun, where she fell asleep. When she awoke, she felt a pain on her breast. Looking at herself, she saw some small incisions on her skin (the kind that lovers make). "Who could have done this?" she wondered. But then, remembering her responsibilities, she went to fetch the dry grass stalks. After cutting some, she tied them together into a large bundle and carried them on her head back toward the house.

But as she walked along she felt a strain in her neck, as if someone were pulling her load back. So, throwing the load aside, she turned to see what had been pulling her back. There stood a youth.

"Who are you?" she asked. "Just me," was the reply.

She explained, "My mother told me to look after the pigs and fetch some dry grass for our hearth."

6ii   "Good," said the youth. "Go back, then. When your mother returns, begin to weep. If she offers you food, do not take it. Later you may wish to follow me, so I'll break off twigs as I go. These will mark a path for you to take."

Having heard this, the daughter went back to her mother's home. There she put the pigs back inside the house and waited. Presently her mother returned. The girl began to weep.

"Why are you crying?" asked the mother. And she held out to her child a bundle of rats she had killed in the garden. The daughter refused the food and continued to weep. Other foods she refused as well.

"Well, do you want to go with a man?" asked the mother.

"Yes," was the daughter's reply.

"Well then, go. One should not weep like that when one marries. Take some food with you and go," said the mother.

In the morning the daughter put on her ornaments. The two women took one of their pigs, named Puramenalasu, and put more white clay on it. The daughter began to lead it off.

"What path will you take?" asked the mother. The daughter replied she would follow a path of broken twigs. Wearing her ornaments and leading her pig, she departed.

6iii   On and on she went. Eventually she looked across a valley, as one can look from Ragera over to Mugiri, and saw a woman and a girl who had donned mourning skirts and were weeping. The trail of broken twigs led her to that place. Nearby was a mortuary platform, and on it lay a dead man.

The two others saw her approach and asked her, "Who are you?" She explained how she came to be there.

Then one of the other two said, "Oh, I see. That one on the platform, whom we are now mourning, is the one who came and talked to you." (These two women were the mother and the sister of the deceased.)

"Oh well, never mind. I'll just stay a while," said the newcomer. "We'll kill and cook this pig of mine, and then I'll leave. Let's gather some firewood." So they split firewood and singed the pig in preparation for the oven cooking.

The mother asked the two younger women to harvest some taro to cook with the pig. "But," she warned them, "you will see a large *kamo* taro. It's my dead son's, so you must not pull it up now. I'll stay here and peel bananas and taro." And she added, "Cut some *muga* leaves to cook with the pork, too."

The young woman went with the dead youth's sister to the mortuary platform, where there were two clumps of *muga* leaves growing. Each of them went to one of the clumps. As she parted the clump and looked down at the base, the woman heard a man's voice say, "What are you doing here?"

"I know you have died, so I'm going to return home," she replied. "But first I will cook my pig."

She heard this reply: "All right. But when you've finished, take the flesh and skin of the pig's neck. Take, too, the *kamo* taro you were told not to pull up. Peel it, cook it, and carry it with your pork. I'll wait for you along the path. When you have finished cooking the pig and have given some pork to my mother and sister, bring some for me."

Then the three women cooked the pig with good *gusede* and *rulu* plantains. When they had divided the pork, she took her portion, as she had been told, and went off. She also took the cooked taro. The pork legs and ribs – all this she gave to the two other women.

As she was leaving, the mother said, "It's almost dark now. Spend the night here with us and then go." But the young woman left with her burden of pork and the cooked taro.

6iv   Presently she met the youth along the path. She spoke, "I have brought your taro and pork. Eat some." But the other said, "No, we shall go along further and then eat."

They did not follow a path but just walked along the stream beds. The woman went where he led her, eating some of the pork and plantains she had brought.

3Di   They came to a hill and there the man said, "Beyond, you see my father's sister's house. Go and sleep there. Meet me tomorrow on the path above the house. But I warn you, my father's sister's husband is a bad man. Watch yourself!"

She went off with her pork and taro. Some of the pork she hid along the path; the rest she carried with her, and only a little did she eat. Reaching the house, she opened the doorway softly and went in. It was a lean-to. She sat in a corner.

Presently she heard noises and felt the ground tremble. Peering through a chink in the door she saw a big old woman, with long sharp teeth, walking toward her holding a stout *walu* walking stick. When the old one reached the house, she paused outside and said, "What smells funny here?"

3Dii   The young woman had prepared some pork and salt to stuff in the old woman's mouth, to ward off an attack from her. So when the old woman opened the door and saw her, she rose and put a piece of pork and salt in her mouth. The old woman ate it quickly. Then she clutched the young woman's wrist and asked her hurriedly, "You, who are you? How did you come?"

"A man told me to go to his father's sister's house."

"Where is he, then?"

"Further up the hill."

3Bi   The old woman then said, "Listen, my husband is a bad man. We must do something, for he will be coming soon." So the old woman dug a hole in the floor, made the young woman sit down in it, and covered it over with a sheet of bark. Only a little opening did she leave in the covering. She put the pork on top of the bark.

"I will drop some cooked sweet potatoes through the hole," said the old woman. "You will want to eat them."

"No, I have eaten enough."

Soon the old man approached. While still outside he said, "Hey, woman, something smells rotten here. What is it?"

3Bii   The old woman had found a rotten rat. Saying, "Here, this is what you smell," she threw it outside. The old man ate it.

The young woman peered through the hole in the bark cover. She saw that the old man had many mushrooms growing down his back, along with leaves and grasses, and many men's legs hung around his anus. She sat still, deeply afraid.

In the morning the old woman showed her the way to go, telling her to go quickly and to place her feet on either side of the path, so the old man would not see her footprints. The young woman did so. She climbed up the hill to where the youth was waiting.

"The old man, your father's sister's husband, almost killed me," she told him. "But I came."

"I warned you he was a bad man," he replied.

"Now take this pork neck and eat," she requested.

3Bi   But the youth replied, "No, I won't eat yet." Instead he asked her, "Do you know my father's sister's husband's name?"

"Yes," she replied, "Kilua Pale."

"My father's sister's name?" he asked.

"Ialibu Lapame," she said.

"The house site?"

"Egapulamiada."

"My father's sister's husband's axe?"

"Adada Ruaro."

"This stick?" which he held, about to strike her dead. She answered correctly (for the old woman had instructed her).

"My father's sister's husband's pig?"

"Puramenalasu."

Each time she had answered correctly. But he questioned her
more. "Which climbing loop do you want, the large or small one?"

"The small one, for I am not heavy." He gave it to her and then
questioned her more:

"This black-palm tree?"

"It's Pualapulamaga yawi."

"This pool?"

"Buna kumi."

"That other one?"

"Lepa kumi."

Then he asked her, "Will you climb that tall palm or the short
one?" She replied, "I'll climb the short one." The man then climbed
up his palm and the woman climbed hers, but more slowly, for she
was not accustomed to climbing.

11i   When she neared the top he kicked her off and she fell into the
pool beneath with a loud splash.

11ii   The man's ghost became the broom-like inflorescence (*painyali*)
of the black-palm tree, and the woman became a *kuri keago,* a kind of
frog.

Tale 33: The Ghosthusband Lost

0 A girl named Saipunyu lived by herself. The way people do in tales,
she made a very large garden extending from Yaro River to Mt.
Keresa and from the Lemako Stream to Kolapi. In it she had planted
many kinds of food crops. In the part close to Amaru and Kuare she
grew sweet potatoes. She also looked after a pig, Puramenalasu, who
stayed with her. Often, when she left for her garden work, she
would ask the pig to fetch firewood or some dry sword-grass stalks,
and the pig would obey.

One day, when it was sunny, she said to Puramenalasu, "I don't
want to stay in the sun, working in an open garden. I think I'll make
a new garden on the far side of Mount Keresa, in the forest at Walu."

She told the pig to fetch some firewood and sweet potatoes from one of the bearing gardens.

Leaving the pig, she crossed Mount Keresa to the land at Walu. She worked hard and cut down much forest, all of it between Keresa and the Sugu River. The next day she went back again. She had several axes—one for travelling, one for ceremony, another for garden work, and a bushknife. On the third day she prepared the garden for burning. On each day the pig brought back food for both of them, as well as twigs and grass stalks to burn.

On the third day, she piled the brush at the tree bases in preparation for burning. The following day she brought with her some coals from her hearth, set the garden afire, and returned home in the evening. On the next day she brought cuttings to plant, and, working until dusk, planted the entire garden. She brought the cuttings from her house in many netbags piled on her head, carried on her back, suspended from her shoulders, and even held in her teeth.

After all the garden was planted, she stayed at her house and did not return, though she occasionally told her pig, Puramenalasu, to have a look. When eventually she did go herself, she found the food plentiful. Some of the Setaria greens were already rotting, but there was much *koba* and *kibita* greens and much taro.

6i   She cut some cucumbers from the vine, sliced them open, and spread them out in the sun to dry. After that, she ate them. Feeling somewhat drowsy now, she reclined on the trunk of a fallen *pora* tree. While lying there, she felt the tree move up and down. Saipunyu guessed that someone must be walking along it. Looking up, she saw a handsome man approaching, wearing a fine bailer shell.

She asked, "Are you a village man (*ada ali*) or a bush man (*raa ali*)?"

"I'm a village man," was the answer.

"Do you see all this food, then?" she asked him. "There's enough here for several people." She took the cucumbers she had dried and salted and offered them to him. He looked tired from journeying, but he ate and was refreshed.

Saipunyu saw that he had brought a very large bundle, of which he had said nothing as yet. But presently he untied it, and she saw that it contained many possums, wrapped in a black-palm sheath. Then he brought out a second bundle and told her, "In the one bundle are young possums and innards, and in the other are large possums." He told her to take both bundles and put them in her netbag. She did so, and with them she put a variety of garden foods. Then she carried the lot back to the house, together with some firewood. The young man went with her.

As they approached the house, they saw smoke rising; the pig had prepared a slow fire of dry twigs. First they cooked and ate the immature possums and innards, leaving the rest aside. The next day they ate the large possums. After that they both stayed there.

6ii   One day Saipunyu asked the man if there were people in the place he had come from. "If there are," she said, "then we must go there." But first, she said, they must kill the pig.

The couple first cut good varieties of plantains, such as *gusede* and *kibame,* along with other foods. Then they killed, cooked, and butchered Puramenalasu. Every odd piece of meat or innards they cut in half and shared between them. Each took a full side of pork and put it in a netbag.

Next, Saipunyu cut a clump of *kabo* sugar cane that was growing near the house and divided it. Some she put in her netbag along with some salt, and some she gave to the man. Each now had three netbags full. All this they did at her place, in Kaluake, and when it was done the girl said, "Let's go now."

They went from Apipalu to Konaka. The youth was carrying his bundle of sugar cane, uncut, on his shoulder along with cuttings for planting. But Saipunyu, who started out carrying the sugar cane on her head, later thought, "This pork I am carrying is heavy and makes me out of breath. I must cut the cane into small lengths and put them in my netbag. When I'm thirsty, I'll chew some." So she cut the cane into pieces.

They went on and eventually reached the Yaro River. The river was high, and there was no bridge. But the youth laid down his lengths of cane on the current and walked on them across the river. He stood on the far shore. Saipunyu called to him to lay down the canes for her to cross, but he threw them into the water and disappeared.

The young woman waited and waited. She wept until her eyes were swollen. Why had she followed him there? she wondered. And why had she killed her pig and brought the pork there? She thought about this and wept. She had seen him cross the river and follow it upstream. But now she did not know what to do.

As she pondered, she rested her chin on her walking stick. Presently she felt the stick move. Looking down, she saw an opening in the earth. So she put her netbags aside and crawled into it. Seeing that it led to a wide path, she retrieved her bags and followed it.

Before, when that man was leading her along, he had said, "If people ask you how you have come, you must say you came along the path of the *pakira* (village rat) and the *repoto* (bush rat)." Saipunyu guessed that this tunnel was what he was talking about, and she continued to follow it.

Presently she encountered an old woman, who asked her, "Who are you?" Saipunyu explained, "I have come along the rats' path," and she offered the old woman some pork and salt. The old woman instructed her to continue along.

6iii   After going on further, the girl came to an old, red-skinned woman, who had long tusks covered in *wabi* wrappings; she stood on the other side of a fence outside a house. Asked once again who she was, Saipunyu explained. This old woman told her that she could stay there, but that an old man, her husband, would be coming along shortly, and she was afraid of what might happen.

So Saipunyu took some pig's belly fat and offered it to the old woman with salt. The old one ate and ate until she was full. "Oh, I've eaten enough now, but this other one will come soon," she said.

"I will see to that," replied Saipunyu.

After they had sat for a while longer they heard a *ruuu* sound. "The one I spoke to you of is coming now," said the old woman.

When she had first come there, Saipunyu saw that the old woman was holding a large bundle bound in black-palm sheaths. The old woman continued to hold it with both hands, even while the girl fed her the pork.

Saipunyu told the old woman, "There's more pork; I shall give some to him as well." So she took some fat, heated it until it began to melt, put some salt on it, and waited.

3Bi   The old man approached saying, "*O sorosoro pua!* What a good smell here!"

"Come quietly," said the old woman. "You can eat!" When he drew near and sat down, Saipunyu took the warm fat and stuffed it in his mouth. "Good!" he exclaimed. Saipunyu gave him more fat, and again he said "Good!" He was full now, and the rest of the pork the girl left aside.

"Usually you eat people," said the old woman to her husband. "But this is a good thing, too, isn't it?" Then she told him to lie down, and he did so.

The old woman kept holding that bundle. Saipunyu saw that the wrappings were soiled from much handling. The two of them sat and recooked the remaining pork.

The next day the old man asked Saipunyu where she had come from, and she replied that she had come along the burrow of the *pakira* and *repoto* rats. "Aha!" was his reply.

10Ai   One day the old woman said, "The two of us are going to visit a pig kill to the south. You must look after things here well." The young woman agreed. The old couple fetched water, firewood, and all sorts of foods for her, and they made her sit down in the middle of it all, inside the house. They told her not to go outside, not even to relieve herself. Everything, they told her, had been left for her, inside. And they told her, too, to hold the palm-sheath bundle carefully. The young woman agreed. She had brought with her all her possessions, her decorations, her *rakia* love potion, and so on. She had everything there with her.

10Aii   They told her, "Even if you see this house burning, do not go outside, for it is just deceiving you. Just stay and hold the bundle. Even if the house burns, just sit." Then the two left her.

10Aiii   After Saipunyu had sat for a while, she saw the house burning toward her from the other end. But she had prepared everything, so she just sat there while the house burned. Everything seemed to be in flames. Soon the fire reached the spot where she had left her *rakia* love potion in a small *karubi* gourd. This *rakia* moved over to where she was sitting. Saipunyu was concerned about it, and she reached over to pick it up. But as she did so, the bundle she had been holding slipped to the ground.

10Aiv   Immediately a large, red-furred dog leapt out of it. Saipunyu trembled as she looked at the dog, which was stretching itself. It trotted away along a path.

The girl followed it. It led her to a good men's house with tall casuarinas and clumps of ornamental grasses growing outside it. The dog walked up to the house. Inside were many compartments tightly fastened with *kalipu* vines. The dog entered and chewed through the vines that secured one of the compartments. Then it dragged out a youth and, with its sharp teeth, bit him in the kidneys and soon chewed him in half.

Saipunyu went inside the house and saw him lying there, eaten in half. Now she realized why the two old people were afraid of the bundle being dropped. She wept. Then, gathering the remains of that man, she put them in her netbag and returned to the burnt-out house site.

The old couple had planted a banana plant and told her to watch for the new leaves: when the leaves were growing out, the couple would be returning. Now Saipunyu saw that the leaves were growing out. She sat and wept, her eyes swelling.

The old man and woman approached. "We smelled the house burning," said the old man. Then he saw that the dog had escaped and had killed the youth. "Ah, you did not look after it well," he continued. "You're not the only one who is sorry! I told you not to release that bundle. Now it is all your doing." The two old people put mud on their faces and mourned. They put on Job's-tears necklaces, mourning skirts, and sat in mourning.

This one who died was their son. He was the same one who had disappeared up the river, and he was a ghost. When the old couple asked Saipunyu how she had come and she had answered "By the rats' burrow," they knew that the youth had led her there. The three of them stayed on.

9Bi   Saipunyu was now a fearfully big woman (*palapi winya*), for her husband had died. She began to tend the gardens there after their mourning had finished. To one of them she took the man's remains. She made a place inside a heap of sugar-cane leavings and placed his head and leg bones there.

9Bii   Later, while sitting outside the house, she would occasionally see lightning glowing near the garden where she had placed the youth's bones. She would sit down outside the house at night in the moonlight. She would sit and roll bark fibers into twine on her thigh. While she did this she would think of the youth, and she would weep. It was then that she would see the lightning glowing.

After about four weeks of this, she went back to this garden, and there she found a boy who, as happens in our tales, grew up quickly. He grew into the youth he was before.

6iv   Saipunyu went to see him secretly. She did not take him back to the old people's house, though; and he warned her not to speak of him to those two. This she agreed not to do. She would go to the garden to meet him, and the two would sing courtship songs for a while before each returned to his or her house. They did this while she continued to live with her mother- and father-in-law.

10Ai   Once Saipunyu said, "We must go sometime to your house, which I have not yet seen. Let us go now."

"No," he replied, "you must go back."

One day, though, she decided to follow him home. So she walked behind him as he returned home along a poor path full of brambles. Soon they came to a large *kero* tree which had fallen across the path. This she could not cross over. "I told you you could not come," said the youth. "Only I can cross."

But when she insisted on following him, he told her to close her eyes. She did so, and when she opened them again she was on the other side. The two went on and eventually reached his house.

The youth gave Saipunyu a bark cloth and a pandanus-leaf mat; he told her to lie on the mat and cover herself with the cloth in a corner of the house. Other ghosts had come to do a *koda* dance, and now that it was dark, they danced.

Since this youth used to dance in the front rank, the others called out to him, "Kama Nebo *aipea!* Kama Nebo *aipea!* What's the front-line dancer doing?"

"Oh, I'm sick," the youth called back. The others remarked, "He's the one who always *koda* dances, and he has never been sick before!"

From her corner, Saipunyu saw that the other ghosts were coming to bring him food. They piled feces on a wooden plate and on top put two ripe *meroka* bananas. She wept, recalling how she was responsible for his being there.

Dawn broke, and he said, "I warned you what this place was like. Now you must return home."

"No," she replied. "What you do I shall do; what you eat I shall eat."

10Aii   "No, you must really go." And he led her back to the garden. There he said, "You can come back here. We'll meet here in this garden, as before. Give some excuse to your parents-in-law, but never tell them why you come here."

10Aiii   The two old ones, however, pressed her. Finally she yielded and told them that she had gone to stay with the one whom the dog had killed, who had been joined together with a piece of bark cloth around his waist.

10Aiv, 11i   Well, that youth had told her not to say anything, and then she spoke to her parents-in-law. She told them how she had gone with him, seen how he lived, and then returned. But this youth heard her saying all this, and he thought, "She will not see me from now on!" He did not return.

11ii   Because that woman spoke to her mother- and father-in-law, now we do not see ghosts. If she had not spoken, village people and ghosts might still marry; but now they do not. That youth was invisible; lost like a needle of flying-fox bone, he was not seen again. And that is why ghosts do not come back.

Tale 34: The Evil Ghostmother

0   Several girls one day went to catch fish. One of them presently grew tired of catching and stringing the small fish, so she sat down on a rock by the water's edge. Feeling drowsy, she lay down to sleep.

6i   A youth wandered along and saw her lying there. He knelt down and cut *pu yapai*, decorative incisions, into her flesh above her breasts while she slept. When eventually the young woman awoke, she felt something on her breast and, looking down, saw the marks. "What made this?" she wondered. Embarrassed to think of how the other girls would view this (since the incisions are made by a boyfriend), she went back directly to the house.

She was like Abuwape now, as she alone sat down inside the house, never coming out. The other girls put fish and other food into the house for her to eat. She refused to leave her room or in any way show herself. And so it went.

One day the others decided to find out why she would not come out in their presence. They decided to put one of them, a very little girl, inside a cooking bamboo and stand this bamboo in a corner of the house while they were away. They did this. When all the others were off, this small girl saw the young woman come out of her room. She was pregnant.

Later, when the others returned, this little girl told the others that their sister was pregnant. "Oh, sister," they called out to her, "you never told us!'

Outside their house, meanwhile, someone was preparing the ground for a new house. First the posts were placed; then, later, the mat walls and a thatched roof were put up. None of the girls knew who was making it. The next day, a sleeping place was made in the house. And when the sisters came back from the garden, the following afternoon, the house had been finished. The pregnant girl went to stay there.

After a while she gave birth to a son. The sisters saw that a pig had been gutted, singed, and left for them. Again and again this occurred; they ate the pork without knowing who had left it. Whoever was leaving it did the killing and cooking unseen: all they saw was cooked taro and cooked pork hung from *walu*-wood posts. Sometimes the food came by day, sometimes by night; but they never saw how.

6iii, 3Di   One day, when the son was now grown to about Miru's age (four years or so), an old woman came and said to the mother, "Woman, you don't look after my son well. I've never seen you tend his pigs; all you ever do is sit in the house and eat my son's pork. Let's go now."

So the girl killed the sisters' pig, Puramenalasu, butchered it, and she carried off a large side.

The three of them went alone – the young woman, her son, and the old woman. They walked along under a hot sun. Presently the younger woman said, "Mother-in-law, I want some water." But the old woman did not allow her to drink, and the three continued on.

After they had gone further, the young woman saw some leaves of the kind used for plugging bamboo water containers. Indicating a pool, the old woman said, "Women such as yourself often drink in this place. Put your child aside and drink." She was a good-looking young woman, this one. "Take your skin and put it aside," said the old woman. This the woman, Abuwape, did, revealing a pale and gleaming skin underneath. Then the old woman pushed her into the pool. In that pool were many women who had drowned this way.

The old woman then put on the young one's skin. She gave the dead woman's bag of pork to the boy to carry. But unseen, the boy had taken some of his mother's hair and placed it inside his bark belt.

The two of them continued on, the boy weeping.

His father heard the weeping from where he was sitting. "My son doesn't know about me," he thought. "He cannot know where to look for me. How is it that he's coming here?" He went to look. Seeing them coming, he called out, "Oh, boy, I didn't call for you. Why have you come?"

"He is crying so much because he misses his mother's sisters," said the woman.

The three of them started off to the man's place. But first the husband told the woman to cut some soft *kabo* sugar cane from a clump, for he was suspicious. While the woman was away, he quickly asked the child what had happened. The boy showed his father his mother's hair and related the events. This woman who had come was not *his* mother, he said.

3Dii   "All right," said the man, and he took the boy to sleep in his house. The next day he told the woman, "Let's go and burn the new garden." They did so, and when the smoke was thick enough to conceal him from her, he took his bow and arrow and killed her. Then he placed her body on top of the fire and burnt it.

Then the two, the father and son, returned to the pool where the young woman drowned, the son showing his father the way. They made a platform on top of it and on this platform they built a small men's house. When the house was finished, the father told his son to do a *rupale* dance along the central corridor. The son sang:

> *Ayama yali wapu ropa ropa winya, aya na ama,*
> *Ayama kili wapu ropa ropa winya, aya na ama.*
> Mother, waving pandanus tree of Ialibu Mountain, mother,
> Mother, waving pandanus tree of Giluwe Mountain, mother.

6iv   Now the mother (her ghost) heard this singing, and through a hole in the floorboards of the house she appeared, her head white like that of the *kaluga* duck. She sang,

> *Kuri aki repalisi mula mula epa, nena pearipula dia, na naki ama.*
> This sister-frog went to catch fish that's all, it (your birth) was not done for you, my son.

11i-ii   The father had readied a noose of rope, and as the head appeared he tightened it around the neck, hoping to pull the woman up. But he could not; she was ashamed to come out. He pulled and pulled, but to no avail. We hear, nowadays, noises from such pools, from dark red-coloured pools that kill men, and that is the sound of that woman struggling. The two others, the father and son, became two *kapipi* tree-ferns by the pool's edge. One is tall, the other short.

Tale 35: The Woman and the Bush Rat

0   There was a girl named Laneame who lived with her father, a man of Kamarepa clan named Ade. The two of them looked after a pig, Puramenalasu. The old man died, and Laneame buried him in Pililiada, where a path leads to the gardens at Raya and Kobea. She put him in a hole, folding his knees up so he would fit. After that she went back to her house and sat in mourning. She did not put him on a platform above the ground but dug a hole and stuffed him in.

3Bi   One day she went to look at this place. She saw that the dead man's knees were protruding from the soil. So she took her axe and, using the side of the blade, knocked the knees back into the ground. Having done that, she returned to sleep at home.

But again the knees came up, and again she had to hammer them back down. And so it went. She would cut heavy pieces of wood, put them on top, and cover them with earth, but still the knees kept coming out of the ground. Things like this happen in tales; the knees kept coming up no matter how hard she tried to keep them down.

Laneame began to worry. "Does he want to come and kill me?" she wondered.

One day she told the pig, "I think he's coming to kill us; his knees keep coming up even though I pound them back and heap timbers and earth on top. I will go to the garden. Watch carefully."

3Bii,6i   She went to fill her netbag with sweet potatoes from the garden. While she was so engaged, a bush rat (*repoto*) approached. It said, "Your father, whom you buried, has come out and is now hiding in the house, on top of the firewood rack. Give me your netbag, your grass skirt, and everything you wear. Then go and cut a tree-fern trunk and carve it, making two breasts, two buttocks, two arms, a head and eyes, and the rest."

So this woman made the carving and put her netbag, skirt, and pearl shell on it. Now the rat said, "This tree-fern trunk will carry the sweet potatoes and give them to the pig. Hide and watch it as it goes." Away went the fern trunk. Laneame followed it, hid, and peered into the house through a hole in the wall. Immediately she saw the red eyes of her father, who was lying in wait on the firewood rack. As the trunk went inside to give the potatoes to the pig, the old man jumped down and bit into the neck of the carving.

"Oh, he would have killed me like that!" thought Laneame.

6ii   Then the rat told her, "Go now and wait there beside the path, further on." Obeying, she left the house and her father's body, walked along the path, and stopped to wait for the rat. Soon a young man arrived carrying a piece of *kayabo* sugar cane. He said, "Your father very nearly killed you! Come with me."

But Laneame replied, "No, I cannot. A rat told me to wait here, and I will."

"But your father will come and find you. We must go." But Laneame insisted on doing what the rat said. Finally the youth left.

She began to worry now, for it was nearly dark. "Ah, I think he's coming to kill me now," she fretted. "Should I have gone with that man?" She decided to walk further along the path.

6iii   Presently she heard the sound of running water. Glancing back, she thought she heard the sound of her father coming. But now, having come to the stream and finding herself thirsty, she bent down to drink.

Yet as she did so, the water receded. When she moved further upstream and bent down to drink, again the water receded. As she went on yet further, she saw a young woman standing in front of her. The woman said, "Your father will kill you if you don't come quickly. This water you wish to drink is not water. I made it." And the young woman led her away.

6iv   They soon came to a place with many bamboos and casuarinas growing. The woman said to Laneame, "Just yesterday did I die, and others have buried me. Now I'll go to sleep in my place. When you see people, do not say anything about me. The *repoto* rat you saw is my brother. While you were waiting on the path, he put the rat skin into a karst hole and came to you." Saying that, she put Laneame into her brother's house.

This man, the youth she had seen earlier, now approached. He rebuked her, "Before, when I saw you, you did not want to come with a rat, even though your father was about to kill you!"

10Ai   The two stayed, and eventually the woman gave birth to a son.

10Aii   Shortly thereafter, the husband began a garden near the Yalo River, a forest garden with cucumbers, *koba* and *kibita* greens, and other crops. One day, as he was leaving for the bush to hunt game, he told Laneame, "Do not go to that garden."

10Aiii-iv   But Laneame did go there to fetch greens and cucumbers. While she worked, she hung the netbag holding her baby son on a branch nearby. Then that ghost, that old man whose knees had kept on coming up, came into the garden, bit the child in the neck and killed it.

11i   When Laneame's husband returned to the garden, he and his wife carried the body of the child back to the house. That night, the ghost came again, wishing to kill his daughter's husband. But the husband was ready. He shot the ghost and burned him in the fire.

11ii   If that old man had not been killed he might still attack us; but now he cannot.

Tale 36: The Woman and the Snake

0,6i In the company of men of Pobarepa and Masigirepa clans, at Kaluake, there lived a woman named Repoto. One day she was working
in the gardens. She had taken off her skirt for her work and a small
snake came and curled up on it. Repoto went to tell this to her
brothers. They killed it, cut it into sections, and cooked it in an earth
oven. But when they opened the oven, they saw the snake had joined
itself together and was alive. So they cut it into pieces and cooked it

*Plate 4. Assisted by his father and his sons, a village leader in Iapi prepares a
snake for cooking in an earth oven.*

a second time, but the same thing happened again, and yet again. Repoto's clansmen said they ought to kill a pig and find out about this snake. So they killed two pigs and gave all the pork to Repoto.

6ii   She put this pork into netbags and went off following the snake. When she paused to catch her breath, for her load was heavy, the snake paused as well. Presently the snake disappeared underneath a clump of *irawapu* grass by the side of the path. She followed it.

After going some distance, they came to a house and a yard in which all sorts of flowers, trees, and bamboos were growing. And not far away was a garden with much *padi, kuni* pitpit, taro, and bananas. It looked as if nothing had been taken from it for eating, though. Repoto went inside the house, put down the bag of pork, and took out a bit of pork backbone to eat. Then she slept in the sleeping room, while the snake curled up on the hearth in the front room. She stayed in that part of the house, first eating and then sleeping.

When she returned to the porch, she saw that all the pork had disappeared. But she had kept a small amount aside and decided to warm it up. She said to the snake, "I have no greens to cook with this pork."

The snake uncoiled and went to a large garden at a good distance from the house. Repoto followed. The snake coiled itself around the base of greens, around a *lobainya* sugar cane, around taro, bananas, *kuni akena* pitpit, and other crops. Each time, the woman took some of the plants thus indicated. Then she followed the snake back to the house. She cooked this food while the snake coiled itself by the fire. The next day—and every day—they did the same.

One day, Repoto thought for a while and then said, "I haven't done any work, though I've eaten the food from this garden. I must do something." She followed the snake to a new garden that had been cut on good land where *yakua* trees had grown. She began to clear away the bush.

When she returned on the following day to continue working, she saw that all this work had been finished. So she started the work of turning the earth for sweet-potato mounds, working until dusk. When she returned the next day, the mounding had been finished. And the same thing happened with the planting.

Now she wondered where she might find firewood. The snake led her to a place in the forest where there was a rock shelter and a stand of *yakua* trees. This shelter was stacked with good dry *muni* logs. Repoto brought some of this wood back to the house in several trips while the snake watched by the cave.

6iv   When she returned after the last trip, the snake was no longer there. Repoto wondered, "Now what shall I do? Where has the snake gone?" As she looked around for it, she heard some rustling in the undergrowth. Turning to look, she saw a tall, thin, pale-skinned young man, whose body was covered with old scars. He was carrying a heavy carcass of pork.

"Your brothers treated me badly," he said, "but I've taken pity on you, and I have brought you this pork."

The two stayed together, and Repoto gave birth to a son, who grew to be about as old as Palusi's son—three years or so. At this time the husband said, "Let us go and give payment for the boy." He arranged a number of sticks, each one representing a pig, shell, or block of salt he would give.

The three of them closed their eyes, and upon opening them, they found themselves at Kaluake. When her brothers saw them, they cried out loudly, "Repoto has come!" Repoto saw that all her relatives were wearing necklaces of Job's-tears seeds and mourning skirts, for they thought she was dead. But now Kaluake was filled with shells and pigs (the snake-youth's bridewealth), enough for every person of those two clans, Pobarepa and Masigirepa.

10Bi   When the three were about to depart, Koke, Repoto's youngest brother, said, "Let us go back together!" Repoto refused, but he insisted. Then Repoto's husband asked his son, "Tell your mother's brother he cannot come." The boy did so, but still Koke insisted upon following them.

10Bii   Halfway back, Repoto's husband said to her "Wait for me, I will go and get some leaves for rolling tobacco." But instead he rejoined them carrying a heavy carcass of pig. This he gave to Koke. But still Koke did not return; he continued to follow them. When they reached the house, the husband said, "Well, you have indeed come. Now you must never go outside this house. Even if we have gone away and closed the door, you must stay inside."

One day, when the sun shone brightly, the husband, wife, and son went to the gardens, closing the door behind them and telling Koke, "You can eat these pork ribs inside the house, but do not go outside."

10Biii   After a little while, though, Koke decided that the pork needed to be cooked with greens, so he opened the door and went outside. Near the side of the house he saw a small garden with many varieties of good food plants. There was taro, *padi, kuni,* and other greens.

So he climbed over the fence, snapped off some *tualepa* greens, went back inside, and cooked the pork and greens in a bamboo.

10Biv   While he was doing this, the three others were returning home. Repoto was coming behind. The husband suddenly felt sick; he slowed down and let his son go ahead. But then the son stumbled, fell, and died. The father saw the boy fall to the ground with a noise like a stem snapping. Then he, too, fell and died. Repoto hurried back to the house. She looked at the garden. Where Koke had broken those plants, many young men lay down dead – good-looking men with bark belts and thick hair.

Angered, Repoto scolded her brother, "Look what you've done! First you insist upon coming; then you don't do what I say!"

He replied, "I wanted to cook the pork, so I cut some greens."

"All right," said Repoto. "Come outside and see what has happened."

Koke looked in the garden. Then she led him along the path and showed him her husband and son. Koke stood there trembling.

11i   The sister told him that he had acted badly and that she was grieved. Picking up a sharp digging stick, she speared him in the side, and then she killed herself in the same way.

11ii   Men, when they marry, might have turned into snakes and then back into men, as this youth did. But Koke killed those men, and now we do not become snakes or vegetables – not *padi* greens, not *rani* greens, not taros, nor bananas. We just stay as humans. We die as well, because Koke killed those men who were greens, bananas, and taros. For this act, his sister made an *ali kalia* revenge killing against her brother, and this is our custom.

Tale 37: The Woman and the Possum

0   Limu and his sister Raguame lived together and looked after many gardens. They had gardens in the area around the house and a new garden in the forest at Putirumu. Shortly after they had planted this forest garden, the brother became sick. Raguame then put on male ornaments: cordylines, belt, breechcloth, and a large headdress with bird feathers. Believing that her brother might have succumbed to *kasa* sickness while they were felling the trees for the garden, she killed a pig to cure him. But the illness remained. Next she made a *rumu wai* ritual for him, but still his sickness continued. Then she made a *ribu* ritual and killed another pig. But the youth died. She put him on a mortuary platform and then sat in mourning.

Who would help her with the gardens and firewood? she wondered. The two of them had been caring for a large pig, Puramen-alasu, and this pig felt pity for the young woman. It said, "Who else is here to help us? *I* will go and fetch firewood." So the pig left, cut a dry *muni* trunk, and pulled it back to the house. The two made a fire and slept. Then the pig dug some sweet potatoes from the gardens, and they cooked and ate them. Because she was still sitting in mourning, the girl stayed inside while the pig fetched the firewood and worked in the garden.

One day after finishing her mourning, she went with the pig to the new garden at Putirumu, where the brother had fallen ill. There she saw many food plants growing. There were many cucumbers, some ripe, some old and tough. She picked some fresh, ripe ones and piled them on the ground, on top of her netbag. Then, seeing how weeds had covered the garden, she decided to clear it.

6i   As she began her work, a small *pakena* possum came along a fallen log and began to eat the cucumbers. She had left the pig outside the garden fence, and now this pig began to squeal, *mmm mmm!* The pig wanted to come and kill this possum that was stealing their food. It jumped over the fence into the garden.

Raguame watched as the possum jumped onto the pig's head, ran down its back, and began to stroke the back of its neck. Soothed, the pig lay down to sleep. When the girl saw this, she took fright. Quickly she roused the pig and led it back to the house. The possum picked a few cucumbers and, holding them in its paws, followed her back while eating them.

When they reached the house, Raguame took some ripe bananas, ate a couple, and gave the peels to the pig. Then the possum came inside and sat down. She offered it some bananas; it took them, peeled them and ate. The woman, the pig, and the possum slept the night.

The next morning the possum said, "Let us kill this pig. Take some firewood down from the rack above the hearth and throw it outside: we will cook the pig." But the young woman replied, "No, this pig helps me in all ways. Why should I kill it?" But the possum simply climbed up to the firewood rack, dragged out some pieces of firewood, and threw them outside. Then, when the fire was blazing, the possum walked over the pig's back. The pig died. Then it pulled the pig into the fire to singe its hide.

Raguame sat and wept for her pig. Meanwhile, the possum cooked first the pig's entrails and then the rest of it. "Come, we will have some pork to eat and then the two of us will go off," the possum said. But the woman kept on weeping.

6ii   Finally the possum took her fine *kaipi* netbag and filled it with pork. It said, "All right, I am going now." Off it went.

"Wait!" Raguame cried out. She gathered her brother's fine "bone" pearl shells, his *wiruapu* bow, his stone axe, and his other possessions. These she threw onto the mortuary platform. Then she got his bird-of-paradise plumes and his *pokai* shells. These she took with her along with the pork. She followed the path the possum had taken and finally she caught up with it. The possum told her, "Wait here. I want to speak to a woman cousin of mine," and it left her. She sat down and waited.

Presently she saw a young man coming along the path. His thick hair was covered with a fine *raguna* hat, and he wore a bright pearl shell on his chest and a good breechcloth. "Come, we'll go now," he said to Raguame.

But she answered, "No, I'm waiting for a *pakena* possum. He hasn't come yet, so I cannot follow you."

"All right," said the other, "stay here, then." And he left.

6iii　　After waiting a while longer, she went further along the path, still carrying her netbag. It was now quite dark, and she had to feel her way with her *walu* stick. After a while she felt the stick strike something; it was the sitting log of the porch of a men's house. From inside she heard a voice saying, "Open the door," and then more softly, "That will be the *pakena's* woman." But after she entered, the same person asked, "Who are you here?" "Oh, this is what happened," said Raguame, and she explained her story. "And I followed this possum, but he did not return; so I came along here by myself. It grew dark on the path."

"Good," was the reply.

She stayed there with this man and his wife, her parents-in-law. Then they gave her a gourd of *yokayo* oil and said, "Go stay with your husband. You will bear many children and look after many pigs. First, you will look after a red-coloured pig. When it comes time to make a ritual, you must throw the cooked liver of this pig in a pool, and you must pour this oil in it as well. Now, when you go you will meet two women on the path. You must speak to them thus: 'Popayame and Popame, go on your way!' And to the next two you see, say: 'Puriri and Pudini, go on your way!'"

Raguame followed these instructions. She greeted two women she met, "Popayame and Popame, go on your way!" After she had passed by, the women turned back, looked at her and said, "The *pakena's* wife!" Raguame went along further and met two more women, whom she greeted by name. They, too, said, "The *pakena* married her!"

The two old people, her in-laws, had also given her a ceremonial staff (*ekepayo*) which she carried. Further on she saw her husband sitting by the path. But when he caught sight of her coming, he rose and walked away. She followed. When he reached a wide blood-red pool, he parted it with his own *ekepayo* and crossed. "Do you see this pool?" he asked her. She approached it and aimed a blow at it with her *ekepayo*, saying, "Blood-red pool, open." The water parted and allowed her to pass through.

6iv　　The two of them stayed together and made gardens; and Raguame soon bore a son, who grew quickly.

11i　　They prepared a sacrifice. After they killed a rufous pig,

Raguame removed its intestines and threw them into the pool along with some of the oil. Then she put on her bird feathers and the two of them danced around the pool.

11ii   Today we kill pigs near such pools and throw pork into it. This is called a *ramu wai* ritual.

Tale 38: The Woman, the Possum, and the Husband

0   There were several girls who lived together, all good-looking ones. One day they prepared some taro, sweet potatoes, edible pitpit, sugar cane and other foods. Then they went to catch fish where Bisipa Stream joins the Sugu River. Carrying their nets, they fished their way upstream to the land at Yawareada and Tigawi.

Some of the girls moved faster than the others. The young woman who was furthest ahead found herself feeling sleepy from constantly peering into the water. So she put down her netbag of sweet potatoes, which also contained her skirt – she had taken it off to wade – and set it on the bank. There, at the confluence of Tigawa Stream and the Sugu River, she found a nice place with many *pai* trees growing. Leaving her things there, she put her hands into the water and felt around for fish.

6i   She found many of them in this small stream and as she worked her way upstream looking for more, she saw an *ekamu* possum sitting on a *pai* branch that overhung the stream.

"Oh good!" she thought. "How good it will be to eat!" And picking up a stick of wood for a club, she went after it. But the possum quickly ran back to the stand of *pai* trees, where she had left her netbag. There it pulled her skirt from the bag and ran off with it. The girl was wearing only a few leaves she had tied around her waist.

She picked up her netbag and gave chase to the possum, thinking she would kill the animal first and then rejoin the other women, whom she heard approaching from downstream. She ran after the animal, carrying her netbag of potatoes and fish.

But then she changed her mind and decided to go back to the river, for she was afraid she might get lost. It would not matter if she gave up the chase, she thought, since she could always make herself another skirt.

6ii   She began to retrace her steps. But then, when she looked behind her, she saw that the possum was following her, looking her in the eye. So she turned and began to follow it again. After going a long distance, she finally came out of the forest to an open place where sword grass was growing.

Then she called to the possum, "If you are a man doing this, stop and give me back the skirt!" But the animal walked on. She followed it. The place looked as though a garden had once been made there, and beyond were many *yakua* trees—a sign of a good garden site. Further away in the distance was a well-kept garden.

On she went following the possum. The narrow path presently widened. Soon she saw footprints in the earth. Reaching the edge of a garden, the one she had seen earlier, she crouched in the bush and looked.

6iv   The garden held all sorts of edible greens, and in their midst was a handsome young man sitting on a log eating cucumbers. The possum trotted up to the man, carrying the skirt in its mouth. "Oh, now I see," thought the girl, "the possum was leading me to him!"

Just then, as she shifted her position, she stepped on a twig, which cracked loudly. The man heard the noise and called out, "Are you someone from far away, or someone from the village?"

"Someone from the village," she called back.

"Come here, then, and eat some cucumbers. This little one, who has your skirt, is my dog."

The woman remained where she was. She asked for her skirt, and the man sent the possum to her with it. As she took off the leaves she was wearing and tied her skirt on, she mused, "Well, maybe I shall marry this man." She walked into the garden.

They sat in the garden for a time and then went along the path to his house. Around the house were many large pigs and various kinds of plants and trees. They stayed there. He told her, "You must make the gardens and look after the pigs. This little "dog" of mine will kill many possums for you to eat."

Eventually the woman became pregnant, and in time she gave birth to a son. Meanwhile that dog killed many possums for her.

One day a small *kau* gecko came and sang, "*Na koda abi!* Our dance is soon!" The young man decided to attend. First, though, he procured strong pieces of *paipala* wood and strong vines. Then he instructed his wife to keep the door fastened tightly at night. "When you go to sleep," he said, "make a large fire first. I say this because my mother and sister were bad women (*koi winya*) before they died, and their ghosts may want to come and kill the two of you, you and our son."

Before he left, he planted a banana cutting and told his wife that when its new leaves started to grow out, he would be coming back. Then he departed.

The *ekamu* possum looked after the mother and son, though it always travelled along paths they could not see. Days passed.

3Di   One day the woman was coming back from the garden when the possum came close to her feet, looking anxious. She pondered this.

Was there someone else on the path, perhaps someone waiting to kill them? She went quickly back to the house with her son and the food she had collected. It was now nearly dusk.

The possum announced, "I shall go and look around, lest some ghosts or men come and kill us." Shortly thereafter – it was now quite dark – the possum returned and said, "We must secure the door, because those who want to kill us are approaching!"

They secured the door. The walls were of strong *raguna* bark. The door they braced with logs of *paipala* wood tied with strong *kalipu* vines. Soon they heard a noise, *ruguuu*, coming first from the direction of Raya, in the west, and then from Kolapi and Tidane in the east. "Ah, they are coming to kill us, surely!" thought the young woman. The little possum decided to watch outside. It dug a small hole underneath the house and left.

Not many weeks had passed since the youth's departure; only one week had he been away.

Soon the little possum returned. "Mother," he said, "Ones with tusks wrapped in *wabi* covers are coming. My father's (i.e., master's) mother, who is a big old woman, is coming with my father's sister. These women are coming to kill us for what my father has once done. They want to kill you two, his wife and his little boy."

She was sorely afraid. The possum told her to build up a bright fire. Soon the two women came, each holding a heavy *walu*-wood staff. With these they quickly broke the door apart, strongly tied though it was. The old woman entered, looking as though she were ready for fighting, her muscles flexed. She put her *walu* stick down, sat on the floor, and said, "Woman, this man is not really your husband; yet you continually eat the food he gives, and you burn his firewood. We have died and now we are ghosts, but still we talk!"

The young woman was afraid. Taking her son under her arm, she added wood to the fire and sat behind it. Across from her she saw the dead sister, daughter of this old woman. She thought, "They will surely kill us."

But the dead sister said, "Oh, mother, we cannot kill her. She is my brother's wife! She doesn't stay with anyone else. This woman and the small boy are my brother's."

But the old woman would not hear of this. She insisted she would kill the two, but then she said, "If I do not kill you, I will at least eat your pig. Kill it for me." The young woman answered, afraid, "Oh, I'll not keep you from killing and eating it. Do so. Just eat it, and take some *aipa* salt there." She hung back.

3Dii   Meanwhile this little *ekamu* was watching unseen. Seeing that the old woman was preparing to kill and eat the two, it sprang onto her face and bit her in both eyes and then in the side. The old woman rose, her arms flailing. "What's biting me?" she managed to cry before she died.

The other ghost woman rose to run away, but the possum bit her as well, in the kidneys on both sides. She, too, fell over, and then the possum tore out her eyes.

Now the wife and the possum pulled these bodies outside the house and then sat down again inside. "I'll look for a well," said the possum. "Get some rope ready to tie their necks."

The possum went off to look around for a well. It returned soon; it had found a deep one, a hole draining into the Yaro River with a small pool at the bottom. The girl and the possum dragged the two dead ghostwomen over to the well and threw them in. "Now let them come back and try to kill and eat us!" said they, returning home.

3Bi But on another occasion, when they were in the garden, they looked back to their house to see reddish smoke rising from the thatch. Returning, they found a tall old man sitting by the fire. He had whiskers like branches of an *u* tree. From his rear spread the legs of men, like cordyline leaves. He told the woman to come inside.

"Are you going now, or are you staying the night?" she asked him.

"I have heard something about you, and I have come," said the old man.

"Oh, what was it you heard?" she asked, "That we were preparing to kill many pigs shortly? That we had many shells? What?"

"Not that. But it's time to sleep now."

"All right," said the young woman, "but in the morning you must leave."

The two of them lay down. The woman, from her sleeping place, looked at the many legs hanging there from his bark belt. But the little possum said, "I will watch out for you, lie down and sleep." The woman lay down to sleep with her son beside her.

3Bii In the middle of the night the old man woke and rose to kill them. But he saw the whites of their eyes shining, so he went back and lay down again. "Tomorrow I will kill them in the garden," he planned, "for now they are not yet asleep."

In the morning the old man departed. He pretended he was leaving, but instead he went to wait for them in the garden. Now, in the vicinity of the garden were many deep holes, but the old man did not know where they lay.

The possum followed the old man. Suddenly it leapt and bit him on the leg. The man jumped and slapped at his leg, but just then the possum jumped and bit him on the other leg. Then it jumped higher and tore out his eyes. The old man writhed and stumbled around until he fell into one of the holes. The possum fell in with him, but it managed to catch hold of a ledge of stone. The old man fell to the bottom, but the possum climbed out.

It returned and said, "He is dead." The woman was overjoyed. "You've done so well," she said gratefully. They stayed on.

One day when they looked at the banana plant they saw that the leaves were growing out. "Oh, mother," said the possum, "I think father is about to come. We must prepare firewood and things to cook with the pork he will surely bring. Stay, and I will go and meet him on the path. Do not worry."

After they had fetched some cooking greens, the possum went off to meet his master and told him of what had occurred. "Aha!" he said simply.

The two came to the house, cooked the pork, and shared it with guests who had come to receive portions. They stayed on. Their house was like that of a white man, containing much wealth in pigs, pearl shells, bailer shells, bows, arrows, and oil. And in time, when their son was about as old as Nika, Driver's child, the mother once again became pregnant.

11i   One day, the husband asked his wife to carry their boy in a net-bag; they would go to catch fish in a nearby stream. He told the possum, "We are going to fish. Stay here and look after the house. If darkness comes and we are not back, sleep here alone. We will sleep in the forest." The possum assented.

The two walked along the path to Mugiri and Amaru, carrying their child and some sweet potatoes. They passed through Nire, Mukatupi, Kogariwala, and Asada, and entered the deep forest. They passed through Asada's dense stand of *karape* trees. Then they came to Tawitali, where they intended to spend the night in a hut that people had built when out gathering pandanus nuts. In the hut the two of them lit a fire and stowed their potatoes. Then they descended to the stream. The stream there is not a large one, and during the dry weather it has pools in which fish collect.

After catching some fish the two returned to the hut. The man said, "Some of these we'll smoke and carry back, and the rest we'll cook now. I'll go find some fern leaves for cooking, and I'll take my bow and arrow in case I see game." Then he went down to an area of old gardens, now overgrown with tree-ferns and a few pandanus palms. There he saw a large *dupa* possum, which he shot.

The woman was happy to see fresh meat. She cleaned out the intestines and cooked the carcass in leaves with some fish and sweet potatoes.

The next morning they fished some more. Then they headed back through Yawireada. Quickly, as things happen in tales, they came to Raliawe, then to Tibi. From there they looked back in the direction of their house and saw billows of smoke coming up. "Hey, is that our house on fire, or are people burning a garden there? I must go quickly and see!" said the man.

He hurried onward and looked again from Porada. He could now see that thick smoke was rising from their house. And it seemed as though the casuarinas, bananas, and sugar cane were also aflame. He came down to Yata and rubbed yellow mud on his face. Then he came closer, to Taraminya and to Kuare. When he reached the burning house he saw to his relief that all his possessions were outside: his pearl shells, pigs and salt; his *raguna* head covering, cowrie-shell rope and nassa-shell headband; his *wiruapu* bow, cassowary-feather ornaments—everything had been saved. That little possum had carried all his possessions outside before the fire could touch them.

Only one thing had been lost: the fire tongs. After safely taking all the valuable possessions out, the possum remembered that the tongs were still in the burning house. But when it went back to fetch it, the possum was badly burnt by flames that had spread from gourds of *yokayo* and *padapi* oil. Badly singed, the possum dragged itself from the house and rolled into a puddle of water, lying there nearly dead.

Now the man came up and clutched the possum, who said, "It will not do to hold me so, I'm nearly dead."

In his sorrow the man seized his axe and lopped a finger off.

"All these things I took from the burning house," said the possum. "But I also wanted to save the tongs we use to cook our sweet potatoes in the hearth, and then the fire burnt me. Now I am dying, but first I wish to see my mother's face."

The man told the possum that the woman was on her way from Yata. He continued to hold the possum to him, weeping. When the woman came, the possum announced it would make its last statement, its *nu yapara moke*. That woman, hearing this, tore at her ears and cut her fingers in sorrow.

"I am dying, you will stay on," said the possum. "It was my mistake to try to fetch this insignificant thing, the tongs." And it died.

Then the man broke his pearl shells, salt, bailer shells, bow, headband, banana plants, all sorts of things. And he buried them all in a hole with the possum.

11ii   I am finishing. If this possum had not been burnt by the house fire, it might still bring young women by fetching their skirts. And when our enemies or ghosts come to kill and eat us, it might help us. But this possum wanted to rescue the tongs from the fire, and it died. This is the story of the woman-taking possum, this *ekamu*. Now that the house burnt with that possum, we no longer see such animals. Away from this burnt house flew two *mumakarubi* quail, the mother and son. As for the man, he took his *wiruapu* bow, broke it in half, stuck the pieces in his rear and flew away as a *walawe* lorikeet.

Tale 39: The Woman and her Elusive Husband

0   A young woman stayed with her pig, Puramenalasu. This pig was like a man; it worked with her, helping her make her gardens. The two of them made many gardens, some with sugar cane, some with sweet potatoes, some with edible pitpit and leafy greens.

6i   One day the woman told the pig, "I'll go to fetch some food from the gardens. And you will prepare firewood." In the garden she gathered some bananas, taro, and other foods, and she put these in netbags. When she was about to return, a heavy rain fell, with a strong wind blowing. She waited, much afraid. Water was running everywhere around her. When the rain had stopped, she prepared to carry the food back to the house. But, feeling wet and cold, she decided to take only some of it with her.

When she reached the hill at Karapere and looked down at Tipuru, she saw her house was nearly covered with water. And she saw something white on the roof. Moving closer, she saw it was a bailer shell that had been put up there.

She waded through the water and fetched the shell. Then she began to look around for hoofprints of her pig. Finding them near a garden fence, she followed them. Soon she came across the pig; it was lying down beside the fence. "*Ama,* dear child, what happened?" she asked. The pig answered, "After the heavy rain fell, a pool covered the house. I ran here. Lie down over there, if you're tired." The woman did so.

6iii   After a while a young woman with uncropped hair came along. The pig woke the sleeping woman. The visitor asked her, "What are you doing there?"

She explained. Then the visitor said, "Come with me. But I must warn you: my mother is a bad woman. I won't look back at you as I approach the house."

Carrying their food with them, the two women and the pig departed. After they had gone on a distance, the woman said, "When we come close to the house I might glance back at you once. If I do so, hide quickly in back of a clump of *irawapu* grass."

And when they were approaching the house, she did indeed glance back. The other two, the woman and the pig, hid themselves.

The woman who had led them there went inside to cook them some sweet potatoes. Her mother watched her doing this and said, "You don't usually do this cooking now."

"I don't always do as I have done before," said the daughter. Then she added, "I have brought an *ada wi,* something I saw and kept."

"Go and bring it," said the mother. So the daughter brought in the young woman and her pig.

Now this house was a long one, extending to the edge of a gulley. Food was offered them. "I won't eat any pork; you eat," said the pig. The mother and daughter put the two—the woman she called Adawi and her pig—at the very back of the house. Then the daughter told the two, "You must not go outside and watch me or my mother. Stay in the house."

The two did as they were asked, but only for a while. Then the pig made a small hole in the wall. They saw the other two take two forked *walu*-wood posts and plant them in the earth near the house. Then they saw them hang netbags filled with bananas, taro, pitpit, and other foods on these posts. When the two looked again, however, the two posts were bare.

The next day the daughter showed Adawi and her pig the gardens that she and her mother were cultivating. Then the daughter and the pig went off to work with the old woman, while the other woman chose to remain in the house. Later the daughter returned and said, "You, Adawi, why do you always stay in the house?"

"Oh, I am afraid of your mother, so I remain inside."

6i   "All right," said the daughter. "But if you are thirsty, there's a stream down there to drink from." She pointed out the path. "Down there the stream flows across stones, but elsewhere it flows through *yarara* grass. Go drink where it goes through the grass."

Adawi did this and returned. Then she slept. Now she felt as though she were pregnant. She told this to her pig, and the two of them wept. But now that she was pregnant, she was no longer afraid of the old woman; so she went to work in the garden with the others.

When she was about to give birth, she asked the pig, "Where will I go to bear the child?" When they looked outside next, there was a new, well-built birth hut. She gave birth to the child there.

From then on, whenever she returned from her garden work she would find cooked possums left for her. The small ones she would eat, and the big ones she would give to the pig. Many months passed.

One day she put the baby in a netbag to sleep, hanging the bag on the house wall. Then she glanced down to where the pig was working very hard in the garden. She felt sorry for the pig, working by itself, so she went down to join it. After helping it for a while, she hurried back to the house. Her child was no longer there! She searched everywhere, and her pig searched too, but they could not find it.

When they told the other young woman, she replied, "Do not say anything. My mother is a bad woman." Adawi wept. The three women and the pig stayed on.

6i   Then once again the daughter said to her, "If you are thirsty, go and drink from the stream where it flows through stones." She went to drink, and the next day she was pregnant again.

"Where will I give birth?" she asked the pig again, since the old birth hut had rotted. But just as before, a new hut appeared. She gave birth, and once again there were many bundles of possums left for her. And once again, too, she went to help the pig in the garden. When she returned, the child was no longer where she left it. Again the four of them stayed as before.

6ii   Some time later, the daughter said, "I have heard they are killing pigs elsewhere. I will procure a pig for you, so that we can go and eat pork. My mother and I shall leave first. Stay here three days or so and then follow us. I will break twigs so you know the path to take. On your way, stay in an old house by the path."

After waiting three days, Adawi told her pig, "I will be going far away, from Kolapi and Tidane, down to Kalawira, and then to sleep at Pulapari, in Wiru land." Then she departed, and on the fourth day she reached an old house.

The floor was strewn with ashes, and pieces of pork and fat lay about. She saw something light within the house and looked closely. It was a small *kau*, a gecko. Picking up a pair of tongs, she was about to strike it when it said, "I will tell you what they have kept from you. Why do you wish to strike me? They lied to you when they told you they would be killing pigs down there. They are killing them very close to here, and I shall show you where. Wait!" Soon it returned with the jawbone of a *pakena*, a possum with very strong teeth.

"Is what you say true?" said the woman. "If you take me there, I shall let you have all this to eat," said the woman, opening her net-bag.

6iv   The two went on, and soon they reached a tall cliff through which it seemed impossible to pass. But with the *pakena* jawbone, they made a hole in the rock. They went through, and on the other side she saw her two children, now grown youths, in the company of a man. This man had just killed a pig, and each of the youths was carrying away a side of pork.

Adawi walked along the edge of the *neada* there. Partly covering herself with her bark cloth cape, she stared at the two youths.

They looked back and shouted. "Look, I think this is my mother coming here!" This man (her husband, the water she drank) looked and said, "True, she is coming."

11ii   She went up to embrace them, but when she reached them, they flew away as *pubu* and *magatya,* two kinds of swallows.

Tale 40: The Wife Breaks Her Word

0   A woman lived with her two children, a son and a daughter. The boy was the older child, and the girl, still very small, was the younger. The mother cultivated their gardens with her son's help.

One day they were burning a garden to prepare it for planting. After they finished, and the mother and son were ready to return home, the girl said she wanted to stay behind. "I will work a little longer," she said to her mother and brother. "You two go back to the house without me, I'll come later." So the two left first, and the daughter returned later.

She did this often. Garden after garden the three of them made, taking food from the new gardens as the old ones were finished. The little girl was growing to be a young woman.

6i   One day they were occupied thus, making a new garden. They had burned it and were planting the cuttings. The mother noticed that the girl's belly seemed to be swollen. After another month had passed, she was clearly pregnant, and, in due course, she was about ready to give birth. Now, the mother and son wondered what to think. "No man has taken her, yet she is pregnant," said one to the other. Not long afterwards she gave birth to a boy.

Some time later, one afternoon, they heard something fall onto the thatch of their house. The three went outside to look, and they found a bundle. After opening it, they saw it contained a freshly killed possum, a *loke.* They cooked and ate it. The same thing happened a second time, and then again and yet again. Many possums did they eat in this way.

The young woman's little boy grew. One day they heard something very heavy fall onto the roof. It was a fine, cooked pig, and this, too, they ate.

6iv   Presently, the one up there (a sky youth) who was throwing down all this meat decided to give payment for this woman. So once, while the young woman was in the garden with the other two, fog blew in, rain fell, and the youth came to her. He said, "I am your husband, and now I am going to give payment for you." To the mother and brother he said, "Close your eyes and shortly you shall receive wealth."

Plate 5. Cloudy weather at Mount Keresa. Rain and fog often herald sky people.

So they shut their eyes and went up to the sky just like that. There they saw many shells and many pigs, some red and some white. They accepted this payment and then shut their eyes again. Reopening them, they saw they had returned to the earth again. The mother and her son continued to live on earth, just as before. As a return payment, the two offered several red and white pigs to the ones up there in the sky, but the husband only asked for one white pig and one red one.

10Ai The new wife and her son stayed up in the sky, while her mother and brother lived below.

Sometimes the husband would give *yagi* payments of shells, pigs, or game to the ones living below.

10Aii Later the wife's father-in-law told her, "If it starts to rain or becomes foggy when you go down to the earth to visit your kin, do not stay below just for that reason. You must always come back here; cover yourself with a mat. When it is very dark, carry a torch to light your way. Never stay down there overnight. You must not sleep there." Thus did her husband's father advise her.

And she obeyed, returning after her visits home whether it was raining or dark. In time her son grew to be a young man.

10Aiii   But on one occasion, after she had left her home in the sky to take some possums from her husband to her old mother, it grew very dark and heavy rain fell. It was so dark and damp that she decided to sleep below, just this once.

10Aiv   In the morning she awoke and tried to return. She closed her eyes, as she had done so many times before. But when she opened them again, she was still on the earth. Again and again she tried closing her eyes and opening them. Still she remained ground. Realizing her mistake, she sang this lament:

> My husband's father told me that to eat the eggs of Ialibu Mountain's *nadi* bird, I must take a torch against the dark. But I, just a girl, did not.
> My husband's father told me that to eat the eggs of Giluwe Mountain's *nadi* bird, I must use a mat against the northwesterly rains. But I, just a girl, did not.

11i-ii   She was sorrowful because she had left her son up there in the sky and could not see him. This woman flew away as a *sakewe* warbler, which sings "*Pe amo, pe amo, pe amo*. Woe, child; woe, child; woe, child." When we hear the *sakewe*, it is this woman who weeps thus.

Tale 41: The Poor Husband

0,6i   There was a woman named Nemono. One day she went to cultivate her sweet-potato garden at Mokoloma, and afterwards she returned home to Karapere. She looked down to where Yarapeara's store stall now stands at the foot of the ceremonial ground, and there she saw a little-man doing a *tama* dance. He was wearing fine ornaments. Nemono went closer to see who it was, but as she did so the man moved further down the hill. She went further down, but so did he. Still further did she follow him, thinking, "He must be going to a pig kill. I'll follow him!"

     First she quickly returned and killed a pig of her own. She did not get good cooking leaves, but tough tree-fern leaves, and she cooked the pig hastily, removing the meat almost raw. Then she bagged the meat and set off to follow the man.

6ii   He was still *tama* dancing. She followed him up the side of the valley, past Ipi Stream up to Yaparapawi. There he disappeared.

     Nemono sat down on the low hill there. She heard a small bird cry out, "Pull up that clump of *ira* grass!" She did so, and saw a path leading down into the earth. Following it, she came to a fine ceremonial ground with a grove of casuarinas. But before she reached this place, she came to an overgrown yard and a house which looked un-inhabited. After putting down her netbag of pork, she began to clear away the growth. Then she sat down inside and lit a fire.

6iv   Presently the little man arrived. He was carrying some *kalere* sugar cane, a tough cane which had grown unstaked. He offered some to her and she chewed it. Then the man recooked some of the pork she had brought. He offered her just a small piece of pork on a bone, putting the remainder in a netbag which he hung up on a forked post of *walu* wood.

Nemono lay down as if to sleep, but she continued to look at him through half-closed eyelids. She saw the little man take the netbag from the post and go off toward the grove of casuarina trees. Nemono went outside to look. Underneath the casuarinas was a long men's house holding many young men. Going closer, she saw that none of them were wearing any ornaments or other apparel. Nemono withdrew and slept the night in the house.

10Ai   The little man returned the next day and asked, "Will you listen to what I have to say?"

"Yes, go on," replied the woman.

"I want you to make breechcloths and head coverings for some men." Thereupon he went to the forest to cut *alipu* fiber and carried it back to the house in massive bundles. Out of this Nemono wove many cloths and hats, enough for that whole clan of men.

Then those men began to plan a *neada* longhouse, marking out the ceremonial ground with sticks. Having finished the house, they donned their tall, red *raguna* hats and prepared to tie their pigs to stakes. The next day they put on their full decorations and began their dance.

10Aii   They gave Nemono a full water container to put in her netbag, telling her, "Do not let a single drop of water pour out." She as-sented.

10Aiii She walked to the top of a rise and watched the men dance under the hot sun. The men were coming toward her from some dis-tance, as far as Tipuru is from here. When they were about as far away as Yarapeara's house, a heavy rain fell briefly. Just then Ne-mono saw that an old woman had come to stand beside her. The old one said, "I'm thirsty. Give me some water!"

"I have none," replied Nemono.

"Well, what's that in your netbag?" asked the old woman.

"It's water, but I must keep it for those men."

"Give me some immediately," demanded the old woman, "lest I kill you."

Nemono was afraid. She drew the bamboo container from her

bag and put it down. The old woman picked it up and poured the water onto the ground. Then she disappeared into the hole in the earth from which she had come.

Nemono was worried now. Seeing some water collected in a nearby pig wallow, she hastily refilled the contained before the men reached her.

10Aiv   When the dancers arrived and asked her for water, Nemono handed over the bamboo without comment. They drank the mud-died water, and their bodies seemed as though on fire. They walked along the ridge to a small pool, and there they immersed themselves. Nemono followed them. They were cooling themselves.

11i-ii   The men made a *duuu* noise when they entered the pool and moved around in it. Today, too, we hear water making such sounds. It is the noise made by those men, who did not want Nemono to follow them because she gave them this bad water. They made the sound to scare her off. Nemono herself became a *keago,* a frog.

Tale 42: The Vengeful Brother and the Poor Husband

0   There were a brother and a sister, Yapara and Nebo, who cultivated gardens and looked after their pig, Puramenalasu. The brother died, and thereafter Nebo had to go by herself to fetch food. She put her brother's body on a mortuary platform close by, in the garden out-side the house.

3Bi   One night she thought she heard some noise in this place, and then on another night she heard it again. It sounded as though the wood of the burial place was creaking. In the morning she rose early and prepared firewood for killing the pig. Then she told the pig, Puramenalasu, "I will not kill you with a club, you will just die." When she had made a fire, she said, "Now I want to burn your bristles. Die!" And the pig died.

Nebo took a stick and broke the block of salt. With the stick she severed the pig's carcass into pieces. After the meat was cooked, she put the salt and the pork in a netbag and set off along a path she did not know. The brother (his ghost) said, "I shall come too! Let's both go," and he kept following her.

She came to the Yaro River, which was in flood. Afraid of the torrent, she rested her chin on her *walu* stick and stood at the river bank.

3Bii,6i   She stared at the water. Then, raising her eyes, she saw standing on the other side, a little-man with unkempt hair. He threw down an arrow and told her, "Walk over on this." She did so.

When she had crossed over, she washed the little-man's skin

well, using *pepe yawe* leaves. She cut up her fine netbag into pieces; one piece she made into a man's head covering and another piece into a breechcloth. She cut and combed his hair, and soon he looked very fine indeed. He then shouldered some of her netbags of pork and salt, and they walked on.

6ii   The little-man told her, "If you go along this path, you will come to a house with a pig lying outside. Say to this pig, 'I am of your father's people.' " Then he took a less-used path and went on.

6iii, 10Ai   She went along the path indicated, and soon she came to a house with a large pig lying outside. The animal looked threateningly at her. But she said, "I am of your father's people," and the pig went to sleep again. She looked over to another side and saw an old man and woman. The two asked her, "Who are you?" She explained how she came to be there. She stayed on with those two; the little-man, she never saw again.

10Aii   One day the old couple announced they were going to a feast, and they asked Nebo to look after a bundle wrapped with palm sheaths. They told her to hold it by both ends in her hands and not to let it touch the ground. Nebo obeyed.

10Aiii-iv   On another occasion, they gave her the same instructions. But this time her arms grew tired, and she shifted her hold on the bundle. It fell down, and a large reddish dog burst from it. The dog ran off and killed that man who had made a bridge over the river for her. Shortly thereafter the old man and woman, her parents-in-law, offered her their dead son's gardens and house, and she lived there.

6iv   One night when she was sitting by herself, she sang in sorrow for this man:

> *Ipa yalo ipa wili matu rikimi lore yago ma molesi yago.*
> At the Yaro River when the mist shrouded, I cleaned the mucus of his nose, my friend.

When she had finished, a bird came to perch on a nearby sugar-cane post. It sang:

> *Yagoma molesi ramua pealena, pora wanome ki paapu apaapu piliyare, pea giala pola pelera.*
> Friend of the mist, he rots, and from there the branches of the *pora* and *wano* trees grow out; forget this, and go on.

11i-ii   But this woman refused to heed this advice to remarry; she continued to mourn her husband. Nowadays some widows and widowers refuse remarriage, and when they do this they are following her behaviour.

Tale 43: The Wife's Journey to the Otherworld I

0   A man named Keapu, of Sangarepa clan, had married a woman from
*   Kamarupa-Aburupa, an enemy clan. One day he went into a forest
     belonging to his wife's group to set possum traps, and the owners of
     that land came across him and killed him.

         Before he had set out, Keapu had told his wife to cook some food
     and to carry it to him in the forest. Accordingly, the woman left for
     the forest, unaware that her husband had been killed by her
     brothers.

6i   She took with her *rani* greens and sweet potatoes to cook in the
     hunting hut. For a long time she waited there for her husband. Fi-
     nally he came in and sat across from her by the fire. "I'm sick," he
     said. "Just give me some *rani* greens to eat."

         When he had eaten the greens, he lay down. The wife noticed
     how pale his skin was and wondered. Apprehensive, she said, "Let's
     go home tomorrow morning. We'll carry the possums back to the
     village."

         In the morning they gathered the possums Keapu had killed and
     they set off, the wife carrying the game in netbags on her head and
     back. They returned toward their home at Kaluake. At the hill of
     Amaru they looked down toward the village. The wife saw that her
     husband's people were gathered on the ceremonial ground; they
     were mourning. The two of them descended along Lemako stream,
     the wife leading the way. Listening to the sound of the mourning, it
     occurred to her that perhaps her husband had been killed during the
     night.

6ii   She turned quickly and looked back. She saw that her husband
     was no longer coming on the path toward Kaluake but was continu-
     ing to follow the watercourse downstream.

         So the wife came alone to Kaluake. There she saw the body
     of her dead husband. When they saw her, some of her husband's
     brothers said they should kill her in revenge; she was, after all, the
     sister of the murderers. But others argued that they ought not kill
     her. Many argued on each side, and in the end they did nothing. As a
     woman does when her husband has died, she sat inside the house in
     mourning, wearing bracelets of Job's-tears seeds on her arms and
     mourning skirts around her waist.

6iv   One night, when there was a bright moon, she felt she had stayed
     indoors enough and went outside. She leaned against a clump of
     kayabo sugar cane in the garden outside her house. Glancing down
     toward Tipuru, she saw what looked like a bailer shell shining in the
     distance. As she watched, it seemed as though the light was ap-
     proaching from the direction of the burial ground. Presently her

husband came and stood beside her. She leaned forward and wrapped her arms around his lower legs. It felt like embracing the thorny buttress roots of a wild pandanus, but she held him fast.

"Put away your mourning skirts and Job's-tears," he said. She did so, and then the two of them climbed up Pipira Hill and followed the crest of the ridge. As they went near watercourses and ravines or sinkholes, she heard the *mata* singing and ululating of countless men and women. "What clans live there?" she asked her husband, and he gave her the long list of clan names.

Now they went down the slopes of Mount Keresa to Potali, and there too they heard weeping. "What place is this?" she asked.

"Urapia (land of the dead)," he replied. "We will soon be there."

One of the houses was newly built, and they went toward it. He took her inside, made her sit by the sleeping place, and told her to stay inside and keep out of sight. She was to lie underneath a piece of bark cloth which he gave her.

"I am a newcomer here," he said. "Take these couple of pieces of cooked taro and eat them." Outside the people continued to sing their dance songs. Time passed.

Near daybreak a man came and called, "Kumiwili (Keapu), I am going to get some food; let's go." But Keapu excused himself, "I have hurt my foot on a stone on the path, so I'll just sit here." Later others came and called, "We must give Kumiwili some food." But he replied, "No, I don't feel like eating anything."

For two days the husband and wife sat, but not once during this time did the wife see him eat. Finally she said, "You must show me the way home now." So the husband stood up and led her back on the path along which they had come, leaving her near her house.

As she went inside, she turned and looked back. She saw the bailer shell shining like a sun in the night. She sang softly to herself,

> *Kumiwili nare pa pua u palu pirainya patape ra.*
> Kumiwili, while the sun shines you must sleep, so good night.

Tale 44: The Wife's Journey to the Otherworld II

0   A man named Amulasi stayed in Ulamada, in the Sugu Valley. He was a young and important man who wore fine ornaments and decorations. He had so many ripe *oda* bananas in his gardens that he often left them unpicked, and they fell to the ground. Nearby, at Sumi, men who were about to kill their pigs called out for their southern neighbours to come; they invited people of Ulumada.

10Ai-ii   Amulasi's mother and father went. They took along something bundled in the sheaths of the black palm, carrying it on a stick over their shoulders. With them went Amulasi's wife, but Amulasi himself remained at home. The parents never put their burden down, not even while eating. They each held one end of the pole under the arm.

Pigs were killed and cooked, and the old man and woman received some pork. They and Amulasi's wife then set off along the path homeward. They carried netbags of pork on the back, and the bundle they carried slung from the shoulder.

10Aiii   After walking a long distance, the old man and woman grew thirsty, so they gave their bundle to a couple of small boys to hold while they walked down to a stream. When they reached the water, the old man and woman argued about who should drink first.

10Aiv   Suddenly the thing in the bundle, whose tail raised up, broke out and ran away. The boys called to the old man and woman, but they did not hear because they were shouting at each other over the noise of the water. This thing that had come out was about to bite the two boys, but they ran off crying "Grandfather, grandmother! The bundled-up thing has run off!" This happened in Ponapeda. They chased that thing all the way back to Ulumada, where they heard that it had come and killed Amulasi.

They put the dead man on a mortuary platform and mourned. Then they buried him in his garden. The woman asked her husband's father to make a house for her near the grave, and they made her one walled with casuarina bark. The woman, who was pregnant, stayed near the grave site. When the grass was growing tall over it, she gave birth to a boy. But every day she still wept for her dead husband, even though small trees were now growing over his grave. She sang:

Nama aama Amulasi yago, nema aama Amulasi yago.
You, important man, Amulasi, friend.

6i   Birds would come and eat the seeds of these casuarinas. One day the woman heard something rustling, so she called her child to her and held it closely. The ghost of the dead Amulasi came and sang:

You do not think of others, you weep for me alone.
Other women go to other men, to other youths.
They make gardens and raise pigs for other men,
But you, you only cry out, "Amulasi."

The woman came and put her arms around his waist. Amulasi said, "Leave me be. I came to tell you this, and now I want to go back." "No!" she said.

"Leave me," he urged her.

"No," she repeated.

6ii   She gathered her netbags, intending to follow him. One of the dead man's arms was short and he carried it slung in a shoulder bag; the other arm was very long. He retreated, followed by his wife with her son. The man said, "You are not walking with a living man, you know. People do not act like you now. Follow my footsteps closely!"

They walked for a long, long time until they came to the base of a huge mountain which seemed too high to climb. The ghost said, "Let's close our eyes." They did so, and when they opened them they were on the top of the mountain.

The woman looked around and she saw that some of the surrounding land was white, some was red, and some dark and blue-black. Men who died in a fight went to the red ground; those who died in a village went to the light ground. In this dark ground there was a good ceremonial ground with metal-roofed houses.

6iv   The man said to his wife and son, "Now you will see how I live, where I sleep, what I eat, what I do." They closed their eyes again and came into the dark ground. The man had a metal-roofed house. He got some sugar cane, some bananas, some taro, and some yams from the garden.

The ghosts came and beat their drums at night. All of them had good ornaments: armbands, bird-of-paradise feathers, breechcloths, cane-wrapped bark belts. The wife stayed inside the house and watched the ghosts dance. She saw two very fat women come and eat many plantains, taro, and yams while sitting in the middle of the dancing men. Then the men brought two large plates and – *buuuu!* – the women defecated onto them. These two women looked after the dead men, who ate their feces. All the men came up and broke off a piece of the feces and ate it. All except for Amulasi, who stayed with his wife and son in the house.

The wife said to her husband, "Why don't you go and dance; I shall stay and look." But the man was slow to go outside, for he was thinking about his wife and child. Some of the men outside were singing.

> Amulasi has a new kind of conduct,
> What he did before he does not do now.
> Amulasi does not walk about with us,
> He has a new kind of thought:
> He thinks of his wife and son,
> He thinks of his gardens and his house,
> He thinks of his brothers and his father.

So Amulasi reluctantly put on his dancing ornaments, locked the double doors of his house, and went to join the others. He told his wife and son to look through the window. He went and danced, singing,

> Now you have seen how I live,
> You have called me often, and now look on.

He did not eat the feces, for he was embarrassed in front of his wife and son—very ashamed. He told them to go back in the morning, but the woman did not want to go. She chopped off a couple of her fingers to show her grief. But the man said, "You must go!"

11ii   So in the morning Amulasi took out a white man's smoking pipe and sat down with the two others on top of the mountain. He turned the pipe bowl upside down, and suddenly the wife and son were again at the base of the mountain. They were two *kipula* possums.

Tale 45: The Wife's Journey to the Otherworld III

0   I will tell a story my mother told me. Puolo and Puolonyu were newly married and lived in Kilipimi. Not long after Puolo gave bridewealth for his wife, he decided to go to the forest to set possum traps. He asked his wife to cook some vegetables and bring them to him in the forest. The wife replied, "I've heard that they are fighting over in that part of the forest. Do not go; they'll kill you. They say that that land is theirs."

But Puolo said he would go anyway. First he went off to Sugukusu, then to Alea and to Ipire, the disputed land. There Puolo's enemies ambushed and killed him. Puolonyu had no way of knowing what happened, so she went up to Kogore and waited in a forest hut for her husband to come. She cooked her vegetables and waited, but the man did not arrive. She waited still. Evening came, but still he did not arrive. She began to worry; perhaps he *had* been killed.

It was now dark. As she lay down to sleep, she heard a noise at the doorway. She was relieved that he had not died, but had simply been delayed. Perhaps he had lost his way or had been disoriented by a cassowary which, unseen, had watched him as he walked through the forest. She rose to open the door. Then she peered outside.

6i   She saw Puolo with blood running down his body, supporting himself with his *dolo* spear. He put the spear down and came inside. He did not eat but went to a corner and lay down.

6ii   In the morning he told his wife, "Go along the path which I have come by. Follow the impressions left in the earth by my spear. I have left possums there. Fetch them here." Having said that, he rose and left by another path.

Puolonyu wondered why her husband did not eat anything, but she went to gather the possums her husband had left near the spear marks. Then she returned to the forest hut, and from there she retraced her steps toward her husband's place in Kilipimi, descending first from Nire to Mupalu. When she looked down from Mupalu to Kilipimi, she saw that her husband's people were mourning over a corpse.

"It *was* a ghost I saw up there!" she thought, sure that the dead man lying there was her husband. In sorrow she cut at a finger with her knife and tore at her ears. Then she stayed indoors in sorrow. She stayed in mourning with her parents-in-law. The Kuri clansmen put Puolo's body on a burial platform, while the wife donned Job's-tears seeds and mourning skirts.

Time passed, but she continued to feel deep grief for her departed husband. Toward the end of the mourning period, she killed and cooked her husband's large pig, Puramenalasa. She took the kidney with attached flesh and fat and wrapped it in a bundle with salt. She took off her mourning attire and put on everyday clothing. She took more salt and more pork and filled her netbag. Then, saying nothing to her father-in-law, she set off to Nire, went on to Kogaire, to Kanare, following the direction her husband had taken from the forest hut.

When she reached Asapili she met a man on the path. When she asked, "Have you seen Puolo?" he answered, "He went on beyond." She gave him some pork and salt, and she continued on. When she came to Kario she again asked a man, "Have you seen Puolo?" She received the same answer, "He has gone on further." And to him, too, she gave salt and pork. The same happened at Kalawira, Yapa, and Mamuane, in Wiru land.

In Mamuane an old man told her, "When you go further along this path, you will see two long-tusked pigs named Kepasura and Kepakikini, one on either side of the path." Then he handed her four round sweet potatoes and an *ekepai,* a ceremonial staff. He told her that when she came to a large patch of *rarua* nettles barring the way, she should say a certain spell and hold aloft the *ekepai;* the nettles would part to either side. The two pigs, he said, would be waiting beside a large pool she could cross. And a high mountain in front of her, called Balibali, would also bar her way but could be crossed.

She went on and came first to the patch of nettles. When she raised the staff and repeated the spell, the plants parted, and she walked through them. Next she came to the pool and the two pigs, which glared at her menacingly. She took two round sweet potatoes and threw one over the head of each pig. As the pigs ran off to eat them, she hurried past. On she went until she met an old woman who told her, "Beyond you will come to a tall and thin old woman with cassowary feathers in her hair. She is strong and will try to spear you with a digging stick. You must dodge aside and go beyond." Puolonyu went on, wondering if she would be killed, but when she came to that old woman she managed to jump aside and the digging stick missed her. So she continued along the path, a wide and well-used one.

Next she came to the mountain Balibali. She ascended it and looked down. At the bottom of a cliff she saw many gardens. Puolonyu had with her two climbing ropes that one of the old people had given her on her journey. Hanging down the side of the cliff below her was a stout vine, blackened by the use of many travellers–dead souls going to the land below.

6iii   Puolonyu put the rope loop around her ankles and climbed down, down, down to the bottom of the chasm. Then she walked one mile, two miles, three, four, five, six, seven, eight. After ten miles she reached a garden fenced with cordyline plants. In it she saw a woman digging sweet potatoes.

"Who are you?" asked the woman.

"I am Puolo's wife, and I have come looking for him. Have you seen him?"

"I am Puolo's cross cousin," she replied. "Wait here by the cordylines. I need to dig some more sweet potatoes."

Puolonyu sat by cordyline fence. Presently the woman came and said, "All right, let's go now. What is it that you are carrying in your netbag?"

"Pork," replied Puolonyu.

"Hah! We do not eat that here," said the other.

Puolonyu considered that. "So. Pork is not something that is eaten here."

"Do you have a needle?" asked the cousin. Puolonyu said she did. She took the object, made of a wing bone of a flying fox, from her *karubi*-gourd ear pendant. Then, as the other indicated, she jabbed it under her fingernail and drew some blood. The blood filled the hollow bone, and she squeezed it into the pig kidney she was carrying. They continued on until they reached a house. It was Puolo's. The two entered it and sat down. As they listened, voices came from outside.

"Goodbye, Puolo; goodbye," people were saying as they walked off in the dark. Puolonyu hid underneath a bark cloth in a corner of Puolo's house. She listened. When men outside received no reply, they called, "Where's Puolo? Where's Puolo?"

Puolonyu hid underneath her blanket and kept silent. Outside the ghosts were *koda* dancing. It was now close to dawn, and she heard many of these dead walk by the house; they were returning to their houses. "Goodnight, Puolo; goodnight," some of the young women called as they passed by.

6iv   Finally Puolo arrived. He stood outside while the others wished him goodnight. Then he sang to himself, not realizing his wife was inside,

> *Imiri na Puolonyu ade nogome na tamere, ni gi piare pulepa.*
> You girls are not Puolonyu speaking to me; I do not care for you, so go off.

Then he entered. His cousin spoke first; she told him that his wife was lying down inside the house. "What? Has she died and come?" asked Puolo.

"No, she has come on her own. She has not died."

Puolo walked quickly into the other room. The wife then heated some *rupi* stones and cooked the pig kidney into which she had earlier introduced some of her blood with the needle. He ate that pork. He did this even though ghosts do not eat cooked foods, but only *pili* and *wakia* tree fruits, and sometimes feces as well.

Then he said, "We must go back, the way you came." By now the daylight had waned, and as it grew dark they followed the path. They came to the base of Balibali Mountain and climbed up with the rope loops. When they came to the woman wearing the cassowary feathers, they dodged the digging stick that she thrust at them. This woman waits for the newly dead, who all come along this path. She spears them with her digging stick and throws them down the cliff.

They went on, and soon came to the large pool where the two pigs waited. The one was named Kepakikini, the other was Kepasura. Puolo warned his wife away, "Ah, those pigs will bite us for sure! What are we to do?" But Puolonyu took out the remaining two round sweet potatoes and threw one to each pig. Then they continued on, coming next to the nettle patch barring their way. The wife raised her staff, spoke the spell, and parted them. The two crossed through.

Soon they were about to reach Kilipimi. Before leaving, the ghost cousin of Puolo's had told Puolonyu, "You must give my cousin only mushrooms to eat." But Puolo wondered why she had said that.

Puolo's parents were overjoyed to see their son and daughter-in-law return, and they embraced both of them. "We put him on the burial platform and now you've brought him back!" They exclaimed about this again and again. Then the couple stayed and made gardens.

Later the wife gave birth to a son. The baby boy cried all the time. This child was born of a woman who cohabited with a ghost, and he cried incessantly. Sometimes the wife would give the boy to the husband to hold, or sometimes she would hold it – the boy just kept crying.

The husband grew tired of all this, and often he would escape into the forest, hunting possums. When he was away hunting, Puolonyu could not go to the gardens to work, for the child kept crying and she had to hold it.

11i   Finally she was exasperated and said angrily to the child, "Hey, your father ate feces with other ghosts, and I married him again and gave birth to you! You cry too much!"

Her ghosthusband heard this, for ghosts hear things even from far away. "All right," he said, "I'll leave." And he did.

11ii   If Puolonyu had not said this, women would be able to bring back their dead husbands. But now we die for good. What she did no longer happens.

(Note: another version of this tale ends differently. After spending the night in the land of the dead, the two return home, as follows:)

10Ai   The two set off the next morning. But the husband said, "We will not go back to the house. We must make a new one in the middle of our sugar-cane garden." They lived there, bore children, and made gardens.

10Aii   The husband said, "I alone shall eat *puti* mushrooms. You may not." The wife agreed.

10Aiii   But one day the woman noticed that there were many mushrooms growing on the trunk of a dead pandanus tree. She collected and ate them, saying nothing to her husband. But he saw her and asked, "What have you eaten?"

10Aiv   She was angry. "You went there to eat feces with other ghosts, and it was through my doing that you came back. Now you're complaining!" After she said that, the man went away and did not return. She looked for him, but without success.

11i-ii   We would be able to revive the ghosts of the dead, but because this woman did not give her husband the mushrooms, and because she insulted him, now people die for good.

Tale 46: The Ghostsister II

0   Moisi had a wife, a woman of Eparepa clan who had borne him no children. Because of this, he married a second woman. But finally the first wife did give birth to a girl child.

One day this wife told her daughter that the two of them might make a visit to her natal place. So the mother and daughter left. When they arrived at the Yaro River bridge, the mother said, "You first, I'll follow. If you should lose your footing, I'll be able to help you. What do you know about crossing bridges?" But when they reached the middle of the bridge, the woman threw the girl into the river and continued on to the other side. She did not return to her husband.

The girl was swept downstream. Struggling to stay afloat, she grasped some plants in the current, and by this means she was able to pull herself to the river bank. The water had by now carried her far downstream, and her body ached painfully. She rested against the roots of a tall tree and sat motionless. It grew dark.

6iii Presently she heard some sounds downstream, and a moment later she saw a number of figures coming up the river bed. She dared not look at them directly, though she did glance at them out of the corner of her eye. She watched the figures as, whistling softly, they moved upstream. After they had passed her, she looked downstream again. Another one was coming behind the others. The girl rubbed her eyes and looked at this last one, who was travelling more slowly: it was a young woman, a girl like herself. This young woman, a ghost like the others, caught the girl's glance.

"Who are you?" asked the ghost, "and why are you here?"

"I was coming with my mother," began the abandoned girl, and then she told her story.

"Come with me," said the other. The two of them went along upstream, following the others at a distance. Because the (human) girl was feeling sick, they made slow progress.

"Granddaughter, hurry up!" the others called back.

"Yes, but my foot hurts, so I'm coming slowly," the ghostgirl replied. She was only recently dead, still fresh and new.

"I didn't come here (die) long ago; just yesterday," said the ghostgirl. "So don't spit because of me; I can't smell that bad yet." Then she took off her skin and put it on the girl, who was feeling cold. Now the girl felt warm, and she was able to go on more quickly. Soon they came to the bridge from which she had fallen.

All the others had gone on further. The ghostgirl explained to the other, "I have no sisters. My mother gave birth only to my brothers and me; I was the only girl. And my house here is a new one, since only yesterday did I come."

Then she added, "When you marry and give birth to a child, or when you make a garden, a *raguna* hair covering, or the like, I will lend you a hand. If you make a forest garden or a sweet-potato garden somewhere, you will only have to start it and I will finish it. Just pile up the cuttings and I will plant them. When you want to

feed the pigs, pile the tubers and I will carry them to the pigs." And
she gave further advice about how she would help.

6iv   Presently the two of them came to a long men's house with a
porch at either end, one that held many men. The ghostwoman led
the girl inside and asked her to lie down in one of the sleeping areas.
Then she disappeared into the night.

One of the young men, who was sleeping close to the doorway,
awoke and found that he was cold; he saw that his fire was nearly
dead and decided to rekindle it. Looking over to where his brother
was sleeping, he saw beneath the edge of a bark-cloth blanket what
seemed to be a woman's skirt. When he got up and tugged at this
skirt, he saw it was worn by a person sleeping there. "What's this?"
he wondered, and woke up his brother. They saw the sleeping girl,
woke her up, and asked her what she was doing there; but she gave
no reply. Morning came and she stayed.

6Ai   The woman and that youth, the one in whose compartment she
awoke, were later married. The girl began to make gardens. All she
ever had to do was carry the cuttings of the crops she wanted to
plant to the garden, and the ghostwoman would do the rest. Or
again, when feeding her pigs all she had to do was put a pile of tubers
out before nightfall. By the next morning, they had been carried out
to the animals. Soon the men were beginning to talk about this.
"How does she make all these forest gardens and these sweet-potato
gardens? How does she look after all her pigs and yet have time to
make netbags and hair coverings?" they wondered.

After a while the woman became pregnant and gave birth to a
child. It was this ghostwoman, the sister of her husband, who helped
her, cutting the umbilical cord and washing the baby with leaves of
kapo, kumama and *epawi*.

The men brought firewood and water for her—for she could not
leave the birth hut immediately after giving birth—but it was the
ghostwoman who worked in the gardens and fed her pigs.

"Ah, this woman, she remains inside, so how does she look after
her gardens and her pigs?" the men wondered.

The child grew and cut its first teeth. It cried very much when
the men held it; in fact, it was always crying. But though the child
was difficult for her, the men noticed how good her gardens and pigs
still looked. It was as if she were not one but two women, they
thought.

6Aii   One day the men conversed among themselves and planned to
spy on her. So they cleared a new garden for her on a mountainside
which happened to adjoin the grave site of their dead sister. After
they had allowed the slash to dry and then burned it, they told the
wife, "We have prepared a large garden for you, but it may be too

large for you alone to plant. So we will plant *kuni* and *kibita* greens, taro, and plantains in part of it, and the rest you can plant with sweet potato and *padi* and *rani* greens."

Accordingly, she went to a bearing garden and gathered some cuttings of *padi, rani,* and sweet potato, loaded them into netbags, and carried them on her back and atop her head to the newly cleared garden. She left most of them there in piles, planting only a few here and there.

That night there was a bright moon. The men went out to the garden to watch, lying down and resting their heads on their axe handles.

In her house, the wife woke in the middle of the night, listened, and was surprised not to hear talking in the men's house. She wondered why.

Meanwhile, the men were waiting in the garden.

Later the woman heard men shouting . . . and a woman weeping.

The men had brought a large woven bag to the woman's burial place after they had caught sight of her moving around in the garden, unclothed, planting the cuttings and runners by moonlight. The ghostwoman was working and talking quietly to herself as she planted the cuttings: "Another two or three here, another two here." Near dawn she had stopped her work and returned to her burial site. She fell into the basket the men had put there. Then all the men had quickly tied on the top and carried the container back to the men's house.

The wife listened attentively. Amid the shouts of the men, she heard the sorrowful song of the ghostwoman:

> *Ipa yalo ralo ria pape nogo raba meawa nogomere, lepi nuri waru lare.*
> I helped this abandoned girl that the flood of the Yalo River had carried; and you, seeing this, have done well for yourselves.

The men carried the bag and hung it in the porch of their house, on the front wall.

11i-ii   When we hear thunder rolling now, what we are hearing is this woman struggling in the bag, which knocks against the wall of that house.

Tale 47: The Ghostsister III

0   In Karapere many Sangarepa youths lived in a long men's house. Only one young woman, their sister Ladanyu, stayed with them. But then she died, and they buried her. Other women of the Kuri group stayed elsewhere; and other women of other groups lived at Rakili, on the far side of the Yaro River.

    Once, the young women of both places decided to hunt frogs by torchlight. Women from Rakili were to hunt downstream, while those from Karapere were to hunt upstream. The two groups did so, and then each went back to its place. But one Rakili woman, named Lopiawane, continued to search for frogs by herself.

6iii   As she walked downstream in the darkness, Lopiawane saw a light approaching. She supposed it would be the Kuri women. But only one figure was approaching. It was a good-looking young woman with long hair. Lopiawane watched in hiding as the other approached her. The woman was eating the frogs she had caught. Staying hidden in an undercut bank of the river until the other woman was opposite her, Lopiawane suddenly rushed out and grasped her arm. She held on, even though the other woman made her feel like she was holding brambles and other things with thorns.

    Then each told the other who she was. "Good enough," said Ladanyu – for this was her ghost Lopiawane had met. "Now let's go to my place at Karapere." So the two walked on through the dark.

    When they were about to reach the village, Ladanyu told Lopiawane, "When you want to weave a head covering or a netbag, you have only to start it. I will finish it; that will be my work. Or, when you go to work in the garden, just start it and I shall do the rest."

6iv   When the two were inside the men's house, Ladanyu led Lopiawane to her brother Peleme's sleeping compartment. Lopiawane lay down beside the sleeping youth, and then Ladanyu knotted a few strings of Lopiawane's skirt to the cordyline leaves her brother wore. Having done that, she departed.

    Later in the night, one of the other youths, Yarapea, awoke and saw the two lying there. He roused the others and exclaimed excitedly, "Look! Peleme has taken this woman!"

    Peleme himself said, "Yes, she will be my wife. I will have this woman, but her work will belong to all of us. She will help us all with what she can do."

6Ai   They stayed. Lopiawane began to net many breechcloths, all of which were secretly finished by Ladanyu. She made enough for all the youths, and then she made them netbags and head coverings as well. She also looked after the gardens and pigs.

One night, when a bright moon was shining, she said to her husband's brothers, "Since I am the only woman to do this work, I must go work in the garden now, by moonlight."

Arriving there, she saw that Ladanyu had brought another young woman. Ladanyu told Lopiawane to take this woman back and leave her beside one of the young men. Lopiawane did so; she put her beside Yarapea. And when the youths awoke, they saw that a second young woman had come. Yarapea said the same as Peleme, "This woman I am taking for myself, but she'll help us all with her work."

Thereafter the ghostwoman brought many other young women for all the Sangarepa youths. She brought them by night, asking Lopiawane to put them beside the sleeping youths. Soon only a couple of the brothers were without wives.

6Aii One day, Peleme decided he would find out how his wife, Lopiawane, brought the women. So he surrounded the garden with traps made of netbags, and one day he found Ladanyu caught in one of them. He held her fast. Though she gave him brambles and spiny vines to hold, he held her fast, for he recognized her to be his sister. Then he brought her back to the men's house and told the other young men how they had come by their women. He tied the woman to a post in the porch of the men's house, and they all sat, looked at her, and conversed. Ladanyu sang sorrowfully,

> *Ainya poremada Kipame Lelewaliri na ipule tamere, ainyara ponora pa.*
> Brother, on top of the mountains they are saying, "Kipame Lelewaliri is not returning." Brother, I want to go.

But they did not let her go. One of them, a man named Karia, saw her weeping and felt sorry for her, however. So when all were asleep in the house and did not wake to his prodding, he cut the rope that held her. When the men rose, some accused Karia. But he denied everything. "I was fast asleep. It must have been you." They all blamed one another and argued.

11i-ii If Peleme had not trapped that ghostwoman we would still be able to bring back other ghostwomen and marry them. But now this has ceased. They would help our wives make gardens and do other work, but now this does not happen.

Tale 48: The Pig Girl

0   There once was a sow which lived by itself, with no men or women about. This pig became pregnant even though there were no boars around either. She became pregnant, just like that. There were of course no sweet potatoes to eat, since no people were around. So she foraged in the forest. Eventually this sow gave birth to a human baby girl. And just as pigs wallow in puddles when it is hot, so did this human baby to whom the mother pig had given birth. The girl followed its mother, wallowing in the mud or sleeping in the grass. In time she grew up and learned how to make herself a bed of dry banana leaves.

As happens in tales, she grew quickly. When she was older she began to make sweet-potato gardens and plant other foods as well. The girl and the pig lived like that.

One day the girl told her mother, "Now I think I shall follow through on an idea of mine."

"What will you do?" said the sow.

"I'll go to look for a husband," she said.

"As you wish."

"I'm leaving you the sweet-potato gardens and the forest gardens I have made," said the daughter. "There is much here to eat. So stay here."

6iii   The girl took her fine *kaipi* netbag, put on her ornaments, and walked on through the forest. In the middle of the forest she came to a place where the light showed through the canopy—it was a clearing, a sugar-cane garden. As she walked along the edge, she saw a pleasing young woman tying sugar cane to stakes. This woman wore a shell around her neck and had long hair down to her shoulders; she was an unmarried woman.

The visitor walked quietly around the edge of the garden to have a better look. Suddenly she stepped on a dry twig. Startled, the woman in the garden looked around with agitation. "Who are you?" she asked.

"I have left home and come looking for a husband," replied the newcomer.

"Oh, good indeed!" said the other, and, taking some food with her, she led the visitor to her house.

It was a long house, divided into two parts. One room was empty; the other was the woman's. So the two women lived in this house and worked in the gardens.

One day the woman who owned the house said to the newcomer, "I am going to receive pork at a ceremony. For three months after I return, you must not speak to me. Find your own food in the gardens, while I sit in my part of the house and find my own food. After three months are over, we shall be able to go about and eat with one another."

The other woman worried when she heard this. "Maybe she's going to kill and eat my mother!" she thought. But she let the woman go without saying anything.

Now when the two women were staying together, the new-comer had seen the other woman do something odd. She would dig sweet potatoes from the garden and bring them back, select the best tubers and put them in a netbag. But later on, by the next morning, those sweet potatoes were always gone. The visiting woman wondered, "What does she do with those sweet potatoes?"

While the other woman was away, she was alone. Later, the other woman returned, and after the three months had passed the two lived as before.

One sunny day the other woman said, "Let us go to eat pork at a pig kill." As the two were leaving, the same woman said, "I will go first, you come along after me."

6iv   So the newcomer followed at some distance. After she had walked for a long time, she met a dark-skinned man on the path. He asked her, "Who are you?"

"Another woman said to follow her, and I'm doing that," she replied.

"So," said the man. "She is my sister." He joined her on the journey.

10Ai   Presently they came to a *neada* longhouse. There they occupied three sections—one for the other woman, one for her brother, and one for the newcomer, who watched the people killing their many pigs.

10Aii   The other woman advised her, "You must never eat the pork that others give you, however much or little they give. Only these two pigs of our own, which we haven't yet killed, shall we eat, later." Then she handed her a *walea*-wood plate; she could receive pork on that plate, but she was not to touch it with her hands.

10Aiii   The people there kept giving her pork, and she accepted all they offered. Each time she asked them to put it on the plate. The plate was piled so high with pork that she had difficulty holding it. Finally, one of them put a fragrant piece of backbone on top. She inhaled the odour, picked it up, and ate it. Even though the other woman had told her to eat no pork, she ate it.

10Aiv   Now she could no longer make human speech, and her hands and legs folded and shrunk. She became hunched over—like a pig. Somewhat later, the brother and sister returned and saw her. "What have you done?" they exclaimed. But she could not answer. The siblings then cut some bark and closed up the doorway to that house.

11i-ii   The woman's skin grew swollen and her body began to rot. When she strained in her effort to speak, liquid ran from her body. This is what we see now as rain. It is water from her swollen body.

CHAPTER 5

Of Tricksters, Little-Men, and Old Men

Tale 49: Keapu and the Little-Man

0,7i One of the clans comprising the Kuri people is Sangarepa. This clan includes Yeritipa and Yawarepa clans, though we sometimes call them Sangarepa as well. Now, one day one of the Sangarepa men, Moisi by name, took his dogs and went to the forest to hunt. He killed many possums, which he carried in his netbag.

On his way back home he passed through Laboko and then into the forest at Tibi. There he met a little-man (*alisi*) who said, "Ah, you are carrying a heavy load! Why not clean and cook your possums here and then carry them on? Many men such as yourself have done this. See, here is the well-used cooking pit, the cooking stones, the firewood and cooking leaves—everything ready for an earth oven."

Moisi agreed. One of the two men cleaned the possums while the other heated the cooking stones. When the stones were hot, they were ready to put the possums in to cook.

Then this poor-man (*riaboali*) said to Moisi, "Go fetch some cooking leaves and some *parara* vines (a weak variety)." Moisi did so. When he returned with them, the other gave him more directions: "Put the leaves down on the stones. I will lie down on top. You must cover me with additional leaves and put a layer of wild pandanus leaves on top. Then tie me up into a bundle and leave me to cook with the rest. When I say 'Turn!' turn me over. When I say 'Remove!' take me out."

Moisi did just as he said. The bundles lay there, cooking. Presently he heard the little-man say "Turn!" and he turned the man over, as well as the possums. Later he heard him say "Remove!" and he bent down to lift out the bundles.

Now, to one side of the cooking place the ground dropped off into a gully. When Moisi went to remove the bundle, the little-man suddenly broke the ropes which bound him, straightened out his legs – which had been folded to fit into a bundle – and kicked Moisi hard on the chest. The blow knocked Moisi into the ditch, where he died. The little-man rose from the earth oven, removed the possums which were by now well done, and ate them.

Back at Moisi's village, his brothers waited for him to return. When he did not, a nephew of his, Purupiasi by name, left to search for him, hunting as he went. Like his uncle, Purupiasi killed many possums in the forest. On his return he met the same little-man on the path.

"What are you carrying?" asked this one.

"Possums I have killed," replied Purupiasi.

"Well, you have a long path in front of you, and uncleaned possums make a heavy load. Why not cook them here and then carry them back the rest of the way?" Purupiasi agreed, and the two of them split firewood, gathered cooking leaves, and prepared the game for cooking. Next the little-man told Purupiasi to fetch more cooking leaves, some *parara* vines, and some wild pandanus leaves, and then to cover and cook him in the earth oven along with the game. After following these instructions, Purupiasi met with the same fate as Moisi. His dogs returned home alone.

Next, a brother of his, Webe, went off in search of the two others. The same thing happened to him. Then Yalanura, another (classificatory) son of Moisi's, went. He also died. Then Thomas, then Kalopa, and then Misi, until all of the men of Moirepa subclan had died.

When there were no more Moirepa men, the Kewarepa subclan went. These too were killed, as were the Kedarepa men. Finally only one Kedarepa youth, named Keapu, was left. What had happened to his brothers, he wondered.

7ii   Keapu, too, went into the forest to look for his brothers and to hunt. His netbag was heavy with possums by the time he headed back. On his way he came across the little-man.

"Give me your hand!" said he, but Keapu declined to do so. Then the little-man made the same talk as before; he persuaded Keapu to stay and cook his possums there.

"All right. We'll cook them," said Keapu. When the little-man gave him instructions about the vines and leaves to bring, however, Keapu brought strong *amape* vines, not the weak *parara* ones, and he bound the little-man so tightly that he groaned in pain. Keapu, you see, had caught sight of the bones and hair of dead men, nearly filling the gully to one side.

When the little one cried "Turn!" Keapu paid no heed. Instead he began to gather the bones and hair of his dead brothers, wrap them in pandanus leaves, and put them into a big netbag. This took some time. When he was finishing this, he heard the little-man call out "Remove!" But Keapu took out only the possums and left the man to cook in the oven.

He returned to his home in Karapere with his burden.

9Bi   When he reached the long men's house, now empty, he put some bones and hair of the dead in every one of the spaces where men used to sit or sleep.

Plate 6. Ceremonial ground of Karapere.

9Bii   Time passed. One day, tired of staying around the house, Keapu crossed the Kuare River and went through Yata to Porada, and from there up along the ridge. He turned to look back at Karapere. It seemed as though there were many men around the men's house, dressed in fine bailer shells and bird feathers, as for a singing.

"Who are they?" he wondered as he hurried back. When he arrived, out of breath and perspiring, he saw that a young man had come forth from each place in the men's house where he had left bones and hair. Keapu was overjoyed and he hugged the men. Once again the men's house was full of youths of the Sangarepa clan.

Sometime later, a pig belonging to one of them, Moiamera, broke into Keapu's garden and caused damage. The pig owner and the garden owner argued heatedly. Finally Keapu said in exasperation, "You men were just a bunch of rotten bones until I fetched you back here. Only thanks to me are you here now!"

Some of them who heard this commented sadly, "Yes, what he says is true!"

11i   That night, while Keapu slept, the bush grew and water flowed around that men's house. When he woke the next morning, he saw no men around. All had left.

11ii   They had become *puluma* pigeons. Keapu became a pigeon, too, and followed the others. He flew somewhat behind the others, for in life he had a bad leg. These pigeons do fly like that, with one bird trailing the rest of the flock.

If Keapu had not argued with Moiamera and said those harsh things, we might nowadays be able to revive the dead with their bones and hair. But since he spoke as he did, and the men left as pigeons, we cannot do so. Those men might have lived together happily, but it was not to last. The pig broke into Keapu's garden, and Keapu, incensed, reminded the men that they had all been rotten and then became men again. Now they are birds.

Tale 50: Lanea and the Little-Man

0,7i   A man named Riba lived at Witapita. One day he went to Walu to collect some tree sap. When he was at Nire, he heard a *rodapia* bird call out, "Who's there?"

"Why do you ask?" Riba replied, and he picked up a stone and threw it at the bird. Then the voice called out again, but this time more like a man, "Come closer!" Riba, curious, approached, and he saw a little poor-man standing in a garden well stocked with food.

The little-man cut some edible pitpit of the *akena* variety and some bananas, and then the two continued along to Kobarema Mountain. After a while they reached a long men's house with a porch at either end. They went inside and talked awhile. Then the little-man said to Riba, "Let's sit down in the porch that faces the ceremonial ground. Later we can sit in the one that faces the mountainside, but we'll do our cooking in this one first. Go now and break some cordylines and cover me up. Cook me in the ashes, having bound me loosely with some thin vines. When I say *perekele* 'turn me,' come and turn me over; when I say *yokale* 'remove me,' do that."

Riba put the little-man in the cooking pit. When he heard him call *perekele,* he turned him; when he heard the call *yokale,* he went to remove him. But just then the little-man broke his bonds and kicked Riba into a gully on the mountainside.

The following day Riba's brother Koke went into the forest, and the *rodapia* bird cried out as before. The bird flew near Koke's face, and Koke picked up a clump of clay and threw it. "Come closer," the bird cried, now talking like a man. "This place has no men, yet you throw these things," it said. Koke came up to Kobarema with the little-man, and the same happened to him: when the little-man said *yokale*, he kicked Koke into the chasm.

7ii All but one of the men at Witapita were killed in this way. The one man left was Lanea. He decided to follow the path the others had taken, and he went into the forest. Like the others he came to the place where the bird cried. Lanea was suspicious, but he followed the little-man up the mountain. He noticed that the path was well used, as though many men had walked over it, and he wondered if all his brothers had come that way. Yet when he arrived at the men's house, he could see no one there. But he did notice many leafless stalks of cordyline plants. Now, when he was going up the mountain, he had taken with him a strong vine, *ra'alipu*.

The little-man broke off some cordyline leaves and told Lanea, "Cover me up with these leaves. Tie me up and cook me in the ashes." Lanea did so, using the stout vines he had brought rather than the thin ones that the other had directed him to use. Then he put him in the fire to cook. When the little-man called out *perekele* and later *yokale*, Lanea ignored him each time. Then he picked up a stick and pitched the cooking bundle into the gulley.

11i-ii When he peered down into the depression, he saw the remains of his dead brothers—hair, bones, breechcloths, bark belts, and armbands—and he understood what had happened. After climbing carefully down into the depression through the rotting flesh and bones, he retrieved his brother Koke's head. He saw that it was still not yet rotten; it was still quite fresh, though broken. He wrapped it in a pandanus sheath and flew away, a *kaima* flying fox, whistling softly while carrying his brother's head.

Tale 51: The Shell-Stealer

0,7i A little-man who was all skin and bones (*kulikama alisi*), named Lawira Kade, lived at the base of a wild pandanus tree (*pima*) growing at Kapolore. One day a man of Eparepa put on his bailer shell and walked along a forest path. Eventually he happened upon Kade, who said, "Oh, you're wearing a nice shell. Let me see it."

So the Eparepa man took off his shell and handed it over to the other to examine. "Let me look at it a bit longer," said Kade. "We'll walk on ahead. I'll continue to look at it and give it back to you further along." So the Eparepa man continued along and Kade followed. After a short while the Eparepa man looked back: the little-man was no longer in sight; he had disappeared completely. Moreover, this Eparepa man, who had worn the shell, was never seen again.

What happened was this. Beside the path where Kade waited there was a clump of tall *ira* grass. When Kade wanted to hide, he would pull up the clump, go into the earth, and then replace the clump.

On another occasion, another man wearing a bailer shell approached. When Kade asked to see the shell, the shell-owner took it off and handed it over. Again the same thing happened. And after those first two, others followed. Eventually there were scarcely any Eparepa men left.

7ii One day, yet another man wearing a bailer shell came. The same thing happened, but this man, turning his head and watching out of the corner of his eye, saw Kade disappear into the ground. He understood and returned to tell the others what had happened. Having done that, he went back to the clump of *ira* grass, lifted it, and went below.

There, in a place underneath the ground, he saw the poor-man wearing good ornaments; he was *koda* dancing beside a pile of bailer shells, chanting:

Kewa rame ayamede adano gida lawade yape.
"Oh brother, let me see your bailer shell," I said.
Ni mea ria puawa lawade yape.
And I put it on and went off.

The man hid and watched.

7i Later he fetched his brothers. These men uprooted the *ira* clump, went below, and fought Kade. "I am only one, and you are many!" he cried out. But he killed them all.

7ii,9Bi All, that is, except for one man, Walupo Romo. Romo, grieving his dead brothers, returned to the scene of the fight. Strewn about were the bones, hair, and bark belts of his dead brothers. Romo took those bones back to the men's house at Walupo, having heaped them in netbags. He walked back slowly with his heavy burden, passing through Kati before arriving home at Walupo. There he divided the bones among the sleeping compartments in the men's house. After securing the door, he went to stay in a house nearby.

9Bii Later he heard much noise from the men's house: the sound of firewood being split and the sound of young men laughing.

11i-ii Once again there were many men there. Romo did this by placing the bones in the house. If he had not done so, this land would be uninhabited.

Tale 52: Keapu and Abuwapale

0,7i   At Kaluake the men had made themselves a long men's house. Upon returning one day from their gardens near the Yaro River, they found an old man sitting in this house. He was sitting in a room next to a hearth, and he was cooking some possums and birds. When the owner of that room arrived, the old man said to him, "Where I live there are many possums and birds, and you can eat like this every day." He talked thus and led this youth away with him when he left. Then he killed and ate him.

Later he coaxed away another youth, and then another and yet another until only one was left, Keapu. And then he led Keapu away, too.

7ii   But Keapu followed him at a distance. Watching the old man climb a rise on the way to his house, he was startled to see many men's legs dangling from the man's back. "Has he eaten those men?" Keapu wondered.

The old one turned and called to Keapu, "Cassowaries sometimes walk along this little path here. Stay and watch." Keapu watched the path, and when the old man drove a cassowary along it, he shot it with an arrow. The old man said, "I will put the cassowary in a pool now (to keep it safe from scavengers). Tomorrow we will fetch it," and he told Keapu to go along another path. But the old man did not put the cassowary in the water at all; he deceived Keapu and ate it all himself.

"Along this other path," the old man told him later, "wild pigs often come. Stay and watch it carefully!" A big wild pig came, and Keapu killed it with one true shot. The two men did this again and again, but always the old man ate the game. Finally the two approached the old man's house. The old man said to Keapu, "Don't follow me along this narrow path. I'm going this way to put the wild pig under water until tomorrow. You must take this wide path."

3Ai   Keapu started along the wide path, but then, without being seen, he crossed over to the narrow one. He followed it to where it rejoined the wide one. Then he turned and looked back along the wide path he was supposed to take. He saw the old man waiting for him — to kill and eat him. The old man was looking for Keapu in the other direction and did not see him now.

3Aii   Keapu looked to one side and saw a house nearby and another one beyond. The closer house was a fine one; the other was reddish and looked as if it were lit by glows of lightning. He went to the second house, and he saw a young woman sitting inside. She was Abuwapale.

"Who are you?" she asked. "Men such as you my father kills and eats. I think you must have deceived my father to come here. Did you see an old man on the way here?"

"Yes!"

"Then you must go back and kill him!"

Keapu agreed to try. He shot the old man with an arrow and struck him with his axe. Then he carried him back to the woman's house. The woman told him to cook him quickly, then set up forked sticks, hang up the flesh, and cook the viscera nearby. Then she told him to gather the cuttings of many kinds of food plants; later they would plant them.

3Ai That afternoon they heard something making noise (*dau ta*) and coming closer. Keapu was frightened, but the woman told him to sit quietly. An old, long-tusked man approached. Keapu trembled with fear as he watched the old man eat the guts hanging outside the house and then remove the flesh from the earth oven. He ate, muttering "Oh, there is no fat on this man, just bones!" When he had eaten, the old man went back to his house and slept.

3Aii Abuwapale then stole over to this house and listened: the man was sound asleep, snoring. She told Keapu to fetch some *katiri* firewood and to lay it around the house. He did this, securely closed the entrance, and then set fire to the wood. Then they swiftly packed up the cuttings Keapu had gathered and fled back towards Keapu's home at Kaluake. As they were going along the path, the woman said, "Listen, later on my father will recover!"

When the two were crossing Paya Mountain they heard a *duuu* sound. "What's that?" Keapu asked. Abuwapale answered, "That's the noise of my father's body burning!"

The two came and stayed in Kaluake, and the woman gave birth to many sons, as many as had been eaten before.

3Ai After some time she said, "Soon I think my father will be coming, so the two of us must build a house in a safer place, on Mount Ialibu." So the couple went there, and after they built their house they planted the food-crop cuttings they had brought with them.

3Aii It was then that the father of this woman brought together all the other old men of that place for an attack. They all came to Mount Ialibu and surrounded it. From the top, Keapu and Abuwapale threw down long vines, each time one of the old men climbed up one of them, they cut it off, and the old man fell down on the rocks below. Many old men tried to reach them this way, but they all died.

Soon only the father of Abuwapale was left. This old man told his daughter to throw down a vine for him. She did this. When the old man was climbing up, the last-born son of Abuwapale and Keapu said, "I'll cut the vine, you watch!" As the old man was nearing the top, the youth tried to cut the vine. But he missed, his hand was shaking so. The old man reached the top, and he killed this youth and all the others. Only the two parents remained, Keapu and Abuwapale. They fled with the old man in pursuit. As they ran Abuwapale told Keapu, "My father has dreamed about the *masa* wild taro. If you uproot one, he'll die!" Keapu uprooted a wild taro and the old one died.

11ii   The two of them became quail, *mumakarubi.*

Tale 53: The Hot Women

0,7i   Several brothers—Numuga, Ogeda, Peagu, Agora, and Pu—stayed with their mother. Pu was the last born. One day Numuga went to the forest to cut bark for a bark belt, but he did not return. So Ogeda left, to cut bark and to look for his brother Numuga. But Ogeda, too, did not return. Then Peagu went to find the two others, but he also did not return. Finally Agora went and also never returned. All were lost except for Pu. The mother of these four then sang,

> *Iminya panuri waru peame, na kama noma wala rabu, kama waru peame.*
> You, whoever you are, did well for yourself, but what about my handsome sons?

7ii   The last brother, Pu, heard this sad song and saw his mother's sorrow. The two of them killed their large pig, Puramenalasu. Then Pu put some pork and salt into netbags and followed his brothers' footprints into the forest. On and on he went, following their tracks. Presently he met an old woman, who was sitting on the side of the path. He gave her some pork and salt, and she in turn gave him a small bundle. Then he went on up a mountainside, and again he met an old woman. He gave her pork and salt, and she gave him a small bundle. He hurried on, and met more old women.

Finally, at the top of a ridge he stopped and looked down to a valley below him; there he saw a wide ceremonial ground with tall casuarina trees and pines growing around it. A tall dark *kebele* bamboo clump grew there as well. "What sort of place would this be?" he wondered. He headed toward it.

Soon he reached a wide pool lying between him and the ceremonial ground. At its edge he saw the footprints of Peagu and others, but he lost them in the mud. At this point he untied a small bundle; it held a frog. He threw this frog into the pool, and the frog parted the water for him. So Pu walked right through the pool and came to the bamboo clump. There he saw a number of bark belts, hair coverings, and breechcloths lying about. There, too, he found Peagu, dying. Pu picked up his brother's body, removed his head-dress, and put it in his netbag. All the others were dead, and their bones, flesh, and hair were rotting. Pu wondered how all had come to die.

He walked up to the men's house on the ceremonial ground, and there he unwrapped another small bundle that he had received. When he opened it, water flowed forth and put out the cooking fire inside the house. Pu then went and hid in the yard outside, behind a clump of bushy *irawapu* grass. Presently he saw two young women coming. Their hair was tightly curled in ringlets falling down the back of their necks, and they wore good shells and skirts. Indeed, they were beautiful women.

When the two women went inside the house, they saw that their fire had died. Pu approached and looked inside: the two had re-moved their skirts and were rubbing their vulvas to rekindle the fire.

"Oh, those two must have killed my brothers!" Pu thought. He sat and reflected for a while.

The next morning the two women left their house and walked over to the lake. There they got into their dugout boat and crossed over to the far shore. "Now I have seen what they do," thought Pu. Taking out some of his pork, he sat and ate. Later when he guessed the two women would be returning home, he rose and went to the water's edge. Using the frog in the bundle, he crossed to the far side and went to the place where the two women had left their canoe. He made a small hole in the bottom with his axe. That done, he crossed the pool again, returned to the two women's house, and hid himself under the grass. He sat there, waiting for the women to return.

Pu had made the hole so that the water would swamp the canoe when it had reached the middle of the pool. And indeed, when the women were halfway across, the boat filled with water, immersing the two women and their netbags of sweet potatoes. As the two sank into the water, Pu heard the hissing sound of steam.

The women abandoned their netbags and swam for shore. There they sat for awhile, feeling very cold. Then the two went back to their house, but Pu had put the fires out there, as he had done earlier. The two women, sick with cold, sat quite still.

Pu approached them, standing before them wearing his good ornaments and holding his stone axe. The two women looked up at him, and he looked down at them.

"Well, what are you up to?" he asked.

"We are sick." "Oh, why is that?" Pu taunted. But then he made a fire, cooked some pork and taro, and gave them something to eat. In the morning they all walked back to Pu's house. He married both of them.

11i   Once before, when men went into the forest to get bark they often did not return. But then Pu went and saw clearly what he had to do; he cut their canoe and made the women feel cold.

11ii   Because Pu did this, many of us live here now.

Tale 54: The Sister's Revenge

0,7i   There were many men in Kuri clan. They lived with one young woman, their sister Tyame. One day one of the men, Keapu, went to the forest to cut bark for bark belts, but he did not return. Yarapea went to search for him, but he, too, did not come back. Then Lopa went in search of the other two. He, too, failed to return. Then Rema, Kusa, Dira, Dira's son, Nayo, Tyamera, Riawa, Mulu, Pasere – all these men went and disappeared.

7ii   Tyame alone was left, and she wept as she strung Job's-tears seeds to wear in mourning. She made bracelets of the seeds, one for each of her lost brothers, calling them by name as she put the bracelets on her arms. Then she mixed some charcoal with pig fat and rubbed it on her skin; and she donned thick mourning skirts.

It was not long before she decided to go in search of the others. First she killed her pig, Puramenalasu, and cooked it. Some of the pork she ate, and the rest she tied up into a bundle. She bound this bundle securely with strong *kalipu* vine, pushing the loose ends of the vine well into it. Having done that, she set off, following the footprints of her Kuri clansmen.

These tracks led her along a wide path that crossed Mount Keresa and dropped toward Walu. Presently she came to a lean-to in the forest. In it she saw the lower jaws of many men. They were strung on a length of vine, just as people string up pig mandibles. She paused and gave this some thought. "Those are the jaw bones of my brothers!" She was afraid, but she pushed that feeling aside, entered the house, and sat down. Placing her netbag beside her, she waited.

After a while she heard a man approaching. He was exhaling his breath in a low whistle as he walked, so she guessed he was carrying a heavy burden. In a moment she heard the sound of a load of firewood fall to the ground. "Mother!" she heard the man call out.

"I am not your mother here," said Tyame. "I am someone who has lost her way. Come inside." The man did so. Tyame rose, took the bundle of pork from her netbag, and tossed it over to him. "Some pork, eat," she said, feeling for the sharp stone axe that she had brought.

The man picked up the bundle and turned it over and over, looking for a way to open it. After a while he gave up and bent over to bite the vine through with his teeth. Immediately Tyame sprung up and brought the axe down hard on the back of his neck. Then she dragged his body out of the house and dumped it in a ditch nearby, in which she saw her dead brothers' bones. Next she threw in a bracelet of Job's-tears, saying, "That's in return for one of you."

Later another man came along, whistling softly. He, too, dropped some firewood and entered. This one was a light-skinned youth of some importance, a headman (*mudu ali*). But she did the same to him, using the bundle of pork once again.

A third youth arrived and called out to his mother. Tyame spoke as before and offered him the pork. She killed him as he bent to bite the bundle open, and then she threw his body and a bracelet into the ditch. Again and again she did this to the others who came, until all but one of the Job's-tears bracelets were used up. She went outside and walked through the piles of firewood to the ditch. She saw that it was now full of dead men.

But still one bracelet was left. She thought to herself, "For each of those who have died, I have killed one. If more come now, they can kill me and I won't care." She went inside and sat down again.

Soon a young man approached. He was about Lopa's age, and the youngest of those who had come. He threw down his wood and called out, "Mother."

"Come inside," said Tyame. She killed that youth the way she had done before, though she did not throw a bracelet in this time.

3Di Finally an old woman, the mother, arrived with many netbags filled with food. She was bringing enough for twenty men. Tyame looked on as the old woman dropped the sweet-potato bags to the ground. And she heard the old one mutter to herself, "Where are those sons of mine? I've never seen them go off like this before."

Then Tyame said, "All your sons went off with some young women who were here. I'm here because I lost my path. Come inside." And when the old woman came inside Tyame threw the pork bundle over to her.

The old woman searched for the end of the vines that held it together. Then, just like the others, she tried to open it with her teeth. Hers were long tusks. As she did so, Tyame broke her tusks with her axe, and then struck her body, but to no avail. "What's this cutting me?" cried out the old woman. "Just blades of grass, that's all!"

Tyame kept striking her, but the axe blade just bounced off her skin. Defeated, Tyame ran back the way she had come. The old woman gave chase.

11i   Seeing a wild pandanus tree (*pima*) at the side of the path, Tyame climbed up it. She heard the woman below, singing sadly,

Go winya nena mone mone nuri pae pe peae,
Na kama nomarabu wa pele peae.
You could well have killed all the others,
And spared the good youth, my Kama Nomarabu.

The old woman was singing thus because she was most saddened by the death of Nomarabu, her youngest son.

11ii   Now we see the large nuts of the wild pandanus, and this is the woman sitting in the tree. As for the white bracts (*kulu*) we see at the top of the tree near the fruit, that is Tyame's mourning skirt.

Tale 55: The Two Brothers and the Little-Men

0   Riba and Koke were two brothers. The two of them cultivated a garden which extended from Koparu Stream to the Kuare River and from there to Madara Stream. This large garden was just for the two of them, and in it they grew all sorts of foods. In its centre was their house, a long one, around which they had planted casuarina trees and a garden of good *kayabo* sugar cane.

One day the two went to the forest to hunt. Coming across a tree with a hole in it, one of the brothers climbed up to see if there was a possum inside. Instead he found two *kea* parrot fledglings, which he brought down.

Riba said, "I think we should take them back to our house. They will guard it for us." They took the birds back and put them inside a hollow casuarina just outside their house. The two birds, as they grew, learned to understand some speech. So the brothers instructed them, "If you see a stranger coming, someone who may want to kill us, cry *keakeakea,* and we shall be warned."

7i   One day while the two brothers were sitting on the grass outside their house, picking lice from each other's hair, they heard the parrots cry *keakeakea.* They guessed that someone was coming and that he was dangerous, for just then a brief but heavy rain fell.

The brothers looked down to the path to the forest, and they saw a little-man approaching. He was a thin, bony man (*kulisi kama*) with dirty reddish hair, and with ashes on his skin. He came and sat down close to the house while the two brothers looked on.

"What are you staring at? Roll me a smoke quickly! I have come a long way," said the stranger.

The two brothers were afraid. Riba went inside to their sleeping place and returned with some tobacco and a leaf for rolling it in. He rolled a smoke for the little-man. They sat smoking. After a while one of the brothers asked, "What are you doing here?"

"Oh," replied the little-man, "It was just an idea of mine to come to spend the night."

"Good enough," replied Koke. "We will sleep here." And to Riba he said, "Go to the garden and fetch some vegetables."

Riba went with his bushknife down to the garden by the Kuare River. He dug up some *kamo* taro, cut two bunches of plantains, and gathered some *padi* greens as well as other foods. As he started back he heard, from the direction of the house, a cry for help: "Hey, brother!"

"Eh!" thought Riba. "My brother is calling out for me." And he adjusted his load so as to be able to move more quickly. Again he heard his brother cry out, "I'm being attacked! I'm being carried off!" Hearing this, Riba dropped his load and rushed back.

When he reached the house, neither Koke nor the other were there. But he heard his brother call out again from a nearby rise, "Help, brother! I'm being carried off!" Riba fetched the axe he used for work, the axe he took on travels, his bows and arrows, and his spears. Armed thus he set off after his brother's captor.

Coming to the top of the rise from which his brother had called, he saw the little-man carrying his brother off on his shoulder. Riba caught up quickly. He swung his work axe and struck the little-man on the back of his leg, but the blade just bounced off. He struck with his other axe, but the blade broke. Then he thrust with his spear, but it, too, glanced off the man's skin.

The little-man said, "You're not hurting me! You might as well be cutting a tree or a stone or something like that!" Riba shot an arrow at him, but to no avail. On and on they went, past Koipu Stream, down to the Yaro River, across this river, up to Tindua, from there up the slopes of Mount Ialibu, and then down the far side. Finally Riba gave up and came back. Smearing mud on his face, he walked slowly and sorrowfully back home. The little-man had told him, "So you are trying to kill me? Well then, in three days I'll come back for you!"

7ii   The next day Riba sat in mourning. On the following day he heard the parrots cry again *keakeakea*. Again a brief but heavy rain fell. And again he saw a little-man with straggly hair and ashes on his skin approach from the main path.

"Roll me a smoke," said the little-man as he stumbled along the path toward the house.

"Yes, all right, I'll make you a smoke," said Riba. "You came back quickly, you who took my brother away!"

"Not I!" said the other. And when Riba looked at him closely, he saw it was true: it was a different little-man who had come.

Riba made him a smoke, and they sat and smoked. After a while the little-man asked Riba, "What were you saying about your brother? I don't understand."

"Well, a little-man like yourself came and carried him off."

"Ah, that must be my enemy," the little-one said. Then he asked, "When did he say he was going to return?"

"On the third day. That was the day before yesterday."

"Tomorrow then," said the little-man. "We must prepare ourselves. Let's get some firewood." So they chopped down a dead casuarina tree standing near the house, split it up and stacked the wood inside the house. They also made a ceremonial digging stick (*ekepayo*), cooked some *ruminya* sweet potatoes, and collected some ants into a bundle.

The little-man advised Riba, "When that person comes back and says, 'Roll me a smoke,' reply 'I won't' and go inside the house. He will follow you in, and I'll be there waiting."

The next morning Riba waited outside in the yard while the other one sat inside the house with the things they had prepared. Presently the parrots cried *keakeakea*, and Riba saw the first little-man approaching, hurrying and stumbling along the path toward the house.

"Hey, don't stare at me! Roll me some tobacco quickly!" he commanded.

Riba refused. "You killed my brother! Why should I give you tobacco?"

"No, I didn't kill and cook him. He's well, staying with me. Make me a smoke."

"All right, then, I'll do so. Come inside."

"Where are you going?" asked the little-man, but he followed him in.

Then the second little-man brought the *ekepayo* stick down on the first one's head, which made him stagger. Then he threw some pulpy cooked sweet potato into his eyes, and then a bundle of ants. As their enemy began to reel and totter about, the two took the firewood and built a huge pyre. They burnt him on top of it.

11i   When that was done, Riba killed the two pigs that he and his brother had kept, and using what was left of the fire, cooked them. When the meat was cooked he butchered it and gave it to the little-man. Then he went and cut some fresh casuarina branches and laid them on the porch floor. On top he laid down the many pearl shells that the brothers owned.

Then Riba said, "I am giving you these things now because you made the *ali kalia* "man-cordyline" revenge for my dead brother."

Having said that, he put the shells in a netbag and gave them to the little-man. This one accepted the gift and broke off a *kalia* cordyline branch, planting it where Riba stood.

11ii   Today we, too, act this way; we follow him in making the "man-cordyline" custom, or "man-cassowary" as it is also called.

Tale 56: The Two Brothers and the Old Man

0   Two youths, Keapu and Lopa, lived together. Their house was in Nire, and they made gardens in distant places like Kuwi, Karapere, and Yarapia.

7i   One day the youths went to fetch food from one of these gardens. Afterwards they returned and put the food in their house in Nire. That afternoon they heard a cockatoo crying from the direction of the forests of Mount Keresa. They talked about what this might mean while they sat and cooked. Then they heard something approaching noisily. It was a big old man with long, tusk-like teeth wrapped in coverings of *wabi*.

Keapu and Lopa asked him, "Where are you going?"

And the old man replied, "My thoughts went to you two. I came because I thought of spending the night here."

"All right," said the youths, "We'll cook some food. Stay the night."

After they had cooked and eaten, the two brothers went outside and conversed. "Whatever we do, we mustn't do it alone. When we sit, eat, relieve ourselves, whatever, we must not separate. And we must not sleep; we must stay awake until morning. Or should we want to go someplace, maybe to fetch leaves for covering an earth oven, we must both go." So they planned.

Later they all lay down to sleep. The old man stretched out on one side of the hearth, the two brothers on the other side. But the young men did not sleep, and when they looked over at the old man they saw that he too was not asleep.

Late in the night, though, Keapu fell asleep. When the old man looked and saw that Keapu slept while Lopa did not, he rose, took hold of Lopa, threw him over his shoulder, and went out through the porch. It was daybreak when he left.

When Keapu woke and saw that his brother and the old man had disappeared, he reached immediately for his axe, spear, and bow and arrows. He pursued the old man and attacked him. But the latter retorted, "You're not hurting me! You're just hacking at stones or trees with your weapons!"

Then Keapu pulled Lopa by the arm, trying to tear him away. But Lopa was stuck fast to that old man, and the old one told Keapu, "He has now joined to my body. You might as well return home!"

Keapu did so and rubbed earth on his face in mourning.

By the side of his house was a large *sawia* tree, whose branches spread in all directions, toward the lands of Wiru, Melpa, Mendi, and South Kewa. Keapu made a hole in its base and from there he worked his way up, inside the tree, to the lowest branch. Then, having killed and cooked his pigs, he carried the pork up there and placed it in that hollowed branch. Finally he himself came to sit there and piled up *rupi* stones to seal the entrance.

7ii   Presently he heard the cockatoo crying again, *kekeke.* Ten old men approached. They sniffed and sniffed around and finally surrounded the base of the tree. Knowing that the youth was inside, they began to cut down the tree with their sharp teeth.

The tree toppled. The branch in which Keapu was hiding broke off and fell into the Yaro River.

The old men sniffed around the branches of the fallen tree, going from one branch to another, and at last they came to the one lying in the water. Since the branch was submerged, they could not come to kill him there. So they watched, waiting for the youth to come out.

But Keapu, who could see their shadows on the surface of the water, did not move.

11i-ii   He would not come out. He stayed there and became a *kara-doali,* a wildman. Today there would be no wildmen were it not for those old men who, trying to kill the youth, trapped him in the water.

Tale 57: The Battle with the Old Men

0   At Kilimi stood a long men's house with many sleeping places on either side of the central corridor. Many men of the Kuri clan lived there. One day some of them went to work in their gardens close to the Yaro River, while others visited their gardens nearer home in Kilimi, Mupalu, and the surroundings. Others went to Mount Keresa to hunt for possums, while yet others went to other parts of the forest to gather the nuts of the pandanus palm. Only the children were left in the village, and they amused themselves by playing in the dirt, mounding the earth, and pretending to make sweet potato gardens.

7i   From the direction of Kalawira some *wata* and *kilira* birds approached crying *rerere.* The children heard the birds calling as they descended among the tree fruits, first at Kolapi, then at Momanimi, Mapeda, Tidane—closer and ever closer to Kilimi. From Nambatu Kilipimi they reached Mupalu Stream and then crossed to Nambawan Kilipimi. Some of the children grew frightened and wanted to run away, but others held them fast. They waited, and soon they saw an old man approaching, a big man with a tall *wakeawi* tree growing up out of the top of his head and with long, sharp tusks in his jaws. On his head and on his back grew *yabala, kata,* and other sorts of mushrooms. The children stared up at him and saw that the birds they had heard were feeding on the flowers and seeds of the tree that grew from his head.

This being looked around and asked the children, "Where are your fathers? When they come back, tell them I have work for them cutting the branches of a tree in my garden. I'm leaving now, but I'll return. Tell your fathers what I have said."

The children watched as he turned and went off. They saw that long lianas were growing from his head and hanging down his back.

When their fathers returned, the boys told them about this tall old man with the mushrooms growing on his back, the tree and lianas coming out of his head, and many birds flocking on that tree. "He said he would come back," the children said. When the men heard this, they got vegetables and pigs ready for cooking, and began to sing *mata* songs.

Three days later they heard the *rerere* cries of the birds, and they knew that the old one was approaching. When he arrived, he said, "I will go now and cook some food for you in an earth oven. In return, you must come and pollard the large tree which stands in the middle of my garden."

Not all the Kuri men went; some men stayed in the village, while the others left with their knives and axes. Upon arriving at the old man's garden, they saw that a tall old tree stood there. One of its branches extended over to the Melpa land, one to Mendi land, one to the mouth of the Sugu River, one toward south Kewa land, and one to Palea (Wiru) land. The Kuri men made a scaffold, climbed the trunk, and then separated, going off in different directions along the branches.

One of the men went along a branch extending toward the Palea land, and when he looked over in that direction, he saw smoke rising in the distance. Many other men belonging to that old man's group were there, and they were preparing for a fight. Immediately, this Kuri man then came back and told the others. After considering their plight, some of them began to hollow out the trunk and branches, while others went down to the Yaro River and carried back some stones from the river bed. After they had dug out the base of the tree and made a cavity there, they filled it in with the stones and wrapped the bark around it so it looked as before. Then they killed some big pigs and quickly—as things always happen in tales—carried this food to the top of the tree and stuffed it into a hollowed branch. Additional boulders, too, they carried up and put inside the hollow branches.

Soon the old men approached. They surrounded the base of the tree and started to bite into the trunk, hoping to cut it down and thereby kill those men. But the Kuri men high up in the tree threw stones down upon them, killing some. Other old men broke their tusk-like teeth on the stones concealed beneath the bark. Some two hundred of them died, and then the others began to fight like dogs over the pork bones that the men above threw down upon them. After many had died in this way, the first old man with the long teeth went back to get more old men. He returned with another hundred.

7ii   Soon the tree began to sway. One branch leaned close to Melpa land, and some men jumped down there. Then as the tree swayed again, another branch leaned toward Wiru land, and some went there. Another branch leaned toward Wapi-Sumi land and toward the mouth of the Sugu River, while a fourth branch fell down to the south Kewa side. By the time the old men reached the top of the tree, the Kuri men had all descended to these different places. Thinking that the Kuri men were still hiding there, the old men began to eat the branches. But there was no one there.

The Kuri men who had left the tree now came back to their place in Kilimi. They considered what to do, for if the old men found them there would be another attack. Indeed, the old men guessed the Kuri men would be there and had set out for Kilimi to kill them.

11i   But this time the Kuri men were ready and waiting for them along the path. Some waited at Tidane, some at Kolapi, some at Mapeda. They attacked the old men and killed them all.

11ii   Old men like these would kill us today, were it not for this. Because the Kuri clan killed them all, there are none left who might kill and eat us now.

Tale 58: The Battle with the Old Tree Man

0,7i   Many youths lived in a long men's house at Kilipimi. One day when they were off in their gardens, a heavy rain came with sunshine. Afraid, they looked back to their house. Dark smoke was rising from the thatch. Hurrying back, they found an old man sitting inside.

This old one said to them, "I have come to ask you to cut some branches for me."

"We'll do it," said they.

That same day they cooked food and made ready to go, for they had promised to do the work on the following day. The next morning they went to where the old man had indicated. There they found a great *sawia* tree, with its branches extending in all directions. The youths cut another, smaller tree and leaned it against the larger one. Then they climbed up. None of them stayed on the ground; they all went up, taking with them cooked food—bananas, sweet potatoes, and others. After leaving these on the lowest branch, they went off to all the other branches. Some went toward Mendi land, some to Palea (Wiru) land, some to Melpa land, some to south Kewa land, some to Pasuma land. One of the youths, Boso, looked after the food which they had left on the bottom branch. All the others went off onto the other branches.

The old man said, "I'll go and cook some food for you in an earth oven. When you finish the pollarding, you'll have something to eat." The youths believed he was indeed going to do this, but instead he went to fetch other old men of his group. Many of them came from their place of hiding in the garden underneath the tree. They approached, baring their long, sharp teeth.

Upon catching sight of them, Boso immediately rose and threw aside that smaller tree they had used to climb up the thick trunk of the *sawia*. The old men could not get up now, but with their sharp tusks they started to hack away at its base. They continued to work at this, and soon the tree began to sway.

Up above, the youths were much afraid. They all came to sit on the thickest, lowest branch, where Boso was sitting. Boso was removing bark and growths on that branch. He uncovered an opening: the thick branch was hollow. He went inside, as one goes inside a house, then came out again and said, "Come now! In here!"

The old men were taunting, "You have no way out! Where will you go now?" And they continued to cut at the base of the tree with their tusk-like teeth, taking turns. The tree was on the point of falling, the branches dipping from side to side.

7ii   The youths all went inside the hollow branch, taking their food with them. And finally, when they were all inside, the tree fell. The branch in which they were hiding broke off from the trunk and landed on the far side of the Yaro River.

After the tree had fallen, the old men began to break apart the branches in search of the young men. But the youths' branch had fallen far away. "Where are they all?" wondered the old ones as they searched. When they met with no success, they departed.

That day, some young women were walking along the Yaro River bed, carrying nets for fishing. Seeing a large dry branch by the side of the river, one of them said, "Sisters, let's carry this branch home for firewood!" So they carried it back. They did not know the youths were inside it. When they arrived home, the women put the branch inside their house in the section where they kept their pigs —for these women lived with very many big pigs, though no men. Having left that branch there, they went to their gardens.

7i   One youth came out, followed by all the others. They saw the pigs in the house, grabbed a large sow, and killed it. "Those women will not be coming back soon," they thought. So they cooked the pig right there inside the women's house. Then they carried all the pork inside their branch and sat down to eat.

As they were eating, the young women returned. They looked around for their missing pig, but could not find it. For three days those youths stayed inside that branch eating this pork.

On a second occasion they came out and did the same thing, retreating into the branch before the women returned. Again the women looked in vain for their missing pig. And so it was. For two weeks the boys stayed there in the branch, taking pigs again and again until nearly all the pigs had gone.

7ii   The young women were perplexed. They conversed a while and decided to hide a small young woman in a pile of netbags while they were away. They did so. When her sisters had gone off, the hidden girl saw the youths emerge one by one from the branch. She saw them take the last pig, kill it, cook it, and carry the pork into the branch again. As happens in tales, the youths were able to make the women's house appear just as before, as if no cooking had been done.

When the rest of the girls returned, they saw that their last pig had disappeared. They searched for it unsuccessfully, and then they took apart the pile of netbags in which the small girl had stayed hidden. She told them, "See this piece of firewood? There are many youths hiding inside it, and they have taken and eaten all our pigs!"

"All right, just wait," said the others. They gathered dry *kati* leaves and piled them around the house. Then, after first removing their netbags and other possessions, they barred the doorways and set fire to the leaves. The house burned.

11i-ii   Those youths became *walawe* lorikeets. Those with black tails are the ones blackened by the smoke; the rest are red from the fire. From the house that burnt, *mumukarubi* quail flew away. These were the girls.

Tale 59: The Battle with the Poor-Man

0 Poamera lived with his son, Neka. One day the two went, as they often did, to their garden. They cooked some food and in the afternoon worked in a place from which they could see their house at Karapere. Once, when they looked back home, they saw smoke rising from it. "There shouldn't be anyone there," said Poamera. "Let's go back quickly and see what's happening."

7i When they returned home they found a poor-man, small and skinny with unkempt hair. Poamera asked him, "Are you a man from the bush (*raa ali*) or from the village (*ada ali*)?"

Plate 7. A father and his young son.

"Oh, I'm from the village. Since I've come, we shall pass the night here together." They ate and then slept.

In the morning the little-man said, "Stay here another day, and on the following day come and meet me at Kapolore." And then he departed. Poamera wondered why he had made such a request. Then he said to his son, "We had better prepare ourselves!"

So the two sharpened their spears, strung their bows, shaped new arrows, and placed them in a bamboo quiver. The next day the father cut some *karape* wood and fashioned a shield, took his spear, bow and arrows, and left.

He waited at Kapolore, as the poor-man had asked him to. Presently he saw the little-man approaching, armed with only two arrows. Poamera hid himself, put an arrow in his bow, and sent the arrow toward the other's back. But the little-man dodged the arrow, crying out "Missed! So you want to fight?"

They began to fight. The little-man drove Poamera all the way back to Kudipa, and then went away after telling him, "On the day after tomorrow, we'll meet again here at Kudipa!"

Upon returning home, Poamera told his son what had happened. "Tomorrow we must prepare more weapons. You must get some food ready for the two of us." The next day, then, Poamera fashioned some new arrows and made a new bowstring. And on the following day he waited at Kudipa for the little-man.

As before, the little-man came carrying just two arrows. And, as before, Poamera waited in an ambush and released an arrow at his back. But the other dodged it again. They fought on, and again Poamera was beaten back.

"I've almost come close enough to burn your house down," cried that poor-man. "The day after tomorrow I'll come even closer. Meet me here at Kaliapore."

On the next day Poamera prepared his things, and on the day following that the two resumed their fighting where they had left off. Again the poor-man beat him back, this time back to Koparu Stream. "Tomorrow I shall really set fire to your house!" he said.

Poamera told this to his son and again said, "We must do something!" So he went to a *sawia* tree growing in the yard outside his house. With a stone chisel he hollowed it out, and then he put food and pigs inside, leaving a space for the boy to sleep and to make a fire. Then he took some resin and covered the hole. The father advised his son, "Should he kill me and burn the house down tomorrow, stay inside this tree. When he has gone away, watch the smoke rising from the burning house, and go in the direction it drifts to." Having said this, he went to resume the battle at Koparu Stream.

The little-man pursued the fatigued Poamera up the hill into the yard of his house, chased him around the house, and finally followed him inside. There he killed him. Then he burned the house down.

7ii   All this while Neka was looking on from inside his tree. He wept as he heard the *buuu* sound of his father's body burning in that house. He watched the smoke rise and drift off in the direction of Mt. Ialibu, beyond the Yaro River. And he watched as that little-man also chopped down some of his father's casuarinas, plantain trees, and other crops planted nearby, all the while crying out, "Tomorrow I'll come back and cut down the rest!" The little-man departed.

Neka watched him disappear over the hill at Raya. Then he took his pig from the *sawia* tree where he had hidden it. He killed it, and with the fire from the burning house, he singed and cooked it. Next he broke a block of salt into pieces, butchered the pig, and put both pork and salt into his netbag.

?*   When all was ready, he set off on the path to Mount Ialibu. After crossing the Yaro River, he ascended the south slope of the mountain. Soon he stood at its summit and looked down over the land beyond.

He saw many dead trees, and he guessed someone might have made gardens underneath them. So he continued on down. Presently he reached a place from which smoke was rising; an old man was there, burning his garden. He had long teeth wrapped in sheaths of *wabi.*

Afraid, Neka took off his netbag—heavy with shells, pork, and salt—and hung it up on the branch of a nearby tree. But the branch broke with a loud snap. The old man looked over and then approached. "Who are you?" he asked.

"Oh, I . . . ," and the boy explained how he came to be there.

The old man was overjoyed. "Oh, good indeed!" he exclaimed, for he had no sons with him. He embraced Neka and led him into his house, carrying the boy's heavy netbag. Then he took out some pork and ate it. The boy watched him eat. The old man chewed the pork well, and Neka was relieved to see this. "He's not a killer of men, then," he thought.

The old man gathered many kinds of food from a nearby garden and returned. The two stayed together, and soon Neka began to call this old man his "father."

Now the old one had a large dog. Often, while the old man and the youth were at work in the gardens, that dog would go by itself into the forest, kill some possums, and bring them back to the house. On other occasions the old man would go off with the dog and bag possums, which they would cook in an earth oven and eat—large possums such as *koyamo* and *pasolo.*

---

*As explained in the introduction, the question mark means that the following part of this tale does not fit any of the eleven sequences.

After some time Neka said, "Father, I've been working in the gardens all this time and I am tired of it. Let me take the dog and hunt possums."

"Don't we eat enough possums here, the ones that I bring back?" replied the old man. "Besides, you can't take this sort of dog to the forest."

But the boy insisted: "Truly, I want to take the dog there."

"You'll get into trouble there. Don't go."

"I won't make trouble," said the boy. "I'll do exactly as you say."

Finally the old man assented. He told the boy, "This dog will kill many possums. But when dusk falls, it will run off. You must let it do so. Don't try to call it back; just let it go. Return here." He told Neka not to call the dog by name or shout for it to come back. "Just come back here on your own," he repeated.

The boy went off and killed many possums in the forest. And just as the old man said, when dusk fell the dog ran off. But the youth started to look for it. He looked and looked, and called for it. Finally, tired, he paused for a rest.

Just then a *kiliwapa* bird called out, "Pull up the *kope* clump! Pull up the *kope* clump!" Neka looked around and saw a clump of *kope* leaves. He pulled it up and saw a hole underneath, and in it he saw a big old woman with white hair. The dog was eating her.

Just then the dog looked up, jumped out of the hole, and bounded toward Neka. The boy sprang up and, leaving his netbag of possums behind, fled with the dog at his heels. Seeing that the dog was about to catch him, he quickly climbed a tree, but the dog chewed at the tree and brought it down. Just before it fell, Neka sprang into another tree top. The dog then attacked the base of that tree, and Neka jumped to the branches of yet another, and on and on they went.

When he drew close to his father's place—as close as Raya is from Karapere—he cried out, "Father, I'm going to be killed!" The old man heard him and guessed what had happened. He was angry with the boy and did not go to help him.

Still pursued, the boy drew even closer. He cried out again, and again the old man did nothing. Finally, when he was closer still, the boy cried out once more. This time the old man felt sorry for his son. He rose and picked up his bow and arrow. As the boy ran up he scolded him severely for forgetting what he was told. Then he shot the attacking dog in the stomach, killing it.

The old man said, "This was not my dog. It was the dog of a cross cousin of mine, who lent him to me for possum hunting, and who said he would return for it. When he comes, he'll expect us to do something, and in any case he'll be angry." Then he and the boy made a mortuary platform for the dog. After that they stayed on, making their gardens.

One morning a brief, heavy rain fell. Then they heard a *buuu* sound, and shortly thereafter an old man approached, his teeth also sheathed in *wabi,* his skin shining and many coloured. "I've come for my dog," he said.

The other old man explained, "Ah, cross cousin, listen to what happened . . . ."

"No, you must really give me back my dog," said the cousin, angry and disbelieving. So Neka's father had to explain why he had killed the dog. Then the old cousin went after the boy, intending to kill him in return.

11i   But the old man, sorry for this boy, whose death appeared close, said, "All right, now I'll compensate you. Come here." So he took some casuarina branches and spread them out on the porch. On top, he arranged pearl shells, some of them the ones that the boy had brought and others those that he himself held. Then he announced, "Cousin, I am compensating you now. Do not kill him." And he gave him all those shells.

11ii Nowadays this manner of compensation exists. If I watch over someone and he kills someone else, the dead person's relatives will want to kill him. In that event, I give them many shells or pigs in compensation. Today we do it thus.

The old man became a *mumakarubi* quail, while the son became a *walawe* lorikeet. The lorikeet's long tail is the boy's bow.

Tale 60: The Girl and the Poor-Man

0,7i One day several girls left their home for their garden. On their way back, they saw thick smoke rising from the thatch of their house. A poor-man was there. He had killed many small *weso* birds, wrapped them in leaves, and was cooking them singly in several hearths of the girls' house. When the girls arrived home and sat down by their fires, they found these parcels, removed them from the ashes, and ate the contents.

The poor-man then said to one of them, "Let's go," and he went off with the girl who usually slept closest to the porch.

The next day he returned and did the same thing again, and again the next day. Each time he took one of the girls off. He was a little poor-man (*riaboalisi*) who did that, and his name was Kikoi.

One of the girls once said to him, "You are a man without much wealth, yet again and again you lead girls off."

"You've seen all the food I bring," replied the poor-man. "That's why they come with me. They eat well!"

The next day he came back with more small *weso* and *ramani* birds in bundles. He cooked them in several hearths, and later he left with another of the girls. And the next day another. Without missing a day, he kept this up until there was only one girl left.

7ii   This last one watched him cook his birds. Then she said, "All the others have gone, and now there's only me."

"Come with me too, then," he asked.

"All right," she agreed. So she killed her pig, cooked it, and put the pork into a netbag with some salt. This she carried with her as they went off.

They went on until it was nearly dark. Finally they stopped, not at a house but at the base of a large *kati* tree and a *pai* tree. The poor-man said, "I will go to sleep on top of that *kati* tree. You sleep at the base of this *pai*."

So she put her netbag down at the base of the *pai* tree, took her walking stick, and walked over to the base of a nearby tall beech tree. She struck the ground repeatedly with it. Someone said from the earth below: "Don't hit my head like that!" Parting the roots, she felt something warm there. "I will sleep here," she thought. And she went back to her netbag, covered it against possible rain, and returned with some pork belly and salt. When she returned to the beech tree, she saw an old woman. On her back, she bore many bruises, made by the many girls who had struck her with their sticks, just as she had done.

This old woman said, "Many young girls like yourself have I seen pass by here, but none have I seen return!"

The girl gave her some pork and salt, and the old woman was pleased. She said again, "No, I don't see them return. But you can go on after sleeping here." The old woman ate some more pork and salt and then said, "That is the way the poor-man does things. In the morning he will come for you." Then the old one got some small bundles and put them into a large netbag. She gave this to the girl, along with a heavy walking stick. Then she fetched a big cooked taro which she had scraped. This too she gave the girl. Then they slept.

Soon it was nearly dawn. The old woman woke the girl and told her, "The *aluba* birds are crying. Get up!" Then she added, "When he tells you to do something, whatever it is, you must do it!" The girl went off with the thick walking stick, the bundles, the taro, and her own netbag of pork and salt.

3Bi   The girl and the poor-man went along for a while, and eventually they came to two wide pools. The girl could not see how they could ever cross them, but the poor-man took an arrow and, holding it out in front of him, walked over the water to the far side of the first pool. Then he aimed this arrow at her and said, "I will shoot you if you do not come across." So she threw down her walking stick onto the water and walked across on it, joining him where he stood.

Then the poor-man said, "We will cross the other pool now, but first tell me your father's name."

She said, "My father's name is Tuaraipara."

"Who is your mother?"

"Menanalapurugi." And then she answered other questions, "My father's axe is Tuaraipara as well. The name of this vine is *awipu*. The name of this lake is Buna Kumi," and so on.

3Bii   The poor-man, hearing her answer so well, said that the two should continue on their way. They went on until they reached a fence enclosing a dancing ground. There he told her, "We shall not both take the same path now. You go on, and I will take the other one. But first give me some pork."

She took some pork from her netbag and gave it to him. "Stay over there at my mother's house, where I have many pigs tethered," he told her. She went where he indicated and found a newly built house. Putting her netbag down inside, she sat and waited. From where she sat she could see, at some distance, another house, an old one with tall grass growing around it; and she saw something shining there.

She went over to this old house and found, sitting there, an old woman.

"Who are you, then?" she asked the little old woman.

The old one said, "Oh, cross cousin, your husband's mother is a bad woman!'

The girl began to clear this old house of some of the rubbish lying around, and then she spread some dry banana leaves down on the ground. She offered the old woman some pork, and then she arranged the old woman's netbags.

"Your husband's mother will come, making much noise," said the old woman. "Prepare yourself. Cut bananas and sugar cane, dig sweet potatoes and taro, and fetch firewood, too. When she asks you for these things, you must have them ready."

3Di   So the young woman went to gather these things, and she returned. Soon she heard a noise—*buuu!*—from some distance. "That's your husband's mother coming!" said the old woman. "All this pork you have brought you will have to give to her. She will eat it all herself! Hang it outside for her."

The young woman did so. The *buuu* sound was drawing nearer;

the ground shook. "Now when she comes here, stay inside and look through the open door."

A tall old woman approached. Her body had branched out into several—her victims' bodies had joined to her own—and each of them carried a netbag loaded with something different. One held *padi* greens, another sweet potatoes, another *rani* greens, yet others sugar cane, taro, yams, and *kuni* pitpit. Many young women branched out from her big body. The old woman herself carried a heavy load of firewood on her head. All of them were saying in unison, "My son's wives don't come to sit by my house. They never stop to help me."

The young woman sat by the door and looked on, much afraid. Then she rose and carried out pieces of pork. She gave a piece to each of the woman-branches. These all put down their netbags, and it was as if many people had stacked them there together for a feast. The young woman gave away all her pork.

Then the old woman with the many branches said, "Good, I have taken some pork and I have brought some vegetables. Do you have taro? Sugar cane? Plantains? *Kuni* pitpit? *Padi?* Yams?" Each time the girl said that she had.

3Dii   "You've brought all these? That's good! Keep them! My son's other wives were not hard workers, yet they said the same thing." It was now dark, and they slept the night.

The next morning the poor-man returned and said, "Hey, I want you to carry some yam posts out to the garden. Come!" When she saw there were many heavy posts to carry, she shrugged and carried them out to the garden, leaving them in a pile. She was about to return when she saw a big *yakua* snake. Seeing the snake approach, she cried out in fear, "Father, help!" and quickly climbed to the top of a tall *yawi* (black palm) tree. The snake was trying to bite or eat her, and it tried again and again on succeeding days. But each time she climbed out of reach to the tree top.

One day the helpful old woman told her, "Beware of them. I'm afraid now they'll kill me soon. When they say they're going to kill a pig and eat pork, what they actually mean is that they will kill and eat *me*. So you must not eat what they offer. Eat instead a piece of pork of your own." She repeated this, "They will kill and cook *me*, but they will say it is pork. Don't eat what they offer. Eat some of your own pork. When the old woman tells you she wants to butcher the pig and asks you to fetch a bushknife, go along this path along which you came. There you will see a house made for the *ribu* cult; the knife will be in the porch." Thus did the old woman tell the younger one everything that would happen later.

Presently the old woman with many branches arrived. She took a length of stout vine and strung the other old woman up, killing her. "My son's new wife must work well. The others didn't obey!" said all the branches in unison. "Now we'll cut up this pig fat and put it in the *ribu* house. My son's other wives didn't behave well. They were all lazy!"

The branched woman said this as she took down the old woman's body. "Now we'll cook this pig." Her many voices sounded together, as in *koda* singing. The young woman saw this and felt sorry for that old woman.

Then the branched woman told her, "Go to the *ribu* house and bring me a bush knife. I want to cut this pork."

7ii   The woman went. She opened the door of the cult house. Inside she saw the same *yakua* snake. Taking down the knife, she chopped the snake into pieces. But when she looked again, it was not a snake but a good-looking young man that lay there. It was this same poor-man; it was he who had been deceiving her by changing into a snake. She had killed this poor-man now, thinking it was a snake; but now a handsome young man lay there dead.

Then the many-branched woman came, all her parts talking and singing in unison. The girl cut at them with her knife. She killed them all.

11i   There, in a depression at the side of the cult house, she saw piles of ornaments and bones of young women and men. She climbed down and picked up beads, armbands, pearl shells, bailer shells, and skirts, some from each pile of bones. Then she walked away with these things and bunches of *kalia* cordylines.

As she went along she met many men and women in mourning, all with Job's-tears necklaces and faces daubed with mud. To each mourner she gave the ornaments belonging to the dead relative, along with a sprig of *kalia* cordylines.

11ii   But when she had finished, she did not return home. When she had given away the last of these things, she turned into a *mumaka-rubi* quail.

Tale 61: The Girl and Her Trickster Husband

0,7i   There once was a poor-man named Baki. That is the name that such men bear, Baki of Kola Baki. Young women always made fun of him. Sometimes he would go over to where several young women lived with their mother, an old woman. He would enter the house and go to sit by the hearth. With other men, these girls might have consented to court. But instead they would throw sticks at him, and ashes from the hearth would cover his skin.

Baki knew that none of these women cared for him, and he often sat and thought about this. Sometimes he would hunt game in the forest, and then he would offer one of the women some possums. But she would not talk to him.

One day he devised a plan. He killed a small *loke*. When he cleaned out the animal's guts, he left some feces in the intestine and put this aside. Then he took the rest of the meat to the young women. They ate it with some sweet potatoes they had cooked, but they did not share any with him. Meanwhile, they made fun of him.

After a while the women tired of mocking him and one by one they dozed off, for it had grown late. Soon the only ones awake were the old mother and Baki himself, who sat covered as usual with ashes. But after a while, the old woman, too, lay down to sleep. Baki stayed awake.

Then, when all were asleep, he took out the feces-filled intestine and rubbed some feces into his hair and on his face. Then he went to sleep beside the young woman he liked most of all, placing his head close by her buttocks.

In the middle of the night, the old woman woke and, feeling cold, built up the fire. As the wood blazed and lit the room, she looked over at the other sleepers. When she saw Baki's hair and face covered with feces, she immediately woke everyone up, and she asked her daughters to see what had happened. They exclaimed in dismay. All the others accused the girl who lay closest to Baki of defecating on him in her sleep. "I slept over there," each of them affirmed. "It must have been you." They were all ashamed, and they offered Baki pork and shells.

But Baki wanted none of these things. "I won't have them," said he.

Finally they asked, "Do you want to take this woman?"

"Yes," he said. And he went off with her to his home. Thus he got himself a wife at last.

The two of them stayed and made forest and sweet-potato gardens. One day Baki found a place where *sawia* and *yakua* trees were growing, and he decided to make a garden there. He cut down the trees and the underbrush, but he had to leave standing one big *sawia* tree, which was too thick to chop down. Instead he leaned a small tree against its trunk, climbed up, and began to pollard it.

7ii   One by one he cut the branches. Only one branch was left, and as he climbed out to cut it, he began to sing to himself:

Loke momo ki kole ka kole.
The *loke* feces, dirty and foul-smelling.

Well, his wife was working on the ground below him, and when she overheard his song, she understood that she had been deceived. Quickly she fetched some sharp sticks, the kind used for digging out pitpit clumps or turning sod. She struck these into the ground, point up, underneath the tree.

Then after changing back into her good skirt and picking up her fine netbag she called out to him, "You there! I am going to my mother's home now!"

Baki cried out, "No!" Hoping to stop her, he jumped down, landed on one of the stakes, and died. The woman looked at him, saw he was dead, and returned home to her mother.

Sometime later she said to her sisters, "Let's go gather some *alipu* vines for netbags. I've seen many in a new garden site." So they all went to that same garden to gather vines and wild greens.

3Bi   By this time all of Baki's body had rotted away except for his head. His skull was lying, like a *kapea* possum, in a hole in the *sawia* tree. When one of the young women drew near that tree, one such possum jumped on her and fastened its teeth to her breast. The sisters ran up and hit the possum on its head, but it would not release its grip. It was the head of that man Baki that was doing this. The remainder of his body had rotted away, and all there was left was his skull, changed now into a *kapea* possum.

The women tried to remove it but could not. Finally one of them got some hard *rogema* nuts from a nearby tree, held one in front of each breast, and said to the head, "Now try eating these!"

Quickly the head went and bit those nuts. The women then climbed up the *rogema* tree, saying, "We'll pick you some more!" But instead they rained these nuts down on that head, trying to break it. But always the head would evade the nuts, rolling from one side to the other.

3Bii,11i   Finally one of the projectiles hit its mark, and the head broke apart. Blood flowed out and covered the bush in a dark blood-red pool.

11ii   But now the women were unable to descend. So after one of them killed a *magatya* swallow, they all took some of its feathers, stuck these in their hair, and flew away as swallows. Now they live on cliffs.

Tale 62: The Girl and the Trickster

0,7i   There was a little-man named Yapi. Elsewhere, in Karapere, there lived a number of young women. One day all of these were away in their gardens except for one named Nebo. Yapi came to her and said, "Let's kill this pig of yours." But Nebo said, "No, it's not yours; it's ours! My sisters will be angry with me if I kill it."

"Let's eat it!" insisted Yapi. Nebo replied, "I can't stop you if you must kill it, but I won't eat any."

Yapi killed the pig, singed off its bristles, and cooked the insides. He offered the girl half, but she refused to take any; she left it untouched. Yapi then heated stones to cook the flesh, and after the cooking was done, he offered her half: a whole side plus half the backbone and half the head. This, too, she left untouched, while Yapi put all the rest of the pork in his netbag.

As he was departing, he said to her, "Well, you've shown your dislike of me. But when the others see what's happened, I think you'll come to me. They'll hit you and drive you away. As you flee them, follow the route marked by broken twigs along the way." And he went off, breaking twigs.

Nebo sat and waited, never touching the pile of pork. Presently the other girls returned from the garden. Nebo explained, "A man I never saw before killed it!" But the others did not believe her. "Oh, no, it was a friend of yours who came. You killed the pig for him! So go and carry your pork off! Follow that man of yours!" Nebo saw she had to leave. She put the pork in a netbag and went off, following the path of broken twigs.

On and on she went, and after a long walk she found the same little-man. He was sitting in the yard outside his house. Tall trees and fine grasses grew there. He had eaten his share of the pork and was resting as she arrived. "Just as I said, you've come!" he said. They ate some more pork. After three days had passed Yapi said, "We'll go to the garden now."

3Bi   Unknown to Nebo, Yapi had been going to that garden during those three days. He had piled firewood and leaves for cooking at a hearth located on a knoll where several *poladi* trees grew beside a ravine. The hearth was heaped high with ashes; Yapi had killed and cooked many women there before.

The two went to that place. Pulling out a pig tether, Yapi suddenly threw her down to the ground, tied her up, and hung her to a *poladi* tree by the feet. Then he raised his bloodied club and prepared to kill her.

3Bii   Now, an old woman whom Nebo had met along the path had given her some advice. She had said, "If the one who wants to kill you asks what his mother's name is, tell him it is Munyu (Sand). If he asks what his father's name is, say it is Muada Rekari (Ficus-tree-at-a-sandy-place). If he asks what his own name is, say it is Puolo (Jew's Harp)."

So now Yapi was about to strike her with his *walu*-wood club. He asked her first, "What's my father's name?"

She answered, "Muada Rekari."

"Tell me, then, my mother's name."

"Munyu."

"Now my own name?"

"Puolo."

At that, Yapi laughed a little, lowered the club, and let her down. He embraced her, singing,

Kepa Kikini repa sa pepa,
Kepa Aipulu repa sa pepa.
The ghost Kikini and his wife are we,
The ghost Aipulu and his wife are we.

11ii   All women might have been killed off, along with Nebo and the others before her, had not the old woman known the answers to give Nebo. From then on the little man killed no more women. If the old woman had not done this, there would still be men like him killing women off.

CHAPTER 6

Of Skin Changing and Other Transformations

Tale 63: The Bad Skin

0   There was a leper (*repono yo wia ali* or *kidimi nea ali*) named Beralo of Kupia, who mostly stayed in his house. He did not go to his gardens much, yet he was rich. In his house he had many pigs and pearl shells. As for his gardens, even though he never seemed to work there, they were full of taro, banana, sugar cane, sweet potato, and other foods. Now a man named Mainasi saw these good gardens, and he said to his daughter, "I would like you to marry this leper, for he clearly must have many pigs, shells, and garden foods."

But the girl replied, "I don't want to." Her father tried to convince her, but she was steadfast in her refusal.

Meanwhile in Alumari men were getting ready to hold a pig kill, and they were dancing *mata* and cooking food. The men of Kupia had been invited and were preparing for the dancing. Beralo the leper readied his ornaments, just like the other men. The others murmured, "Why is he doing this?" for lepers are poor. "He has no sons; for whom could he be preparing these ornaments?" they wondered.

8ii   When the others had gotten themselves ready to dance, they left for Alumari. Beralo waited. After they had all gone, he went down to a clump of cordylines and took off his leper's skin. Immediately he had the appearance of a handsome young man. He hung a good "bone" pearl shell from his neck, and he put on fine plumes and other ornaments. Then he set off.

By the time he reached the dancing ground, the others were already dancing. He joined them and took a position in the front row. Mainasi's daughter was also there, finely decorated. She went up to him, gripped the handle of the axe he was holding, and paraded by his side.

"Ah," thought Beralo, "your father wanted you to marry me, but you refused. But now you come and dance by my side!" The two did the *mata* dancing together.

Later in the day the people began to remove food from the earth ovens. Beralo made a hasty departure, returned home, and changed back into his ordinary leper's skin. When the others returned, they found him there, just as they had left him.

8i Persistent, Mainasi kept telling his daughter, "You must marry this leper. I've seen his house, and he has much wealth and excellent gardens." Finally he was successful in persuading his daughter to marry the man.

But Beralo said, 'I don't have anything to marry your daughter with."

"It doesn't matter," replied Mainasi. "I've seen your gardens. I know what sort of person you must be: a hard worker. So I'm giving her to you."

Upon hearing this, Beralo went into his house and took a large netbag of shells. He arranged the shells in two rows on the ground outside his house. Then he went out to a grassy area beyond his house and struck the ground several times with the flat of his hand. Out of an opening in the earth in front of him emerged many long-tusked pigs. He planted a long row of stakes for these pigs.

Then he told Mainasi, "Well, I offered you nothing, but since you were willing to sit in my house anyway, I consent." He handed over all the shells and pigs to Mainasi, and on the following day he gave two more pigs and three more shells. Then he killed and cooked a pig and gave the pork to his wife, who carried it to her parents. Thereafter she stayed with him and made gardens on his land.

8ii At Alumari, meanwhile, they had been preparing a second dance. The leper now told his wife, "They are preparing to kill pigs in Alumari. Cook some food and take it with you there." So the woman brought some food from the garden, cooked it, and prepared to carry it to Alumari. Meanwhile her husband secretly prepared his ornaments. He said to his wife, "Take these two pigs with you; you will tie them to the stakes at Alumari." And he sent her away.

The next morning he put on his decorations and went along the path that led to Alumari. When he had gone as far as Kauware, he waited for the Kuri clan to approach, and when they did so he joined them and danced in their front ranks. Again the same woman, the one who now was his wife, came and joined him, grasping the handle of his axe.

8iii On the first occasion, she did not know that this man was none other than the leper, but this time she looked carefully at his face and wondered, "Could this possibly be my husband?" They continued to dance, and once again when it was nearly time for people to remove food from the earth ovens, she saw him depart. But the instant the woman saw he was leaving, she, too, hurried home. She walked very swiftly and succeeded in reaching their house before her husband.

Searching around, she found the leprous skin at the base of some *kasua* cordylines. So, gathering a pile of firewood, she made a fire around the cordylines and incinerated the skin.

11ii When Beralo returned he saw what she had done. Feeling suddenly painful and tired, he sat down. Today we act in this same way: we marry a wife, and the wife makes gardens. Because that man's skin was burned, our skins are now good. And when we marry, our wives bear many sons. Many of us are here now. This is not a tale (*lidi*); it is a true story (*ramani*).* This woman burnt that man's skin and then she bore him sons, our ancestors.

Tale 64: The Cannibal Women

0 There were three siblings; a brother, a sister, and their little brother. There were no other people around.

? One day the older brother said to his sister, "It's no good for us to stay in the house. Go to the garden; I'll go hunting in the forest." He set out immediately. The sister wanted to cook some food before leaving, but when she looked in the hearth she saw that the fire had gone completely out. She got a piece of rattan cane and a split stick and tried to kindle a new flame; but though she tried several times, the cane always broke. Annoyed, she put her hand in the ashes, but there was really no fire to be found.

Thinking her brother would be angry with her, she went outside and looked around. In the distance—as far as Kopere is from Koiari—she saw a plume of smoke.

She got some ripe bananas, put them in her netbag, and departed with her little brother. When they reached the place where they thought the fire was, they saw it was still further away. So they kept on going, on and on. When night fell and they still had not reached the fire, they slept.

The next morning they got up and continued walking. Soon they came up to a place where many men and women used to live. It was now deserted, so they continued on. Truly it was not close! On the second night they slept in a cave. The little boy complained, "I'm really hungry."

* However, this narrative clearly conforms to the *lidi* genre. See *Fabricated World.*

It was about then that the older brother returned home. Seeing that no one was there and that the hearth was cold, he looked around, found two pairs of footprints, and followed them for some distance. Then he put a stick in the ground to mark the spot, and came back to sleep.

The little brother and his sister were far away. They walked on and on, and finally they reached a garden. The sister picked four ripe bananas and gave them to her little brother. Then she saw some women singing and dancing. Hiding the boy in the bush, she told him she was going to have a look at their men's house (*tapada*, literally "platform house"). But when she approached, she saw that there were no men at all, only women. But these women surrounded her and rejoiced. They took her to the porch of their house.

"Don't you have any men here?" she asked one young woman. She replied, "Don't say the word 'man' here!" Then she looked at the visitor's forehead and saw the mark of a netbag. "Did you come alone?" she asked.

"No, I didn't," the sister replied, wondering why she had brought her little brother to that place.

3Ci   The same woman asked the sister if she had men in her place. She had left her older brother at home, she replied, and had brought her younger one along and left him nearby in the bush. All the women rejoiced and told her to bring him in. She did so.

The women took the boy and sat him in a hearth beside another little boy who had come the same way. Then they took bamboo knives, cut through the other boy's skin, sliced off bits of his flesh, cooked them, and ate. They did this until there was no flesh left on the boy. The sister fearing for her own child, said, "If you do the same to my brother, you'll have to kill me, first!"

Upon hearing this, one of the women said, "Look, this isn't a place for men. These fruit-bearing pandanus trees, these casuarinas, these cordylines and plantains—they weren't planted by men; *we* planted them! When men or boys come here, we eat them." So they started to cut up her little brother. The sister lay down and refused to watch.

8i   But while this was happening, the first boy whispered to the other, "It's all right, it doesn't matter, they can eat everything, let them eat you, too!"

The next day the women went to look at a singing sponsored by pig killers from another village. They put on the decorations, closed the doors of their house, and left.

Then the first "all-bones" boy (*kuli kama si*) said, "Look at me, I'm only bones, no flesh, but I'll get up anyway!"

8ii   And he stood up, fell down, got up, fell down, got up and fell down until he reached the door and took something that had been tied up. It was a young man's skin. He put the skin over his bones and became a fine-looking young man. Then he gave another skin to the little brother, and he too took on a fine appearance. Having done this, the two of them got axes, put on bark belts, cordyline leaves, and cockatoo feathers, picked up bows and arrows and a spear, and went where the women had gone.

When the women saw them arrive, they asked others who these two young men were, but no one knew. One young one said, "I want to marry you," and another said the same, and soon all the women were saying they wanted to marry them. When the dancing was over, the young men hurried back to the women's house. Arriving there well before the others, they took off their skins, rolled them up, hid them, and lay down in the ashes.

Soon the women came back, laughing and in high spirits. They entered the house, sat down in front of their hearths, and got out their bamboo knives. Again they cut pieces of flesh from the boys and ate them. The sister did not eat. All the women told her to do so, but she just said, "Ah, you are all bad women!"

Later some visitors came from the village which had held the singing; they had come to announce the date for the pig kill. On the appointed day the women once again put on their ornaments and departed. When all of them had left, the two all-bones youths rose, put on their skins, and went outside.

8iii Later that same day, they watched the women returning home with their pork, talking and laughing. One said to the other, "Those women are always against us. We must kill them." So the two of them went to spend the night in the forest.

When the women came into the house and looked for the two all-bones youths, they could not find them. They ate their pork instead, and then they slept.

Towards morning one of the youths came in the front door while the other entered by the back. The two of them shot all the women.

3Cii Then they walked along a path leading through the forest. After following it a long way, they met an old woman sitting in front of her house. She asked the two where they had come from, and they told her.

She said that yes, she had heard about those bad women. Then she asked the young men to put down their bows and arrows and to sit down. They did so. She told them to shut their eyes. While they did, she fetched a small bundle for them. After telling them to open their eyes, she gave them the bundle. It held two bird skins. She directed them to put the skins on, which they did. They flew away.

11i-ii   If the two young men had not killed those women, there would be only women here now. But they are dead, so today both men and women live here.

Tale 65: The Skin-Changer Wives

0   Nemera lived alone. One day he took his dogs and went hunting in the forest at Raipala. On the path he came across two little girls. They had mucus running from their noses. He asked them who they were, and the two girls answered, "Our parents have gone to a garden along the Yaro River, and we are waiting for them here."

Looking at the yard outside the house, he saw that many plantains, sugar cane, and other crops grew there. "All right, I'm going," he said, and he walked on. He wondered if that good house and garden might belong to those girls alone, but then he decided that no children could make so fine a place.

After three days he decided to return. Concealing himself, he watched the two girls as they worked. Swiftly they fetched their pigs from the house and put them outside, cut fence posts for the garden, dug up sword-grass clumps, and did other such jobs.

On another day he returned carrying possums. He asked them, "Can I leave these with you?" The girls replied, "Our parents have again gone down to the Yaro River. But yes, you can leave them with us."

8i   The next day he again hid and watched them cut bananas and sugar cane and carry heavy netbags back to the house. He approached them and asked, "Where have your parents gone, leaving you to work so hard?" They answered, "If we go away with you, our parents will come looking for us. Then you'll see them." So the two girls went with Nemera to his house.

The two girls stayed with him, worked in the garden and looked after his pigs. Although Nemera was pleased with their work, he found them unattractive. For this reason he disliked them, which made the two girls a little angry with him.

One day, when the two girls were hard at work pulling out the sword-grass clumps in a garden, a small gecko came and chirped, "A *koda* dance now!" The two girls told this to Nemera, so he prepared his ornaments, body paint, ceremonial axe, and everything else he needed for a singing. When he had finished, he left for the village where the ceremony was taking place.

8ii   The two girls went to where several *ragua* plantains were growing and recited a spell, "*Mone daga, one kai;* here ornaments, there

Plate 8. Two girls, painted for a singing.

ashes." And the two turned into fine young women. They attended the same *koda* dancing as Nemera, and they danced in the first row to either side of him. Nemera looked at them and thought how good it would be to have these two as wives. But soon, while the earth ovens were still being opened, the two young women quickly departed.

When Nemera reached home, he saw the two little girls putting the pigs back in the houses, feeding them, and cooking. "Hey, I saw two beautiful young women at the dance," he told them. "If I took them for wives, that would be good indeed." He watched them closely.

8iii   On another occasion, a gecko came to give the same message. This time Nemera told a little-man named Moiloma to hide and watch the two women while he was away. So after Nemera had departed, Moiloma hid and spied on the two. He saw them go to the plantain trees, say the spell, take off their skins, and depart as good-looking young women. He took these skins and threw them in the Yaro River.

Later in the day the two young women came back from their *mata* dancing, but now they could not put on their other skin. Many times they repeated the spell, "Here ashes, there ornaments," but the skins did not appear. They went back to Nemera's house and, embarrassed, lay down there in his room.

11i   When Nemera returned home, he was not surprised to see them, for Moiloma had told him that he had disposed of those skins. Content, he lay down with one woman at either side.

11ii   Now we see rainbows in the sky. They have red colours on either edge: these are the two girls with their red body paint. And they have a dark colour in the centre: this is Nemera. Today we might be able to change our skins and appear youthful at singings, like those girls did, but we cannot because those skins burned.

Tale 66: The Orphan Wife

0   I am going to tell a story about a snake that ate men, a story my mother told me. Nokali lived with his wife, who was just about to give birth. She was feeling early labour pains, yet her husband said, "They are killing pigs not far away. Let's go and receive some of their pork." She agreed and they set off.

As they were walking along the path, the wife had to stop. She gave birth to a girl child. After she did so the couple left the infant in the forest and continued on their way. They arrived at the pig kill, received gifts of pork, and returned home. Back at their house they recooked the pork and ate it.

Elsewhere some men were working on a forest garden for a man and his wife, who in return were cooking food for them. The men who were working had left their belongings—axe, shoulder bags, tobacco, comb and the like—at the edge of the garden, lest they be damaged during the work.

8i   Now this baby girl, the one who had been abandoned in the forest, survived. She was a short, thin little girl with reddish skin around her mouth. Her uncut umbilical cord still dangled from her belly. She approached the place where the men were working, picked up one of the young men's shoulder bags, and hid it in the brush nearby.

When the sun was getting low, the men ceased their work. One of them, a youth named Keapu, could not find his bag, though he looked all over. "Did someone take my bag?" he asked the others. "I put it here but now I can't find it." No one knew. Finally he told them, "Go on ahead without me. Start eating. I'll stay and look." He continued to look, went to rejoin the others, ate, and then returned to look some more. But he could not find it.

Finally the little girl brought him the bag and said, "You there, is this what you are looking for? I took it, and here it is!"

Keapu was startled. "You, with your red mouth, what did you do that for? Give it back!" he said sharply. And he left for home with his bag.

He was surprised to see the same little girl sitting on his sleeping place when he reached the house. He thought to himself, "Why did she go and sit there? How did she know it was my place?" She stayed with him, sharing his house.

One day the youth thought for a while and said, "I'm going to a place where they're gathering for a singing."

"All right," said the girl. "I'll stay here and cook food for you. It'll be ready for your return," she replied. So he left.

8ii   She quickly prepared plantains, sweet potatoes, taro, pitpit, and pork. She put the food into an earth oven to cook. Then she took off her hair and skin, those of an ugly little girl, and became a good-looking young woman. When she had put aside the bad skin, she looked very beautiful indeed. Then she put red pigment on her face, stuck cockatoo feathers into her hair, and decorated herself with other ornaments. That done, she walked swiftly to where they were dancing. She danced at Keapu's side, grasping the handle of his axe.

When the dancing was nearly over, she let go of his axe, left his side, and hurried back to the house. There she put her ugly-little-girl skin back on. Then she began to remove the food from the earth oven.

Keapu returned, and when he saw her, he spoke unkindly, "You with your red mouth and that thing dangling from your stomach, what kind of woman are you? I saw a good-looking one at the singing."

"Oh well," she replied, "here I am, and I've been cooking food for you. Never mind her, come and eat."

"Some woman you are, to come and stay in my house," he muttered. But they stayed on.

Another time a gecko came into their house and chirped, "*Na koda abi; koda* dancing now." The girl said to Keapu, "Go by yourself. Put on your ornaments and go. I'm not the type to go to that sort of thing." She helped him put on his decorations, and he departed.

She prepared food just as she did earlier. Then she took off her bad skin and set off. When she reached the dance ground, the singing had already begun. She once again danced at Keapu's side. "Ah, woman," thought Keapu, "before you came and danced with me. This time I'll not let you go!" But once again she released her grip on his axe and went quickly back to the house. There she took off her nice skin, removed the cooked food, and waited for his return.

When Keapu returned, he said contemptuously, "Oh you, if only you were the woman who looked so nice at that dance. I saw her again. Give me something to eat!"

"Say whatever you will, I'm going to stay here with you. You can't get rid of me!" she replied.

8iii   Later on, another singing was announced. But this time Keapu told a poor-man named Weabi to spy on her after he had left. Weabi did so. After Keapu departed, the girl put the food in to cook as usual, then went to the foot of a wild plantain tree, took off her bad skin, and hid it there. Weabi looked on as she wrapped her little-girl skin in dry pandanus leaves. Good-looking now, she set off for the dance.

Weabi came out of his hiding place and burnt that skin. Then he hurried off to Keapu. "Brother," he said, "that good-looking one is your wife! I've burnt her other skin. Hold on to her tightly during the dancing!" When the young woman arrived on the dance ground, she did just as she had done twice before. She danced *yasa* with Keapu.

Late in the afternoon she rushed off back home, removed the cooked food, and went to change into her other skin. She searched hard for the skin, but she couldn't find it. Resigned, she went and sat down on Keapu's sleeping place inside the house.

After the dancing was over, Keapu's brothers returned and sat around eating. They were very pleased that their brother had taken that beautiful young woman. When Keapu saw her sitting in the house, he said, "You tried to deceive me, didn't you?"

So he took her as his wife, and after a while she gave birth to a son. They lived on.

One day the wife left the infant at home with her husband while she went to work in that distant garden. She did not return quickly, and the boy began to cry. When finally she returned, very late, Keapu rebuked her. "You who were such a sorry-looking girl, with your red mouth, why didn't you come home sooner?"

"Look," she replied, "I have returned with all this food, and the garden is a long way off. Why do you bring up these old ideas?" She was angry. "From now on I won't nurse your son, and I'll sleep on the other side of the house." So she went to sleep in another room.

9Ai   The next morning a pool of water had surrounded the house; it was choked with tall grasses, a real swamp. She had turned everything there into wild forest, and then she had disappeared. When the father and son saw what she had done, that morning, they hurried to look at their gardens. They, too, were overgrown and in ruin. All their pigs had gone wild as well.

9Aii   Nothing had they to eat now, those two. They began to consume their bark belts, hair, and fingernails. Then the father said, "Let's go to the forest. We'll be able to eat the buds and shoots of trees." So he led his son into the forest, where they ate the tender new leaves. But still they were sick with hunger, foraging over the mountainsides. When the boy could no longer walk, Keapu took some black palm sheaths and rolled him up in them, tied the bundle with vines, and carried him on his shoulder.

Some time later during his wandering, Keapu saw smoke rising from the slopes of Mount Ialibu. He set off to see who was there. After several days he came to a forest garden, and he sat down at its edge. Seeing two ripe cucumbers, he cut them and gave one to the boy. They ate and fell asleep.

They had not seen that in the middle of the garden there stood a tall old woman, with a stone axe stuck in her belt. She was standing on a forked stake tying up bananas. When she had finished, she walked along the edge of the garden, checking the fence. She found the father and son, asleep and covered with buzzing flies.

The woman prodded Keapu with her foot and he awoke. "What are you doing here?" she asked. "Get up and let's go," she ordered them. "Look, there's much sugar cane growing here. You must go and cut stakes and tie the cane to them. And don't take the broken canes and eat them. Tie them up, too, and mend them with gum."

Keapu took an axe, cut posts, and staked up the sugar cane. Then she commanded him, "As for the canes that rats have gnawed, you must tie them up and cover the marks with gum." Next she told him to split a dry *walu* log for firewood and carry it into the house. While he was doing that, she gathered several sorts of food from the garden and carried it back.

The three of them went to her house. She took a dish of *walea* wood, put cucumbers and other food on it, sprinkled some salt on top, and ate it all herself. Then she made a large earth oven, but she alone finished off all the food in it, giving none to the two who looked on. The next day it was the same, and the next. All she ever gave them was more work.

"Go and fetch water," she ordered. Then later, "You see this new forest garden. You must enclose it with a fence today." He finished it that day.

9Aiii   One day the man said, "Listen, I've done all this work for you, but now I'm dying of hunger, for you give me nothing to eat. How can I do more work for you?"

"You won't die right away," she replied. "Continue to work for me!" And she told him to go and carry back the stump of a big *walu* tree, for firewood. But he found he could not lift it by himself, and he called for her help. When he got it on his shoulder he asked her, "And the boy, how will I carry him?"

"Put him on top of the wood," she told him. When he had done so, she told him to fetch some water on his way back.

While he was doing all this she put some cucumbers on her dish, sprinkled some salt on them, and ate. But this time, she got some more cucumbers and spread them on the plate along with some ripe bananas.

When Keapu returned, she said to him, "Do you understand now? Before you called me all kinds of things and insulted me. Don't ever speak like that again. Now I have my son with me and I am content. Sit and eat." Having said that she took off her old-woman skin and gave them both food. She was indeed the wife who had left him.

"I have many pigs and gardens," she told the father and son. And indeed from then on the two ate well and regained their strength. Both father and son looked well, and the two seemed like brothers.

11i   One day Keapu said to his wife and son, "You two stay here and cook some vegetables. I'll go to the forest and hunt possums." He went off, but he did not return. So the next day the woman said to her son, "Let's go, we must look for your father." They followed his footprints and soon came to the ridge at Kunabalo. They saw that Keapu's footprints led toward something like a greenish-blue stone. When they drew closer, they saw a huge *yakua* snake lying there, its two jaws open wide.

11ii   Too late. They were swallowed. Nowadays, too, this snake on Mount Ialibu eats people, the way it did those three.

Tale 67: The Girls Who Grew from Fingers

0   A man lived alone after his wife died. The widower worked in his gardens, cultivating sweet potatoes. One fine, sunny day he sat in his house and thought, "What shall I do? With whom am I going to stay now?"

9Bi   He rose and walked to his forest garden, where he had built a hut of sugar-cane posts. Resting one hand on a log, he took his axe in the other hand and chopped off one finger and then another: his little finger and his index finger. These he buried in a *kubura,* a brush heap in that garden.

9Bii   Not in the habit of going to that garden often, he did not return that day or the next or for some time. But once, when he was about as far from this garden as Poreada is from Karapere, he looked there and saw flashes of sheet lightning. Often thereafter, when he looked through the open door of his house toward that garden, he would see these glows of lightning. So one day, after some four months had passed, he decided to go and have a look at the garden.

When he entered it he went directly over to the brush heap. In it were two baby girls moving around. After looking at them for awhile, he gathered some dry plantain leaves and covered them up, so they would be warmer. By the sixth month, when he returned again, the two girls were crawling around on all fours. Then he cut some ripe bananas, pumpkins, and other soft foods; and he fetched some wildfowl eggs for them. As happens in tales, the children grew up very quickly. Soon the two were as grown as Ewa and Robame are now, and then he made ornaments for them to wear. It was not long before they were fully grown young women.

8i   One day the man said to the two women, "Since a time of hunger is approaching, we must go and make a new garden, a large one." So they all went to work on a new garden. He had named the two women Egalinyu and Malanyu, after the two fingers he had cut off.* "The two of you will stay together with me in my house," he told them. He took them as his wives, these two women who had grown from his fingers.

8ii   Some time later a gecko came to the house and said, "There's a singing now; there's a singing now!" Having decided to go, the man got out his ornaments and put them on. He told the two women to stay home and prepare food for his return. They agreed. But after he left, the two decided to put on ornaments and go, too. So they hastily put some food into an earth oven and, leaving it to cook, began to decorate themselves.

Meanwhile many people had already gathered for the singing. They much admired this man who had come onto the dance ground and stood in the first row of dancers.

Back at their house, the two girls were preparing themselves, imagining how people would see them come to the singing and exclaim, "Egalinyu has come; Malanyu has come!" Finally they were ready, and they set out.

As they were going along the path, they met an old woman who gave them a small bundle. This they took with them.

Just before arriving at the dance ground, they stopped to put on the last and finest of their decorations. Then they walked out and broke into the first row of dancers. Each woman took a place beside the husband, gripping the axe or weapons he was holding. Adorned and painted as they were, the man did not recognize them to be the same two women he had left at home. But he had heard the people

*From *egali* ("one") and *mala* ("four") plus -*nyu* (ending for female names).

cry out "Egalinyu has come; Malanyu has come!" when the two had arrived.

The dancing went on for some time. When it was over, young men drifted off in different directions, some of them to court the young women, others to converse among themselves. But the two girls did not stay. They began their walk home.

On the way they again met the old woman who had given them the bundle. They asked her, "What are we to do with this bundle?" The woman replied, "When you come to two wild plantains at the side of the path, take aim at them with this bundle and say, '*Ne daga, ni daga;* you ashes, I ashes.' You'll see what it does."

The two women continued on their way. When they came to the two wild plantains, they repeated the spell just as the old woman had told them to. Then they resumed their journey home.

When the husband returned home, he found the two girls sitting by the hearth, just as before, with face and skin covered with ash–from the cooking they had done, he supposed. As the two women removed the food from the earth oven he said to them, "Well, everyone at the singing was admiring two young women who had come. And you know, the two had the same names as you!"

"We know nothing about it," said the two women. But the husband was suspicious.

So the three of them stayed on. One day, during the time of hunger, they went to the garden to tie up the sugar cane and to harvest some of it as well as some greens. The husband had prepared some stakes for the cane, and these he gave to the two women to carry. All three walked along the path toward the garden.

8iii,11i   On their way they had to cross a low fence and a ditch constructed to keep pigs out of the garden. The girl in front was carrying her load on top of her head, the way women do. She threw the bundle of posts across to the other side of the ditch, climbed over the fence, and then bent down to pick up her bundle. When she reached down, the husband caught sight of some body paint in her armpit. "Ha, now I know you two have deceived me!" he thought. He tightened his bow and let two arrows fly, shooting each woman in the breast and killing her.

11ii   The two girls flew away as *mumakarubi* quail. As for the husband, he broke his *wiruapu* bow in two, stuck the pieces in his rear, and flew away as a *walawe* lorikeet. This is the end of my tale.

Tale 68: A Youth Trapped and Rescued

0   A small boy lived with his mother.

?   One day the boy was splitting firewood outside the house. The sun being hot, he left his work and followed a stream with the intention of catching fish. Several times he put his hand into the water, but he could find no fish. Then he went a bit further and, seeing a pool in the stream, decided to drain it by diverting the water. He did so, and when the pool was dry, he gathered many fish.

While wondering if his mother would be angry with him for staying away and not splitting more firewood, he saw a pile of pig intestines lying nearby. They were uncooked, and looked as if they had just been removed. To another side he saw a piece of pork belly. "Who could have left that there?" he wondered. Seeing some bamboo growing nearby, he fashioned himself a bamboo knife, cut and cleaned the intestines, and carried them back home.

He cooked them outside his mother's house, having first wrapped them in *wakia* greens and other edible leaves. While he was doing this, his mother returned from the garden. She brought back sweet potatoes, which the two then fed to their many pigs, including Puramenalasu. Then the boy said to his mother, "I want to tell you something, but first let us take out the food."

"Son, I thought you had gone to catch fish, but you've pig intestines, skin, and fat here as well!" exclaimed the mother when she saw what he had cooked. The son explained that he had found the meat in the bush. "No, son," said the mother, "don't lie. How did you get it? Did you steal it?" But then she relented, "It doesn't matter; we'll cut up these intestines and this fat and eat." They did so, and they found it all very good. The food lasted them for a second and third day.

Days later the boy said, "Since that pork was so good, I think I'll go and look around along that stream." Then he added, "Whether or not they'll kill me there, I can't say. You, mother, stay and think about me. If I don't come back, you'll know I am lost."

He went along the stream, following it upstream. Near the headwaters, beside a pile of *rupi* stones, he saw a path. He followed it, and presently he came to a place where pines, casuarinas, and other trees grew, and, underneath them, sugar cane and plantains. There he saw a huge old man with arms, legs, and a head, but no face. He was there heating stones to cook a pig.

The boy hid and looked on. "What? Has he no eyes or nose?" he wondered. The old man indeed had none. He was cooking many pig livers, and he was eating them, but not by putting them in his mouth. Instead he was stuffing the food into a hole in the top of his head.

The boy watched while this man took the innards and put them into his head. The rest of the pork was cooking in an earth oven nearby.

After having cooked and eaten the pig guts, the old man waited. When the rest of the food had cooked and the old man was removing it, the boy crept closer to the cooking pit. Since he had no eyes, the old one could not see him. After the old man had cut a big piece of pork in two and had put one piece into his head, the boy stole the other. Then, becoming bolder, he stole more: part of the neck and one hindquarter; then he went to hide. The old man continued to down the pork, plantains, and greens through his head. He did not eat as we do.

The boy was afraid. "Oh I'm sure he would eat me, too," he said to himself, while walking back to his mother's house. When his mother saw what he had brought she asked him, "Where did you get that pig? Did you steal it?"

"I saw an old man of an odd sort, with no eyes, mouth, or face, only legs and arms. He eats by stuffing pork into the top of his head. It was his pig intestines that we ate before. You see this pork I have here: I stole it from him, and he couldn't see me!"

Thereafter the boy often went to get meat this way, every fourth day or so. Once he said, "I'm going to go back once more. Will the old man kill me this time? I don't know. You must stay and think about me." Then he set off.

Meanwhile the old one had been pondering, "Ah, I used to really eat a lot of pork, but now some of it seems to disappear." So he got some twine and netted a large netbag, and with it he made a trap which he placed on the path. One end of a rope he tied to the mouth of the bag, and the other end he tied to his leg. Having thus prepared himself, he continued to cook his pork.

The boy came along. He did not see the trap and sprung it. It carried him off the ground and left him dangling. The rope tightened and pulled against the man's leg.

3Ai, 9Ai   "Aha!" cried the old man. "So you're the one who has been deceiving me!" Then he took several netbags and put them one inside another with the boy inside. He carried him down to the Yaro River, where a large *u* tree grew above the gorge. He hung the boy from a branch. Leaving him suspended high above the river, he returned to his pork.

9Aii   The boy was unable to free himself. Without food, he ate his armbands, his bark belt, and his breechcloth, then his fingernails and toenails, he was so hungry. Eventually all the netbags rotted except the innermost one in which the old man had first trapped him, and even it was nearly broken. The boy was almost dead by now, but still he hung in this netbag above the river.

9Aiii   Presently he saw some flying foxes flying toward him. They dropped him a ripe plantain, then another, and yet another. Flying foxes came by night and *sai* birds came by day to bring him plantains to eat.

His mother, meanwhile, was weeping for him. One night the flying foxes carried the netbag with the boy to the mother's house. They let it fall. Hearing a noise outside, the woman lit a torch and went to look. There was her son. The flying foxes told her they had carried her child there. The mother was overjoyed but also worried. "Oh, whatever can I give you in return, for I live here alone," she said.

"Well, you must give us something; get it ready," said the flying foxes as they flew away.

11i   The woman put together valuables such as salt, bailer shells, palm oil, pigs, and shells. But when the flying foxes returned, they wanted none of these things. Then the old woman got some white wood fiber with which she was intending to make twine for a netbag, and she offered this. The flying foxes said, "Yes, we'd like that. Prepare more of it for us!" They flew off and returned later to collect the gift.

Now, as things happen in tales, the boy grew quickly into a young man. Thinking of revenge, he sat down and sharpened his axe, picked up his bow and arrows, and followed that same stream. When he came to a pile of *rupi* stones beside the path, he took a large one with him.

3Aii, 11i   The old man was there as before, killing pigs and heating cooking stones. The youth approached and put his own stone there to heat up. Then he withdrew and looked on, though not without first cutting himself a piece of pork to eat while he waited. Meanwhile the old man was cooking his pork liver. Soon the youth's stone was glowing hot. As the old one opened up his head to stuff the liver down, the boy lifted the stone with a pair of tongs and dropped it into the head. The old man reeled about and ran down to the Yaro River. The stone was so hot it sizzled and steamed in the water. Thus the boy made an *ali kalia* revenge killing.

11ii   When this old man ran into the river, wind and fog arose from the hot stone in his head. Today, the mist we see comes from this old man. That is the story about mist and also about the flying foxes and the white fiber they took. That is why the flesh of the flying fox is so white; it is just like that fiber.

Tale 69: Revival and Revenge

0,3Bi A brother and a sister lived alone and looked after their pig, Pura-menalasu. One day an old man came and said he would marry that girl. After he had gone, the brother said to her, "You must go to his house." Again and again the old man returned to the siblings' house, each time saying, "I want to take her with me." The brother was apprehensive about the old man, and he said to his sister, "Let us kill our pig now. Lest he kill the two of us, you must go with him." So they killed the pig, butchered it, and cooked it. Only the back of the pig's neck did the brother keep for himself; the rest, including the two sides and backbone, his sister took with her in her netbag. The old man led her away. As they went, she saw him give the pork away to people they met on the road.

Soon they came to a fork in the path, and the old man told her, "I'll go this way, but you must take the other path." But then he added, "Wait, I'm thirsty. Wait here for me while I get a drink of water." But he was deceiving her, for while she waited he went back and killed and ate her brother, who was sitting at home eating his share of pork. He cut him into pieces and then came back with them. The sister guessed what had happened, and she wept copiously for her brother.

9Ai Then the old man told her to go off in the direction he had indicated, on the other path. The path led her onto a fallen log. While she was walking along it, the old man suddenly appeared and shoved her into a deep well underneath. Down and down she tumbled, bouncing–*kilikili tatatata*–down to the bottom.

9Aii She lay at the bottom, her head reeling from her fall. After a while she got up slowly. She heard people groaning: "Don't hold my arm." "Let go of my head." "Get off me." Lying beside her were other young women who had been thrown down there. Some were dead, others only half dead.

The sister saw that one young red-skinned girl, who was sitting beneath some casuarinas and pines, appeared to be well. She asked her, "Are all these women alive, or have some died?"

"Some are dead, mostly from hunger; but others are still alive," was the answer.

9Aiii Now, the brother had given his sister many bundles, which she had put in her netbag. She opened one and found some glowing embers; in another were a bushknife and axe. So the sister took the axe, cut a dry *walu* pine, and made fires in different places. Then she asked the other girl to help her put the others by the fires, so they would be warm.

Then the sister took a stake of *kagu* wood, skewered a pig kidney she had brought, and cooked it. Then she shared it out to the other women. She cooked all her pork and gave most of it away. The remainder they recooked later. Those young women's bodies soon fattened up.

Later the sister looked inside the other bundles her brother had given her. In them she found cuttings of sweet potato, *rani* and *padi* greens, and other crops. She planted the cuttings here and there at the bottom of the well, and crops grew from them. Presently all the young women were quite recovered.

One day the sister said to the others, "Listen now, I want to say something." She reminded them about the old man. They should do something in return, she urged. So they chopped down trees and began to make a ladder of forked sticks and crosspieces. They worked their way to the top of the well, laughing and joking all the while.

One day a young man passed by the well and heard the sound of women laughing. He came and listened at the edge. Realizing that the women were engaged in constructing a ladder, the youth put some logs down and climbed downward to see. Then he returned to his village and told others what he had discovered. An old man there said, "Hey, they are mine! Why did you go there? They are mine!"

"Yes," said the youth, "but I did see them there, those women."

When the women had almost reached the top of the hole, the youth returned and climbed down to them. They asked him who he was. "I heard your voices," he answered, "and I've come to tell you that a villager up there is preparing a feast for some people, who will be bringing him pandanus leaves for thatch. And I also heard an old man say you all belong to him." The young women replied that they knew nothing about any of this.

When they had come out of the well and put on their ornaments, the youth advised them to arrive with bundles of pandanus leaves, and he offered them a bush-knife and axe to use while collecting them. "We have our own!" the women told him.

They made their way to the ceremonial ground. People were surprised to see all these fine young women approaching. So many of them: could this one old man have thrown so many into that well? The youth heard that old one say with satisfaction, "All these women are mine!"

3Bii, 11i   People were heating the stones for the earth ovens. When smoke had filled the ceremonial ground, the young women ran over to the old man, surrounded him, beat him with their *walu* sticks, and threw him into the fire. The sister took the axe her brother had given her and cut him through the middle. His body burned unnoticed in the smoke.

11ii   The young women turned into *kope* leaves, which we use for cooking. Nowadays people still kill one another with axes, and they make scaffolds the way those ones did.

Tale 70: The Broken Siblings

0   A man named Kilimi Wi had married two wives, one of whom was from south Kewa land while the other one was from the north. The two of them became pregnant. One day, when Wi was about to go off to a ceremonial gathering in a southern village, he told them, "If either of you gives birth to a girl child, abandon it. If you bear a son, care for it." In his absence, the wife from the south gave birth to a daughter, and the one from the north gave birth to a son.

Now Wi had planted a banana cutting and told them, "When the leaves start to grow out and down, I will be returning. When you have borne your child, prepare things and await my return." Each of the women looked after her child, for the wife who bore the daughter had not killed her. Time passed, and both children had already grown considerably, when their mothers saw that the banana leaves had grown out, announcing their husband's return. The two children ran off to meet him.

When Wi encountered them, he ignored the girl. To his son he gave a piece of cooked pork liver, but to his daughter only some soiled pig fat. He did not care for her. Back at the house he told them both to fetch greens for cooking with the pork. But when the meat was done, he gave the pig hoofs to the girl, while to his son he gave a good piece from the hindquarter.

3Bi   Then he sent the two children to fetch water. To the daughter he gave bamboos with the nodes knocked out, to the son he gave bamboos with nodes intact. The two went off down to the stream. The boy filled his bamboos quickly, but the girl's containers did not fill. They did no more than gurgle, and as her brother was leaving she cried out to him,

> *Ainya ya kulukulu ta, adoara;*
> *Ainya ya kalakala ta, adoara.*
> Brother, it gurgles still, wait for me;
> Brother, it burbles still, wait for me.

But, tired of waiting, the son went back. The girl continued to wait for her bamboos to fill. Finally she left them and returned, but when

Plate 9. A young mother with her daughter and her pig.

she arrived there was no one there. The house and yard were deserted. Near the door of the house, however, she found a small net-bag containing some pig's hoofs for her to eat. She took the bag and, weeping, followed the others' tracks.

She caught up to them when they had just crossed over the vine bridge to the far side of the Yaro River. She cried out to them, "Wait!" Her mother looked back and saw her daughter, covered with mud from the journey. She told her husband, "I know you don't care for her, but now you really must go back and get her."

So Wi took a netbag from his wife and recrossed the bridge. He put the girl inside the bag, cut the bundle in two, and threw it into the river.

9Bi   The water carried her downstream to the edge of a hill, depositing her in a pile of branches and debris. Her body stayed there and eventually it grew again.

After some time the mother, feeling sorry for her daughter, set off to follow the river downstream from the bridge. She did so, and presently she reached the spot where the child had been washed to the bank. There, on the side of a hill, she saw a new large garden. In the midst of the garden was a house, empty but not deserted. She approached. Before the doorway lay a pig, huge as Puramenalasa, which rose and barred her path. But when the old woman went to the pig, it allowed her to enter the house. She went to lie down in the back, awaiting the occupant's return.

9Bii   After she had been cut in two, the two parts of that girl had grown up into a young man and a young woman, both named Ruguli ("Broken"). As those two came back to the house, their pig squealed excitedly.

"Ruguli," said one of the two, "I have not seen our pig behave like this before!" This Ruguli, the girl, went inside. Beside the pig she saw a *kura* skirt, and when she looked more closely, she saw the old woman. "Ruguli," she said, "I think I see our mother here. Come and look."

"It *is* our mother!" exclaimed the other. The woman stayed with them.

Said one Ruguli to the other, "Now we must kill our pig for her." And they did so. After they had given some pork to the woman, they said, "Now you may go."

11ii   The mother went a short distance and then turned around to look back. Her thoughts returned to her two children. The moment she turned, she became a *pudina* tree, a wild pandanus. Nowadays we see these *pudina* trees bearing their nuts. The daughter and son became cassowaries.

Tale 71: The Blood Girl

0   Rube and his wife lived with their daughter, Torepeame. The father, who was aged, would go with his daughter to work in the gardens and feed the pigs, while the wife would go off to kill and eat people.

9Bi   One afternoon, while Rube was working hard in the gardens making sugar cane stakes, his axe slipped and gashed his hand. He let the blood run on some sugar-cane peelings, wiped the rest off his hand, and covered the peels over with sugar-cane leaves.

9Bii Considerably later he went to this garden again. When he looked down at the pile of sugar-cane peels, he saw something moving. Peering closer, he saw a baby girl there. Happy to discover this, he made a small hut for her in the garden and placed her inside. When he returned home to his daughter, he said nothing to her about this, nor anything to his wife.

After a month had elapsed he returned to the garden. The baby girl was now crawling around. He enlarged the hut, cut some sugar cane and ripe bananas, peeled them, and put them inside. Then he went home. Thereafter, each time he went to this garden he would give her sugar cane, ripe bananas, or cooked sweet potatoes.

When the girl had grown more, he made her a larger house in the same garden. Later he got some tree oil for her skin.

One day he fetched her from her garden house and led her a long way off to the other side of the Yaro River where he built her a house in the middle of the forest. He also gave her a sow to look after. Not once did Rube say anything to Torepeame, for fear that she might mention it to her mother. After working in his own gardens, he would carry food to this girl or clear a garden for her, returning home barely before nightfall. He was always going back and forth between the two places.

Torepeame noticed his absences. One day she said, "Let me go with you." Rube refused. The girl insisted and finally Rube gave in. So the girl followed her father through the forest watching while he killed a couple of possums on the way. When they came to the Yaro River, Rube took from a hiding place a ceremonial staff (*ekepai*). With it he parted the river and the two were able to cross.

On they went through the forest. Torepeame thought that the two of them were just hunting possums, for she knew nothing of the other girl's existence. On and on they went, until they came to a large garden. They walked through it and came to a house at the centre. There, mounding earth for sweet potatoes, was a young woman with long hair falling down to her shoulders. Torepeame embraced her and wept with gladness. The girl was keeping many pigs there now, and Rube killed one of them.

They cooked the pig in an earth oven, and then Rube divided it in half. The head and two forequarters he gave to Torepeame, and the hindquarters he gave to the other girl, whom he named Yapiame. The remainder he divided in half, along with the possums he had killed.

10Ai After they ate, Torepeame and her father returned home.

10Aii Rube warned his daughter, "I know that you are fond at *mena* *maada,* * playing at sharing out pork. But you must be careful not to say anything about Yapiame to your mother."

10Aiii   One day the father went to a pig kill in a distant southern village. "Say nothing; remember what I said," he warned Torepeame before leaving. But one rainy day, when she and her mother were both in the house, Torepeame was playing at *mena maada.* She was saying to herself, "This piece I'll give to that girl over there, this other piece I'll give to my father, and this piece I'll keep for myself," while she drew the cuts of pig in the sand.

The old woman overheard her. "What was that, Torepeame?" she asked.

"Nothing," replied the daughter.

"But you did say something. You said that you would give a piece to some girl." Still Torepeame did not reply. "I'll swallow you down if you don't talk." When Torepeame still did not answer, the mother opened her mouth and swallowed her down, until only her feet were sticking out.

"All right mother," cried Torepeame, giving in. "Cough me out! I'll talk." And after her mother had coughed her up, she admitted she had said, "I'll give this piece to that girl over there." She explained further.

"Let's go, then. Show me where she is!" said her mother.

The two reached the bank of the Yaro River. Torepeame said, "There's no bridge here; my father simply crosses through the water." The old woman tried this, but the river nearly carried her downstream. When she came back, she demanded, "And just what does your father do here that I haven't done?" Torepeame, after some reluctance, told her about the *ekepai.* The two then crossed the river with it.

10Aiv,   When they arrived where Yapiame was, they found her mound-
3Di   ing earth for sweet patatoes. "Come with us," the old woman or- dered.

Yapiame put her hair covering and her good skirt into a netbag and hung the bag on the wall. Then she followed the old one, who led her to her natal village. Her people, who were about to start a pig feast, took the young woman, tied her hands and put her inside one of the houses. Then they fetched more cooking greens and split some more firewood, intending to cook and eat her with the pigs.

3Dii   Meanwhile the old man, Torepeame's father, had returned home. When he saw that neither Torepeame nor his wife were there, he became suspicious. Dropping his pork he hurried quickly to Yapiame's house on the far side of the river.

*The game of *mena maada* consists of drawing a side of pork on the ground and pretending to share its pieces among kinsmen.

When he arrived, he saw that she was nowhere about and that the house looked abandoned. But he found her netbag hanging on the wall. Inside he saw the girl's hair net, her fine skirt, and a small *karubi*-gourd container. He took out the gourd, opened it, and looked inside. In it were two small things, which said in a diminutive voice, "Put decorations on the two of us, and we'll find her for you." They were *ali rakia,* a love potion or charm.

Rube understood what this *rakia* charm was saying, so he put a bark belt and cordylines on each of the two things. He anointed them with tree oil, and the two left.

They came to the house where Yapiame was held captive. They began to sing *mata* songs:

> Rakia kubade mokede, wita kubade mokede.
> One *rakia* star divides, another star divides.

So the men there divided: some of them were attracted and approached to hear the singing, while others were afraid and retired indoors. Then one of the two *rakia* continued to sing, while the other loosened the ropes around Yapiame and led her away. The first continued to sing until all the men had gone inside and were asleep.

11i Back at the house, Yapiame put the two *rakia* back inside the gourd. The father spoke to her, "If we stay here this woman will come back and she'll try to eat you again. We must go away." So, leaving Torepeame, he led Yapiame away.

11ii Some time later the two continued to fear the old woman's return. So they set fire to their house. The father took his *wiruapu* bow, broke it in two, and stuck it in his anus. He flew off as a *walawe* parrot. The girl Yapiame turned into a *mumakarubi* quail.

Tale 72: The Blood Girl's Escape

0 I am going to tell the story of how a woman brought us the Kuare *ribu* ritual. A big-boned man lived with his son. He grew much more sugar cane than other men. When the canes were broken by the wind or gnawed by mice, he would usually tie them up again or patch them, rather than cut and eat them.

9Bi One day he saw that a cane, broken and gnawed by mice, had wilted from the sun. This one he decided to eat. But while he was removing the skin with his axe, he accidentally sliced his little finger. Blood flowed like water from his wound. He sponged it with some sugar-cane leaves, which he buried right there in the garden. Then he bound up his finger and went back along the path to his house.

9Bii   After two weeks had passed, he went back to his sugar-cane garden. His work took him to the place where he had sponged up his blood. Something was moving about underneath the heap of leaves. When he removed some of the leaves he saw an infant, a baby girl. He pondered this a while, and then he recalled that this was the place where he had wiped off his blood. Guessing that the baby grew from that blood, he named the girl Yapi ("Blood").

As happens in tales, Yapi grew up quickly. Soon she was a fine young woman. She lived right there in that sugar-cane garden, in a house her father had made for her. One day the father heard that a singing was to be held in Kuare. A *kiliwapili* bird had come to his garden and sung out, "A *koda* dance now, a *koda* dance now." So he told his daughter, Yapi, that she should attend that ceremony in Kuare. He prepared some ornaments for her: shells, a skirt, netbag, red pigment, and other things. He also prepared some male ornaments—a bailer shell, a head covering, cassowary feathers.

Then he took a long *alipu* vine and told her, "I shall send you off now. While you are there, you must not eat any food they give you." Tying one end of the vine to her wrist, he told her, "While the rope is still being pulled out, I'll know you're still on the way; while it remains tight, I'll know you are there; if I can pull it back, I'll know you are returning."

Then he told his son to take some salt and ginger and to accompany her. "Take these things," he told him, "lest she feel thirsty and accept other people's ginger, salt, and water." So the two went off, while the father stayed holding onto his end of the vine.

3Bi   They arrived at the dance ground and joined in the ceremony. When the two grew tired from the *mata* dancing, the youth gave Yapi some salt and ginger. But while she was eating some crumbs of the salt and ginger fell to the earth. An old man came and ate them. This old one had rocks covering his back, and leaves and grasses growing on his stomach.

When the dancing was over, the youth said, "Sister, it's almost dark now. We must go back home." Now although that old man who had eaten the crumbs had not said a word to her, she decided to follow him. And so she did. The youth followed her closely, urging her to turn back. On and on they went, the three of them—the old man, Yapi, and the youth.

Finally they reached Pulumakana mountain, beyond which there was no path. "How will we two proceed here?" she wondered, but the old man took out a ceremonial stick (*ekepayo*) which he had hidden by the side of the path. Then he said, "Open, Pulumakana, open," holding the staff and aiming a blow with it at the rock. When the rock divided, the old man led the sister through. The rock closed together before the youth could follow.

Back at the house, at that moment, the end of the vine ran out of the father's hands. Realizing his daughter was lost, he cut at his fingers and ears, set fire to his house, and ruined his gardens.

When his son returned home, the father asked him what had happened. "What about the ginger and salt I gave you?" he asked the youth.

"It was not my doing," replied the other. "I gave it to her, but an old man came and ate the crumbs."

"Ah!" said the father, and he shattered his bone pearl shells, axed his garden crops, and remained in mourning.

Meanwhile the old man had taken Yapi to a small house in which an old woman lived, his wife. He made the girl stay there and told the old woman, "I've brought this pig back from my journey. Lest it run away, look after it carefully. I won't be back quickly." He went away.

The old woman explained, "This old one always does this sort of thing, but for you I feel especially sorry. Go and sit over there," she said indicating a corner.

3Bii   The next morning she told the girl, "Now he has gone off searching for others like yourself. Do you see those crippled young women over there? Later he will come and eat one of them. And when he has done that, you will take your place among them and wait your turn. But now let's go to the gardens." They went to a place where sword-grass clumps were piled up in a newly cleared garden. They saw that rodents had made their burrows underneath. Covering the openings with their netbags, the old woman poked into the piles of roots with a stick. A small *kapea* possum ran out. They killed it, returned to the house, cleaned out the intestines, singed its fur off, and finally cooked the possum in the fireplace.

Then the old woman said, "Stand up!" and she took lengths of dry *pora* wood, measured them, and broke them into pieces. Then she placed them inside the young woman's arms and legs, parallel to the bones. "Now you must remember to crouch down when the old man comes to cripple you," she said.

3Bi   Presently the old man returned with another young woman and said to his wife, "Here's a new one. Is the one I brought yesterday still here?"

"You made her stay here, and here she still is," replied the old woman.

"Get one of the ones brought earlier," said the old man.

He killed one of the crippled women and left her to cook. Then he returned to break Yapi's limbs and put her with the others. He clubbed her arms, legs, and back; but unknown to him it was only the pieces of wood that he heard snapping, not the bones themselves. Then he left her, taunting, "Sit down now! How do you feel?"

Yapi sat hunched over in a crumpled position, pretending her bones had really been broken like the others. Going over to where he had left the other woman cooking, the old man took the intestines and gave them to the old woman, saying, "Share this with the pig whose bones I have just broken." But the old woman slipped Yapi the possum intestines to eat, while she herself ate the dead woman's.

"Is she eating?" asked the old man, to which the woman replied that she was.

Then he began to cut up the flesh and bones from the woman he had cooked in the oven, giving some of this to the two to share. But the old woman again passed Yapi some possum flesh, saying, "He is gone. Straighten up now and eat." The old woman took out the pieces of wood, now broken, from her arms, legs, and back, and Yapi was as before. The young woman ate the possum meat while the old woman ate the human flesh.

3Bii   The next day, when the old man had left the house again, his wife said, "I must think of some way to help you. Wait." She rose and took all the male ornaments that Yapi had brought—bailer shell, breechcloth, hat—and put them in a netbag. She gave her a skirt to put on and other decorations for women.

"Was the *ekepayo* staff still there when you came through?" she asked. Yapi affirmed that it was. "Then do as the old man did. Say 'Open, Pulumakana, open.'" Then she gave her another instruction, "Outside this house you will see a ring of *kalia* cordylines. In the middle there is something for you to take home."

Yapi went out and took this thing. Then she walked back to Pulumakana mountain, took the staff, parted the rock with it, passed through, and returned home.

"How is it that you've come back?" the rejoicing farther asked. She recounted what had happened, and the man said, "Ah, I fear he will return. We must leave here and move further away."

"But since I took his staff, he will not be able to come back," she said.

11i   They killed a pig and cooked it. Then she placed the bundle she had brought on the ground outside, and she ringed it with *kalia* cordylines. While they were asleep that night, she woke to hear a low whistling and these words: "*puawale, nawale;* I have gone, I have eaten," spoken through flutes of bamboo. When she came out the next morning to look, she saw two short bamboo flutes where she had left the bundle.

11ii   This woman, who went beyond Pulumakana and managed to return, brought the Kuare *ribu* ritual back. Now we have the "short" *ribu* ritual, but before it were others, such as the "long" ritual. When, in the short ritual, the women carry their netbags on their heads, they recall the fact that the old man ate the heads of women, and that it was a woman who brought the ritual to Kuare.

CHAPTER 7

Of Broken Promises and Angry Ghosts

Tale 73: The Husband Breaks His Word

0,5i* A youth named Lewe lived at Nire. Near his house was a large *yamo* tree whose branches reached out in all directions, to south Kewa land, to Sumi land in the west, and to Mendi land in the northwest. Lewe and his mother were making a garden where this tree grew. Lewe climbed it to lop off its branches, while his mother placed pandanus-leaf mats on the ground underneath, lest he should fall. Lewe cut away the branches except for one which grew in the direction of Mendi land. He walked out on this branch, sat down, and began to whistle a tune softly.

His mother heard the sad tune and asked, "What are you thinking about?"

"Oh, I see smoke rising in the distance. A woman must be burning her garden there," said the son.

"Go to her, then," replied the mother. "But first we must get some cooking leaves and some firewood and kill a pig." So the two killed one of their pigs, and then they cooked and butchered it. Lewe put some of the pork in a netbag and set off.

He went up to Toranamapu, and there he saw a dark-skinned woman and her daughter. But the younger woman was not the one he was looking for. However, he took some pork from his netbag and gave it to them, saying, "When I come back I want you to go with me. Stay here now."

Then he went on to Modada, where he saw a light-skinned woman and her daughter. Nor was this the woman he was looking for, but he gave them pork and promised to return, just as before.

*Tales 73, 74, and 76 start with the first function of sequence 5 but do not develop the sequence further.

On he went, until he drew close to the place where Ialibu Raguame and her father were burning their garden. He did not go to the garden, though. He sat down by a stream where, he guessed, the woman would be coming to drink. And, indeed, soon she came to get some water. From his place of concealment, Lewe picked up some tree nuts and threw them at her. She started and exclaimed, "By Ialibu Rasa's backside, who did that!"

Then Lewe rose and spoke to her. "You mention the name of Ialibu Rasa, the youth you await. That's me! I threw the nuts."* Then the woman said, "I'll come with you, then. But my father, who is nearby burning a garden, is a bad man; we must be careful. The smoke will conceal us as we leave, but first I shall take him this pork you have brought."

Raguame went up to the garden to talk to her father while Lewe stayed below by the stream. She said to the old man, "You and I have been working hard in the gardens, and I am tired. I need a rest. Here, I've put some food for you on that mat over there. Eat some and then come back to the house." Then she left him and went down to where the young man waited.

3Ai The father began to think about this, for never had his daughter done anything similar before. First, he examined the netbag full of pork. Then, looking up, he saw his daughter hastening away with a youth.

"Someone's carrying her off!" he cried out, and he began to chase after the couple. On and on he pursued them.

3Aii Raguame and Lewe were soon tired and winded from their flight. Then the woman said, "Listen, I told you that my father is a bad one. He is about to catch us and kill us! But do you see that clump of *kope* leaves? You must uproot it, for my father's liver lies concealed beneath it!"

Lewe uprooted the clump, and just after he did so, the old man slowed his pace, stopped, fell down and soon died. The two others went on.

Soon they came to Modada. There Lewe went up to the two light-skinned women, the daughter and mother, and asked them to accompany him. The four went on together.

"I thought he was taking me alone," said Raguame to herself, "and now these two are coming as well!" But she continued to follow him.

---

*Raguame is a name sometimes given to attractive young women, and Rasa is a similar alias for handsome young men. Hence Lewe's assuming of this name. As for Raguame's exclamation, it seems that such comments are made when one is startled or surprised.

When they reached Toranamapu, Lewe said to the two dark-skinned women, "Let us go!" Once again Raguame was worried, for she had thought that she and Lewe would be going alone. Why had she helped him kill her father, she wondered. She began to weep.

10Bi Presently they arrived at Lewe's house.

10Bii Raguame said to him, "You've done well for yourself, taking so many women. But when we killed my father, I thought you were taking me alone, not two others as well. Now you must listen to what I have to say. Those other women shall have their own gardens and houses. You must not go to where they live. You and I will live away from them."

Lewe agreed, and the two of them lived away from where the other women had their houses.

10Biii One day Lewe decided to wrap up a bunch of plantains which were maturing. The plantains were growing in a garden cultivated by one of the other wives. As it happened, this wife was there with the others. They were talking, so Lewe joined their conversation for a while.

10Biv But Raguame saw him. She got some greens, taro, and plantains from her garden and took these back to her house. But she did not cook them; she sat, wept, and wondered what to do. Presently, she heard a noise on the thatch. When she went outside, she saw that the end of a root of the *kaipa* plant had made the noise. She looked to see where it had fallen from. The root was dangling like a rope from the sky, and at the other end was her father. It was he who had thrown the rope down. She climbed up.

When Lewe returned to the house and saw that Raguame was no longer there, he searched for her everywhere, in the bark walls, in the thatch, underneath the floor. Realizing that she really was not there, he pulled at his hair, broke his armbands and legbands—such was his sorrow. He sat, growing thinner as the days went by, nearly dying and unable to move because of his great sorrow.

10Bi Eventually he heard a noise on the thatch as the *kaipa* rope fell a second time. Lewe went outside to see what it was. He looked up and saw the woman with her father. She spoke to him, "I am here with my father. You can come up, if you want to. But if you do, you must never go back to that place again, as I warned you already." Consenting, Lewe climbed up the rope to join them in the sky.

But now Lewe's old mother was alone. From his place in the sky, Lewe saw that she had to work hard at fetching firewood and cultivating the gardens. He saw, too, that she believed her son was lost, for she had cut her ears and fingers in sorrow.

One day Raguame and her father allowed him to go down to the earth. They threw the *kaipa* rope down and Lewe climbed down it.

Raguame and her father had told him, "Go stack firewood for your mother, but only when she is not at home. Do not show her your face." This Lewe did. He stacked piles of firewood and then left.

When his mother returned home she saw chips of wood in the yard, and inside she saw the stack of firewood. After thinking about this, she decided it must have been her son who did it. From time to time Lewe did this work for her, but she never saw him.

10Bii   Raguame had reminded Lewe of his promise: "You must never go back to those other women," she had said. "There'll be no more warnings."

10Biii   But one day, when he was down on the earth to cut firewood for his mother, he looked at his wives' gardens and saw some maturing plantains that needed to be wrapped. "Well," he thought, "I'll just go and wrap them before returning."

Again Raguame was watching. "Once again he has not listened to me!" she thought. "I told him not to go there, but he did."

10Biv   When Lewe finished his work, he went back to his house, closed his eyes, and waited for the *kaipa* rope to fall. It did not. And try as he might, now he could not go up to the sky.

11i-ii   Today we might be able to marry sky women or go up to the sky and then come back. But this man, Lewe, did not heed the woman's word, so now we cannot go up there. Because he was stubborn and did not listen to the woman's words, the rope fell no longer. And thus there is no more marriage with sky women.

Tale 74: The Sky Women and the Broken Promise

0,5i   A man lived alone. One fine day he went into the forest at Kolo Mountain. As he walked through the trees he saw some pieces of earth and ochre lying on some leaves. He thought about this. Had some men from around there left it, or had women from the sky (*yaa sone winya*) dropped it? Looking around, he saw a large *walu* tree whose bark was worn off along the trunk. On the surrounding earth were footprints.

He followed the tracks a short distance until he came to where some *kapipi* tree-ferns were growing. There on the ground he saw more earth with ochre which, from the look of it, had been dug up recently.

"I must find out about this," he said to himself, so he made a small hut which he walled and covered with the mosses that grew on trees around there. Then he sat down inside the house. As the weather was good, he was quite content just to sit there, keeping his eye on the *walu* tree.

Presently he heard some women laughing, and he looked up to the tree top. Several young women were descending; they had come to collect the coloured earth. Frightened to see them, he remained still, trembling slightly. Then one by one, the girls started to climb the tree to return to the sky. Soon only two remained below, and the first of these climbed up while the other, a good-looking girl, waited her turn.

Quickly he ran over to her and held her fast. The woman tried to twist free, but without success. "I have you now!" he said, holding her tightly by the wrists. Finally, when she saw she could not escape, she asked him, "Are you a man of the bush (*raa*) or a man of the village?"

"I'm a man of the village," he assured her, but he continued to hold her. All the others had gone, and it was now dusk. Then he took her back to his house.

10Bi-ii   She told him, "I see you are indeed a man of the village. Now I will tell you something. Wherever you make a garden, there you must make a garden house for me. Others up there (in the sky) will look down at me, keeping watch. I cannot be seen outside the house by myself, so you must always accompany me. You must not leave me alone while you go somewhere on a journey; the two of us must go together. When we make a new garden, we must first make a hut and then the garden." So she spoke.

He followed her instructions and made a hut for her in each of his gardens, whether a forest garden or sweet-potato one. One day he told her that a ceremony was being planned in another village and that he was going to attend. So, in a new garden, he made the woman a new house of strong materials. But he had not yet given valuables for her, and she was wondering whether he was going to do so. She said nothing to him about this, however. Others in the sky were looking down at them and also wondering about the bride-wealth.

And indeed he did prepare things to give for her: shells and pigs. When he had assembled everything, however, it did not seem like much. But the woman said, "Never mind, that's enough; we will close our eyes now." They did so, and when they opened them again they were up in her place, in the sky. Having given the payment, they came down again the same way.

10Biii   "Now," he thought, "I've given wealth for her. Who would dare to carry her off?" So he told her to stay inside the new house, behind a strongly fastened door, while he went off to look at the dancing. The woman objected; she wanted to go with him. But the husband insisted that she should stay home.

10Biv   After he left, she sat lost in thought. Why did he disregard what he had promised earlier? So she closed her eyes, so as to go back to her place up in the sky. When she opened her eyes, she found herself there.

After the ceremony was over, the man came back and saw that his wife was not there. He was at a loss; how could he get her back? If he had followed what she said, we might still marry these women from the sky. But it was not to be. The woman spoke justly, and at the beginning he listened to her. But later he forgot her wish. As a result, we no longer marry such women.

11i-ii

Tale 75: The Journey to the Underworld

0   Pisimi lived with his clansmen.

?   One day he went to Walu to clear a forest garden, taking with him an axe and bush-knife to cut and pile the brush. Before leaving, he said nothing to his brothers, his wife, or children. He simply went.

When the bush was well piled and dry, he took some embers to burn it. But first he put his axe down beside another brush pile while he collected some more debris. While doing so, he saw that a large tree was casting too much shade. Deciding to cut it down, he returned to retrieve his axe from the brush pile where he had left it. But just as he reached down to pick it up, it disappeared. He looked around but could not find it. He returned to the tree he was intending to cut, thinking it might be there. It wasn't. But when he looked back at the brush pile, there was the axe again. Yet when he went to pick it up, it disappeared a second time

Four times this happened, and after the fifth, he began to pull the brush pile apart and search it. In the pile grew a *kope* plant, whose broad leaf is used for cooking. He looked around it without luck and then stood up to catch his breath. At that moment he heard a small *kiliwapili* bird cry, "*Kope repa yoka!* Pull up the *kope* clump!" Indeed, that was the only thing he had not pulled apart in that brush pile. He uprooted it and looked underneath. He saw a tunnel descending.

He followed it, and was led down into a deep well. After walking for some time in the dark, he saw some light in the distance. Continuing, he came to a fork in the path where it joined a wider track. The wider path took him to the vicinity of a house. Many plantains were growing around a long men's house, which had porches at both front and back.

Pisimi hid behind a clump of *irawapu* grass. His face was flushed, and he was afraid. He saw no one there, but presently an old man approached with a load of firewood. Pisimi looked closely and thought

he recognized his axe sticking out of that man's bark belt. This was
the one who had taken it, he thought. Quite afraid, he looked on as
more and more men arrived. Soon both porches were full.

The first old man began to chop his firewood, and when he did
so, one piece of firewood flew up and landed in the clump of
irawapu grass where Pisimi was hiding. Muttering, "I have fetched
this firewood from some distance, so I might as well retrieve this
piece," the old man went to fetch it. When he did so, he saw Pisimi.
"Are you a man of the bush (*raa ali*) or a man of the village (*ada ali*)?"
he asked.

"A village man," replied Pisimi.

10Bi   "Well, then, if you are not a ghost you should not have to sit
down in the sword grass. Come inside."

"I was afraid," said Pisimi.

The old man brought him forward and told the others that a
traveller had arrived. He suggested that they should cook some food
for him. They did so. Looking at those men, Pisimi thought he recognized some of his clansmen who had died. "Have they come here?"
he wondered.

Several days later they asked him, "Are you thinking of returning
to your home?"

"Yes, I came here for a purpose; I lost my axe and came looking
for it," Pisimi replied.

10Bii   Then they brought him axes, nassa-bead headbands, strings of
cowrie, pearl shells, salt, and other valuables, instructing him to take
these with him. They advised him, though, that when he took these
things and distributed them among his clansmen, he should not say
where they came from, nor even should he give a false answer—he
should say nothing at all. If he kept his word, he might return to
receive more valuables.

Pisimi put the things into a netbag. The old man he met first told
him to come back again the same way, by pulling up that clump of
kope leaves. Then they told him to shut his eyes. He did so, and when
he opened them again, he found himself outside his house.

10Biii   All the people there cried out, "Pisimi has come!" They were
surprised to see him carrying all these valuables. Pisimi did not notice that the old man whom he had met had followed him home. Unaware that the old man was there, he told all who had assembled,
"You with ash on your faces and in your hair (you poor-men), you
could not do as I have done, for I have gotten these things from the
dead of our clan. Look on!" And he shared all the things out, leaving
none for himself.

"Why don't you keep anything for yourself?" Pisimi was asked.
"Oh I'll go and get some more!" Pisimi replied. That is why he shared
all these things out.

10Biv   After a month had passed he decided to go back to the same place. So he returned to the spot where he had removed the *kope* clump. But that old man had heard what Pisimi had told the others, and when Pisimi came to this spot he found a big rock there, covered over with vegetation.

11i-ii   How could he go back, with that stone there? Now, too, we might be able to do as Pisimi had done once. We might be able to get our wealth from the dead. But because Pisimi did not listen to what that old man had said, that opening in the earth is blocked by a stone, and we can get nothing.

Tale 76: The Angry In-Laws

0   Keresa Pale lived alone and made many gardens. He had chosen to live alone, not in an open grassy place but in the middle of the forest at Mount Keresa.

5i   One day, when he was weary of working in the gardens, he went hunting in the forest. Catching a faint odour of smoke, he paused to look around. Wondering where the smoke might be coming from, he climbed first one tree and then another, but in vain: he saw nothing. Finally he found a tall beech tree (*karape*) on the top of a ridge. He climbed it and saw a column of smoke rising far away on the slopes of Mount Ialibu. After a long deliberation, he made up his mind to go there. Having arrived at this decision, he returned home and slept.

The next morning he combed his hair, and in it he hid a fine pearl shell. Next he killed, butchered, and cooked one of his pigs, and he put the pork in a netbag. That done, he followed a path into unknown parts of the forest.

As he went along he met an old man. "What are you doing?" he asked. Pale explained and continued on. Later he met an old woman. She questioned him and he answered as before. She pointed ahead and said, "There's a fire burning in a garden up there." Pale reached with his hand as if to scratch his head, but instead he pulled out the pearl shell. This he gave to the old woman. In return, she gave him a cooked *mata* taro as well as a bundle.

Then she said, "A young woman is up there making a garden. Soon she'll come down to the stream to fill her water containers. Wait for her there."

"Good," replied Pale.

"If you go and watch," the woman continued, "you will see her slip on a slick log and exclaim, "*Na Keresa Palena ke masa!* My Keresa Pale's backside!" When you hear her say that, tell her, 'I am here. Come!'" She told Pale to offer the woman the cooked taro. If she refused it, that was all right; and if she accepted, she would eat it. "When you see her go to fill her bamboos with water, you must unwrap this bundle and pour its contents (*rakia,* love potion) in the water."

Pale went to wait at the stream, and presently he saw a young woman come down the slope, carrying empty water containers of bamboo. She put her foot on a slippery piece of wood, lost her footing, and cried out, "*Na Keresa Pale ke masa, yare!* Oh dear! My Keresa Pale's backside!"

Pale said, "Hey! I'm over here. Come!" The two looked and smiled at each other with embarrassment. After a moment she went to draw water, and the man opened the bundle, rubbed the *rakia* between his fingers, and dropped it into the stream; it flowed into the bamboo.

The woman filled her bamboos and then drank some water. "Won't you eat some taro?" Pale asked, offering her the food. "Yes, I have been working hard. Give me some!" she replied. She added, "My mother is a bad woman. Stay here, and in a while I'll come to fetch you." Pale agreed, and the woman left with her bamboos of water.

Back in the garden, she said to her mother, "Mother, I want to go off now, so I will just get some food together." She took some taro and sugar cane and put them in netbags. She took also some greens, some *padi* of the *kusaru* variety, and some *opa* sweet potatoes.

3Ci   Then she returned, led Pale to a corner of her house, and put him inside a coil of bark in which she was accustomed to keep sweet potatoes. She killed a pig, and having singed off the hair and hoofs, she threw these out the open doorway. Having cooked all the food, she gave some to Pale.

Now the mother arrived and asked her daughter, "Ialibu Ragu-ame, what are you doing? What is all this?" The mother was about to come inside, but she saw the singed bristles that had been scraped and thrown outside; and she saw, too, the pig hoofs. She began to devour it all. Pale trembled. But Raguame sat down in the entrance, blocking it. Then she removed the pork from the oven and gave a leg to her mother. She continued to throw pieces of bone and meat to the old woman outside. Then they slept the night.

In the early morning the mother left. Raguame told Pale, "This woman is a bad one. She goes off to kill men. Go now." And she repeated, "Go now. Shut your eyes." Pale did as he was instructed. When he opened his eyes he saw he was back home on Mount Keresa.

"Tomorrow I'll return," he thought, and he killed his biggest pig, Puramenalasu. He singed, cooked, and butchered it, keeping aside the choice cuts of meat, which he stuffed into a separate netbag. At dusk he barricaded the doorway with a large, flat block of salt.

In the night Pale felt that the house was heavy, like a weight pressing on him, so he built up a large fire in the hearth. He sat. The door was pressed inward, but it held. On the roof, too, and on the walls there was great weight. He sat there trembling, adding wood to the fire. "They are coming now to kill me," he thought. He took a piece of pork kidney and ate it.

They were indeed trying to kill him, and they tried all night long to enter the house. Finally, toward dawn, Pale lay down, but he did not close his eyes.

3Cii   The fire lit the house dimly. He looked over at one of the bark walls and saw a small thing come down from a hole; it looked like a small tree frog. Taking a piece of fat, Pale heated it until the fat melted over the fire.

"Do something lest the fat drip away," said the frog—this "frog" was Pale's father's sister's ghost.

"Open your mouth," said Pale, and when the frog did this he squeezed the fat into its mouth. Then the man fed it kidney and also some pork leg, until the frog could eat no more and had to leave the rest aside.

The frog said, "You have all this meat here, but I see only one net-bag. How will you carry it?"

"I have no other netbags," said Pale. "I can only pile the pork here on the floor." The frog then left through the chink in the wall, and Pale went to sleep.

In the morning he saw only one netbag, the one in which he put a hindquarter of pork. He did not know where the rest had gone. Then that frog came and said, "It's daylight. Let's go." It had hung up the rest of the pork in netbags outside the house. "All the pork is there," it said.

Pale left one piece of pork for the frog. "I suppose you will not be back soon," it said.

"No," replied Pale. "You must stay and tend my gardens and pig." The frog agreed. Then Pale shouldered the bags of pork and closed his eyes. When he opened them again, he found himself by that stream where Raguame had drawn her water. He sat down and waited, and presently Raguame came.

"Oh," she said, "You're here! I'll tell my mother. Let her kill you!" But when she told the old woman, she only replied, "Oh well, before you did not say anything to me about any of this, but now I am content." And she held the young woman and man close.

The three brought the netbags of pork into the house, and the mother ate the meat. Then she killed her own pig and gave it to Raguame and Pale, after which they stayed on there.

10Bi   Presently Pale decided to give payment for his wife. So he returned home to get his valuables. He got a sow and tethered one leg.
Then, with the pig tether in his hand and a large bag of pearl shells
over his shoulder, he closed his eyes again. Outside Raguame's mother's house he planted a pig stake, and set out his shells and blocks
of salt. The old woman, too, gave many pigs to the couple, after
which Pale and Raguame went back to Mount Keresa. She bore him
a son.

10Biii   Now all this time Raguame had said nothing about her father.
And of all this payment that Pale had given for her, none went to
him.

One day Pale heard that people in the distant village were going
to kill their pigs. Men there were already cutting sugar cane to give
those who would be receiving the pork. So Pale went to attend with
his wife and son.

10Biv   When they got there, they sat inside the house, but because a lot
of smoke was coming from the fire, Pale took his son outside,
leaving Raguame inside. In the yard, Pale looked over to one side
and saw something profusely covered with grass and looking as
though clothed in *pai* leaves. The two rubbed their eyes and looked
again. This thing came toward them and tore out their eyes. Pale and
his son both died. When Raguame came outside, she saw the two
bodies lying there with their eyes torn out.

11i-ii   Upon taking his wife, Pale had not given payment to his wife's
father; the mother took it all. Raguame, too, had said nothing to her
husband about her father. So that woman's father's ghost came and
took out the eyes of that man and his son. And that is why, nowadays, our eyes are sometimes bad or are torn out in accidents. If that
marriage payment had been well shared with the father, then our
eyesight would not be affected like this.

Tale 77: The Grandparents Outsmarted

0,?   An old man and an old woman stayed and looked after a young boy.
They would tell him to collect dry pitpit for firewood, and then they
would leave for the gardens. The boy was always hungry, but he
would go to collect pitpit or draw water for the old couple. When
they came back from the gardens, the old man and woman would
give him very little food, and that is why he was always hungry.

When he went to the old man's house the old man would say,
"I'm eating *kabo* sugar cane. Go down to the other house." But when
the boy did so, the old woman would say, "I'm eating *yapo* sugar
cane. Go up to the other house where that man will give you some-

thing to eat." They always did this, and the boy stayed hungry.

One day the old man and woman went to the forest to visit an old garden. Knowing that they would return with no food for him, the youth went into the forest to find some *rani, rakia,* and *rulupa* greens. He gathered some leaves here and there, tied them into a bundle, and wandered around.

Eventually he approached a good garden with cucumbers and bananas. Crouching down at the garden's edge where the dry brush was piled, he peered into the garden and saw an old man with a huge headdress and a beard. The boy saw that the man was weaving a *ropa* armband.

The man looked up, saw the boy, and asked, "What are you doing?"

The boy told him that he stayed with an old man and woman and that they did not feed him well. He told how when he went to one house the man said he was eating one kind of sugar cane and sent him off, and when he went to the other house the old woman said she was eating another kind of sugar cane and also sent him off. Feeling sorry for the boy, the old man led him home and gave him some ripe *oda* bananas. Then he took some cockatoo feathers and told the boy to try them on, to put the feathers over his body, and to fly up into a nearby tree. The boy squawked *"Aaaa!"* like a cockatoo and flew up. Then the old man told the boy to perch at the top of the tall casuarina tree which grew nearby, which the boy did.

The man said, "Good, come down now, and I'll tell you something." So the boy flew down. The man asked, "From where you were sitting in the tree top, could you see the old man and the woman in their garden?" The boy assented. "Then fly now and sit in the branches of a tree in that garden," the man instructed. "Fly down slowly; fly onto the heads of the two old people, first one, then the other. Then if one of the two tries to hit you, each will only hit the other, provided you are quick!"

So the boy, squawking *"Aaaa!"* once again, flew off and perched in a tree in that garden.

3Ai   The old woman, who was digging in the garden, cried out, "Look, there's a cockatoo!"

"Yes, but I have no bow and arrow. Too bad!" replied the old man.

Then the boy flew down closer. The woman exclaimed, "Look, it's coming close!"

Next the boy flew onto the head of the old woman. The man picked up a stick which he was using to plant taro and tried to hit the bird, but he only succeeded in striking the woman on the head, for the boy had jumped off.

Next the boy perched on the man's head, and the woman said, "Ah, you've hit me and there's blood, but now I'll try!" But in her attempt to hit the cockatoo with her digging stick, she, too, struck her husband in the head.

3Aii   The boy perched again on the old woman's back, and then on the old man's back, again and again. The two were badly hurt and collapsed on the ground while the boy flew up into the tree again, and then flew away.

The old man who had given the feathers asked the boy what had happened. When the boy told him how the two had struck each other, the old man approved. Then he took all the cockatoo feathers off the youth and told him to go home with the greens he had gathered.

The boy did so, made a fire, and sat down. A heavy rain was falling, and the boy wondered whether trouble was afoot.

Soon the couple came back to the house. The boy asked what had happened, and the two related their story.

"Oh grandfather! Oh grandmother!" the boy exclaimed, pretending to sympathize with them.

3Ai   They asked the boy to fetch some water and nettle leaves with which to wash their wounds. He agreed, but when he reached for the bamboo container the old woman saw some white feathers in his armpit. After the boy had left the house, she told the old man, and she asked him what they should do.

"I will see if feathers are really there," said the old man. "If they are, tomorrow you will take the boy into the new garden and then cut his neck with your knife. There are lots of greens in that garden. Cut plenty of them and cook the boy and we shall eat him. I'll go to the old garden and come later."

The boy returned to the house and gave them the nettles and the water. The man asked him to reach for some firewood underneath the roof, and when the boy did so he, too, saw the white feathers. So he said to his wife, significantly, "Oh! the boy has given me some red nettles," and asked her for some of hers.

The next day the old woman took the boy to the garden. There she prepared piles of firewood and greens. Then she said to the boy, "Hey, I see a louse in your hair! Let me pick it out." She had hidden a knife in her netbag.

"Oh, grandmother, leave it be," said the boy, "I'll look through your hair first!"

3Aii   When he did so, he saw the old woman's knife. He drew it from her bag and thrust it into her neck, killing her. Then he took off her skin and put it over his own. Seeing a small well in the garden, he made a trap by concealing the mouth with sticks and leaves. Then he cooked the old woman's body and put some of the flesh over the hole.

The old man came up. The boy—now disguised as the old woman—said, "Ah, this is no good, the boy has no fat! But I've put some meat over there for you," and he pointed to the place.

The old man went over there and fell into the hole in the ground. He fell down and down.

11i-ii Then the boy took off the old woman's skin and threw it into the hole with all their things. He picked up an arrow, broke it in two and put it into his anus. He became an *oleyamu*, a lorikeet.

Tale 78: The Father, the Son, and Their Good Dog

0 A father and son lived with their little dog and their big pig, which slept in the hearth of an abandoned house.

? One hot day, finding the heat of the sun oppressive, the father and son decided to go hunting in the forest. They took their dog and shot some possums sleeping in the tree tops. But then, going deep into the forest, they lost the path they had taken. Further into the forest they went.

Presently they came to a dark pool which barred their path. On the other side they saw a tall *nema* tree in fruit. Many birds had gathered to eat the fruit of this tree.

Father and son deliberated what to do. They could go and shoot these birds, but how would they cross the pool? As they stood and talked, a dark object came swimming toward them. It was a duck (*sipi*). The bird asked them, "What are you talking about?"

"Oh, we would like to shoot the birds in that *nema* tree, but we do not know how to get across," said the man.

"No difficulty," said the duck. "I'll carry you across." But the two were afraid of this and held back. "I won't let you sink. I'll take you straight across," the duck reassured them. But still the father and son hesitated.

Then the duck said, "If you don't believe me, fetch a heavy piece of wood and put it on my back. I'll show you." The son did so, and the duck swam across the pool with it, depositing the log on the other side.

Then the dog spoke to its masters, "That looks all right. The duck can take me across first. If it abandons me in the pool, you two can return." But the duck carried the dog across and then returned for the son and then again for the father.

3Ai The father, the son, and the dog then approached the tree, eager to kill some birds. They walked around its base, looking for an opening through the foliage of the lower branches. But at that moment they heard someone shout, "Ay ya!" An old, tall man came up, with his long tusk-like teeth sheathed in *wabi*. He shouted, "People always come to shoot my birds. Now I see you're doing it."

The father replied, "We just came wandering through the forest, and we saw them, that's all."

"Well then," said the old man, "we'll all go and spend the night in my house nearby, but first you may shoot some of the birds." After the father and son bagged a few, the old man said, "Now we'll go home for the night."

The others followed the old man for some distance, and soon they all reached his house. The old one urged the other two to sit down and rest while he went to fetch some food from the gardens close to hand. But the father replied, "When I stay somewhere on a journey, I usually like to walk around a bit, have a look at what trees are growing, locate the toilet, and only then sit down. So he and his son went outside and looked around. The son saw a small house nearby and approached it. He hid when he saw a little old woman inside, but she caught sight of him, too.

"Who are you?" she asked him, and the boy explained how he had come there.

"I never see them return, the likes of you," she said. "How many of you have come?"

"Three of us," said the boy. "I came to have a look around and saw you here."

"Then I'll give you something before you go back," said the old woman. She gave him first one little bundle and then a second.

The son returned and told his father what he had seen. The father put the two bundles into his netbag. Then the dog announced, "I'll go now and see what this old man is up to. Stay here." And the dog went off, sniffing the path the old one had taken. It came to a house and, hearing talking from within, went to listen at the wall.

"I have brought three pigs," the old man was saying, "and tomorrow I'll go and fetch all my clansmen. We must bring food to cook them with." He was talking to an old woman (his wife). "My brothers will bring *rani* greens, firewood, and cooking bamboos. You, too, must bring some tomorrow." The dog heard him say all this, and then: "Now I'm going to take them some food, and I'll stay the night there." The old man went off to cut some plantains to take back, along with the sweet potatoes he received from his wife.

The dog returned and told the father and son what it had seen. Now they saw what was being planned for them. Not long after, the man returned, apologized for being slow, and urged them to eat and then sleep. So the father and son cooked the potatoes, ate, and lay down. "Tomorrow you'll go back home. Sleep now," said the old man.

3Aii   After the old man had gone to sleep the others opened the first bundle. In it were three pairs of little things shining like stars; they were fireflies. They put these over their eyelids and slept. When they were sound asleep the old man rose and crept toward them. He was surprised to see their eyes shining. "Why don't they sleep?" he wondered. So he went back and dozed for a while. He got up a second time; still they were not asleep, it seemed. "Ah, one cannot even kill people here," he muttered, "Why aren't they asleep?" But they had put these fireflies on top of their eyelids, and their eyes still shone when dawn broke. Then they awoke.

The old man said to them, "I'll go to see the old woman about sweet potatoes. I'll be back shortly, so wait for me."

But the three decided to flee immediately. But first they opened the second bundle. In it they found a *wiruapu* bow and a *sapalu* arrow. They wrapped the bundle up again, happy to see these things. Off they went.

When they had gone some distance, they heard the others come following. They were crying out, "Our pigs have escaped!" Some were coming from distant places like Kaimare, Porada, and Kuwi. The three pressed on, hearing the cries of that old man: "Oh, why didn't I kill them sooner?"

The dog said, "You two go quickly. I'll stay behind to fight them." And the dog waited for the old men. When they appeared, he attacked and bit them on the legs and testicles. Many died, but the old man who had tried to kill them during the night said, "Ah, these are just fleas biting me." He barely felt the dog's bites and continued his pursuit. When the father and son saw the old man, they unwrapped the bow and arrows and shot an arrow at him, but still he came on. As for the others, the dog bit them on the calves, thighs, and testicles, and they all died. But that old man continued to give chase.

Presently they came to the shore of that pool, and once again they saw the duck. The dog told the bird, "I'll watch here at the shore. Carry the other two across first!" The duck then took the father and then the son across, returning finally for the dog. When the old man came to the edge of the pool, he could not cross.

11i   The three of them sat down to rest. The dog said, "I have helped you greatly, for without me you would have surely perished. When we reach home, you must kill your big pig. You can eat it all, but save me the kidney. This you must give me."

When they arrived back home, they found their pig sleeping as usual in the ashes of an old house. They split firewood, killed the pig, singed it, and butchered it. They cooked the innards in one earth oven and put the rest of the carcass into a second.

When the food was cooked, the father opened the first earth oven and shared out the pork. Some he gave to his son, some he gave to the little dog, and some he kept for himself. But the dog did not eat, for the kidneys were not there. Then the father and son opened the other oven, and the father cut the pig into quarters. But still he did not offer the dog the kidneys. The dog whimpered, lowering its head.

Finally the father scolded the dog, "Look at the meat and fat I have offered you. Why do you whine? Have I not shared it well?" But the little dog did not reply; it had spoken earlier, and now it just sat and whimpered. Again the father questioned the dog. And this time, exasperated, he struck the dog with a pork leg. Blood flowed from its head and the dog whined even more.

The man, who had totally forgotten he promised to give his dog the kidneys, struck the dog a second time. And this time the dog died. Later they buried it.

11ii   Nowadays, when we go to where our enemies are, dogs do not help us. That is because this man did not do as the little dog requested. When the dogs go after possums, they kill and eat them, for dogs know well how to fight. But against our enemies they do not fight.

This dog went off as Kilua Kapi Yana, a wild dog of Mt. Giluwe, and now there are wild dogs on Mt. Giluwe and on Mt. Ialibu as well. The father and son broke their *wiruapu* bow and became *walawe* lorikeets.

Tale 79: The Angry Ghostfather

0   A man lived with his daughter, Ipirinyu, and with her he cultivated forest and sweet-potato gardens. But then the father fell sick and was no longer able to work. The daughter continued to go every day. One day the father said, "For once, you must stay here and look after me." But the young woman did not listen to him, for she always went out to the gardens.

"If you must go, come back quickly," he said. "I am dying and we must kill this pig." Ipirinyu did not come back quickly, however, and by the time she did return, her father had died. On her return she heard the pig squealing. Looking inside the house, she saw her father's lifeless body.

Not being able to make a proper mortuary platform for her father's body, she immediately pulled the body not far from the house, dug a hole in the earth, and buried him. Having done that, she made a fire in the house.

3Bi   As she sat, her father's face appeared in her imagination. From fear, she did not sleep that night, while the pig kept squealing *suuu! suuu!* until morning. Her father's ghost had gone inside the snout of that pig.

That morning she decided to kill the pig and leave the house, so she cut some *weliako* plantains and peeled them. Laying down some fresh leaves, she piled the plantains on them. On top, she put some pig fat and kidneys. Meanwhile the pig's head, which she had severed from the rest, continued to squeal. So Ipirinyu stuck it on the picket fence that surrounded the house, while she continued to cook the rest of the pig. Then she put all the meat and bananas into her netbag and set off. She took with her a good skirt and a *walu* staff as well.

She went down to Labogo, crossed Kema mountain, and descended into Kelowala. As she walked along, she continued to hear the pig's squealing, for the pig's head was still following her. On she went to Pupiri, to Puriri, and finally to the bank of the Pore River. She was unable to cross it, since it was in flood, and she walked upstream, then downstream, then upstream again, looking for a place to ford.

3Bii   A young man was standing on the other side. When he saw her, he took a long sugar cane and lay it down across the river. So Ipirinyu put down her netbag and—in the way things happen in tales—walked along the cane to the other bank.

There she told the man, "My dead father went inside the pig's snout. I was afraid it would kill me, so I left my netbag over there." The youth immediately swam across and retrieved the bag.

It was only then that the pig's head reached the river. It, too, went upstream and downstream looking for a crossing. The young man called out to it, "If you are a devil or ghost, you'll be able to cross on this bridge of sugar cane!" And he threw the cane across the river with a splash. The pig's head started to cross on the cane, and when it had reached the halfway point, the man pulled the cane away from under it. The head was swept away downstream.

Ipirinyu and the man went on to Wamulu Pai. There in the forest she saw a large garden. The trees in it were not pollarded; they simply stood there dead. Many bananas grew in it, and enclosing it was a high fence protected by many deadfall traps, all of them plastered with possum fur.

3Bi   The young man had been going to fetch water when he had seen Ipirinyu, and now in a garden house the two recooked the pork she had brought. He told her, "My father is a bad man, so we had better not eat any of this pork."

3Bii   Ipirinyu told him, "I'm not a man, I'm actually a woman. But if your father sees that we are just alike, he may not kill me. Let's try it." Ipirinyu put her skirt aside and put on a bark belt, cane belt-loops, and a breechcloth. And she picked up a *keroga* stone axe and held it in her hand. Now the two young people looked much alike.

They carried their cooked pork and possums from the garden hut to the main house, which was surrounded by a high pallisade of *kalo* wood topped with dry *kati* leaves. The fence ringed the house and its stand of fruit-bearing pandanus palms.

3Bi   The youth then told her, "My father made this fence. Everyone in Papua New Guinea wants to kill him, because he kills and eats men with his long teeth. You'll see. When they come from one side, my father kills them with his teeth; when they come from the other side, I kill them with my bow and arrow. They die, and my father eats them.

Then, having left the pork in the porch, they went inside and lay down underneath a bark-cloth blanket. They slept, leaving all the cooked meat in the front of the house. "It's about time for my father to come," said the youth. Indeed, the old man approached not long after.

"A fine smell here, good child of mine!" he said.

3Bii   Raising his torch, he looked underneath the bark cloth and saw the two: their legs, their bark belts, their hair, their axes – all were the same. "My good sons!" he exclaimed, and he began to eat the meat left in the other room. His long teeth were crusted with dried blood of many men. So they stayed.

One day the old man said, "I've killed many people from all places, but tomorrow I fear they'll try to kill us. Prepare your bows and arrows, and I'll get my own ready." The following day they cooked food in the garden house and brought it back.

Meanwhile, many southern clans were preparing for battle, as were the Polopa men of Keba. They were saying, "It's no great matter; this time we'll kill him!"

Men of Kanarepa and Waluaperepa arrived along one path, and those from Erave approached from another side. All those men came and made fires outside the old man's fence.

11i   Now the old man worried that the men might kill his two sons, so he picked them up and threw them into the tops of two pandanus trees. As for himself, he fled into a hole in the earth.

11ii   He became a *kagi* possum, which sleeps in holes in the ground. Those two young people, the youth and the girl whom he had thrown into the pandanus trees, became *basa,* Raggiana birds of paradise. Because the old man had eaten so many men, he no longer dares to go about in daylight. Instead, he fetches *mara* leaves and makes himself a house in karst holes. *Kagi* do this still. That is the story of how the pig's head tried to kill the woman, Ipirinyu.

Tale 80: The Old Man with Fire (Version 1)

0   This is a story my mother, Kekoinyu, tells. A girl stayed with her pig, Puramenalasu, and cultivated gardens in the valley at Kumiali. Their house was on Yole Ridge, which is near Mount Limba high above the Yaro River. Their gardens in Kumiali were all on the slope of the mountain facing the river.

?   One sunny day the girl and the pig left as usual for their gardens. First, though, the girl buried the glowing firebrands deep in the ashes so they would continue to smolder. Then she poured some water around the edge of the hearth. That done, she and the pig departed.

It was late, near dark, when they returned home, for the day had been fine. They found that the embers in the hearth had died and grown cold.

"What shall I do? Since I am not a man, I do not know how to make a fire by friction," she thought. But as she and her pig stood on the slope of the hill and looked over toward Kuwi, she saw smoke rising. She thought that the smoke was over in Waneloma, which is near Kuwi and thus not far away. So she set out to get some fire. She walked to Taguada and from there to Munire, crossed Yopene Stream, went on, and came to Waneloma. But the smoke was not rising there at all. Now she saw that it was coming from Kanayari. Yet when she reached Kanayari and Mapire there was still no fire or smoke; it was further still. So she followed the smoke to Mugiri, Amaru, Kaluake, Kilimi, Gai, Kabeasa, Mapeda, and Kolapi. This was strenuous going.

Finally she came to Wanera and Kalawira. And there in Kalawira she found several small fires burning. She thought to herself, "It's not really stealing something important, if I take some fire; I'll just take a couple of brands."

3Bi   But just then an old man with long teeth wrapped in sheaths of *wabi* appeared and cried out to her, "What are you doing with my fire?"

"But this is not something important. It's just for starting a fire, nothing more!" she replied.

"Well then," said the old man, "you may take it, it doesn't matter. But first come and eat some *koba* greens with me." She agreed.

But unseen by her, that man who had led her there (for he had made the smoke recede) cut off his testicles and his lips, wrapped them up in *koba* greens, and cooked the lot in his hearth. After the girl had eaten this, the old man said "Good. Go off now with your firebrands."

The girl set off for her home at Yole. But she had gone no further than Leparini Stream when the old man cried out "Wakulu!" (another name for *koba* greens). From her stomach came the answer "Yes!"

Well! When she reached Momanimi again the old man cried out "Wakulu!" And once again came the reply, "Yes!" from her stomach. The same thing happened at Gai, Mugiri, Kaimare, Kuwi, Yopene Stream, and Taguada. Finally she reached her home.

"There is something bad in my stomach," she said, telling her pig what had happened. "I'm afraid that it will kill me." Indeed, as she spoke the testicle and mouth in her stomach began to eat her. They ate and ate until all that was left of her was her stomach, which rolled down into a clump of raspberries.

3Bii   Now in the forest nearby, at Yole and Limba, lived many cassowaries. For a while Puramenalasu pig stayed alone, mourning its mother. But one day it went by itself to work in the garden at Kumi-ali, returning home late in the day. And on the next day it went again. While the pig was in the garden this second time, two cassowaries came to the raspberry patch to eat the berries. They saw some flies buzzing there. "It's the stomach of a man or woman," they thought. The two cassowaries licked it all over and then rolled it to the base of a tree. There they looked after it.

Soon a head, arms and feet came from it. Soon it had made itself back into a girl.

But then again the old man was heard to call out "Wakulu!" "Yes," came the reply once again.

"Help!" thought the girl, "I thought it had died, but now it's crying out again." This time, though, the cassowaries heard the cry. And now many cassowaries came together, group after group of them. And many red bees of all kinds came, some two hundred of them. Puramenalasu pig, too, was there, a huge pig. All these animals arranged themselves along the path. The pig went furthest and stationed itself at Leparini Stream. The bees and cassowaries waited behind, spacing themselves out along the path all the way back to Yopene Stream, preparing to fight the old man when he came. The girl remained at Yole.

"Wakulu!" cried the man a last time. "Yes!" came the reply from Yole. And the man started out. When he reached the stream, the pig attacked him and bit him with its tusks, but the old man simply commented, "Just fleas biting me!" Then the bees attacked, biting him in the face around the eyes, but he kept on. The cassowaries then attacked him with their claws, but still he went on, crying "Soee! Soee!" Pursued by the pig and the bees and the cassowaries, he came to Kuwi, then to Yopene Stream, and on to Porawiteme. By now he was feeling considerable pain.

Yopene Stream was in flood, but he struggled across up to Taguada. There he died. As he expired steam rose from his body. The cassowaries and bees continued to strike and bite their foe. Then the girl took dry casuarina wood and burnt him until nothing remained.

11i "Now I will give you payment," she said to the cassowaries and bees, bringing them together. She brought out her pigs, salt, and "bone" pearl shells, and she laid these out in rows. With them she put her *wiruapu* bow and ripe bananas. In addition she put down nuts of *pima* and *pudina* trees (both wild pandanus) which she had gathered from the valley at Kumiali.

The cassowaries said, "That's what we'll eat, these wild pandanus nuts; and the bees can have the ripe bananas as their food. It's good."

Addressing herself to the bees, she said, "I will divide you in two." To some she said, "Go stay in sorcery bundles." And she got various kinds of leavings: corn cobs, pieces of ornamental plumes, ornament wrappings, pieces of feces, and so on. These would be the food of those sorcery-making bees, all one hundred of them. "You must go to the tree bases in the forest. Don't stay here," she said to them. Some went to Wiru land, some to south Kewa land—all these bees that would later be used for sorcery she sent to live in the tree bases. "I'm making your path now," she told them. "Some of you will stay in rock crevices. I do not give you shells and pigs, but I give as your food the things which people use to kill other men."

To the other bees she said, "Your place is in leaves of trees and cordyline bushes. Your food you will find on bark, leaves, and flowers." That was for the other hundred bees.

11ii Today the red wasps (*yada sipira*) are in the bush, and they still bite us in the face the way they did when they were fighting with that old man. This is because the girl gave the wasps this work to do.

Then the cassowaries said to her, "We must see you married off." And the woman replied, "You have helped me much. Because of this, I'll go and live with the *pima* pandanus and bear its children. When these sons drop down, you can eat them. Now I'll go to stay with that tree."

So today, when we see cassowaries eating wild pandanus nuts, they are taking the sons that the woman has born. In just the same way as women of the village bear sons, so did that woman marry the tree and bear nuts. The white bracts (*kulu*) near the ripening nuts are that woman's white skirt.

Tale 80: The Old Man with Fire (Version 2)

0   A brother and sister stayed in Wapopa, near Asumai.

?   The brother decided to go to Orokane to bring back *tigaso* palm oil, and he asked his sister to look after the pigs. He left; his sister, too, left the house and went to the garden. After a while she came back to the house. The fire in the hearth had completely died. She went outside the house and looked around, and in the distance she saw a glow of flames. So, taking her netbag, she set off in that direction. First she went to Wapeapi, from there to Ndi, and from Ndi to Orokane, and from there to Kurupu.

3Bi   At Kurupu she found a big old man sitting by a fire – the one she had seen. The old man asked what she wanted, and she told him that her fire had gone out. He replied that she could take some fire-brands back in the morning if she wanted to stay the night. That evening he cooked a huge *ma* taro, which he gave the woman to eat. But she could finish only half of it then. She slept the night, and in the morning she ate the other half, took some glowing embers, and left. When she had retraced her path back to her house, she took sick.

That woman's stomach was soon swollen as though she were pregnant. But fortunately the siblings' pig, Puriminalasa, did her garden work and fetched her firewood. This pig of theirs was as large as a cow.

Presently the fire glowed again in Wapeapi, and that old man cried out, "Is the taro there in Wapopa?" And from inside the woman's stomach, the taro cried out in response, "Yes, we two are here. Come!"

The woman was very much afraid. "I thought it was a taro I ate there," she thought, "but it must have been something else!" The old man arrived at the siblings' house, took out pieces of vine, and tied one around her stomach below her breasts and another lower down around her waist. He pulled them both tight and knotted them securely. Then he left her and went back to his house, having told her he would return three days hence.

3Bii   The sister wept in pain and anger. In the morning she crawled outside. A small cassowary had come up to the house to eat pig feces. The sister, reclining beneath a banana tree, asked the bird to help her.

"What's the matter?" the cassowary asked. She told it what her trouble was, recounting the story. The cassowary then asked her, "When will he come back?" and the woman replied, "He will return in three days time."

Then the cassowary said, "I'll get all my brothers, and together we'll help you. But what will you give us in return?" Said the sister, "I have stones on this land, the seeds of trees, wild plants, the fruits of *toba* and *wakia* trees, ripe bananas, and the streams named Alapita, Ula, and Ekere. I will make decorations on your neck with red and white earth."

The cassowary clapped its wings in delight and went off. It got all its brothers, big and little alike, and it got Ekere Duku, a very large and strong one. All of them came and encircled the house, parading around it. They approached an *ula* wild plantain and attacked it with their claws. The plant fell over, broken in the middle. The cassowaries announced they would do the same to the old man.

Ekere Duku went to watch for him by the door of the house, and the little cassowary that had come first went and stayed inside the house, filing its claws on a sharpening stone. It waited in a pig compartment and held its claws outstretched in readiness.

From Wapeapi the old man cried out, "Who's there in Wapopa? Is the woman still alive?" He came with a very large vine, which he wanted to tighten around the middle of the woman's stomach. But as he neared the house, the little cassowary gouged out one of his eyes with its claws, and then Ekere Duku came and dragged him outside and gouged out the other. Next all the other cassowaries came and clawed at him, surrounding him like flies on open skin. Then they pulled him away and threw him into a well.

11i-ii   Having finished with him, all of them came and danced around the house to celebrate the old man's death. The woman put body paint on the cassowaries' heads and necks, and she gave them plantains to eat. Then she told them to eat the fruits of the wild trees and drink the water of the streams of that land. The cassowaries kicked the woman's stomach and the taro came out. They took this thing and cooked it in the fire, and then they went off into the forest.

Tale 81: The Angry Ghostwife

0   A man named Boso lived with his wife at Taguada. The two were childless, but they looked after their pig, Puramenalasu. One day Boso's wife took sick. She said, "I'm going to die; you must kill this pig of ours now."

But Boso replied, "I can't kill this pig just for you." "Good enough," said his wife resignedly. After a while she died. Boso now lived by himself.

3Ci   During the night that woman (her ghost) came again and again, trying to open the door to get in and kill Boso. He put a fence of sharpened stakes in the front of his house, and he ringed it with a pallisade, taking refuge in the back. She came and tried to break through the fence, but never could she manage to go all the way through before dawn broke. Boso made many such fences; but that ghost would come along with others and tear each one down. Yet by the time they got through to the last fence daylight would break. Again and again this happened.

3Cii   One morning Boso went to his garden and saw that much of the food – plantains, sugar cane, sweet potato and taro – had been taken. He cried out, "Who has stolen food from my garden?" A thin voice responded from the other side of the garden. It was a little-man who was answering, "Why are you yelling so?"

"Someone has stolen from my garden, I'm shouting because of that," replied Boso.

"Maybe a ghost took them," said the little-man.

"Ah, I'm afraid of a ghost and I've been staying around the house building barricades. That's why I haven't come here often. You must help me watch out." He explained what had been happening.

"All right, I'll watch with you," said the other. And the two of them went back to prepare food. The little-man said, "You must cook food for me while I do something." He took a tree-fern stalk, fashioned it into the likeness of a man, and stood it outside by the fence.

That night when the ghosts came to kill Boso, they thought they saw him standing alone outside the house, and they attacked. The ghost of Boso's wife battled with the tree-fern stalk. The struggle took her toward a deep well, into which she eventually fell.

11i   Boso was thankful. He killed his pig, cooked it, and gave half to the little-man. But this one told him, "I won't eat that." So Boso brought all sorts of cooked vegetables and put these with the pork, along with salt and shells. But these too were refused. "What can I give him?" wondered Boso. He went to the side of his house, broke a branch off a *kenoa* tree, and asked, "Will you take this?"

"I will," said the other. Boso had thought that the other would roll a smoke with it – for *kenoa* leaves are used for this – but instead he ate it; he was a *loke* possum. He had refused all these other gifts – pork, shells or garden foods – and only the *kenoa* leaves would he take.

11ii   That is now what they eat, those *loke* possums. As for Boso, he became a *muma* quail, living among the *muma kibita* plants where new gardens are made.

Appendix 1

LIST OF NARRATORS

A. Men

Name	*Residence*	*Tales*
Malu	Karapere	2, 9, 11, 12, 19, 24, 30, 35, 38, 45, 57, 67, 68, 80 (version 1)
Wasape	Karapere	10, 20, 48, 72
Melepa	"	1, 4, 49
Pepana	"	5, 47, 73
Tisi	Iapi	7, 13, 18
Parea	"	8, 31, 77
Rugi	Koiari	16, 17, 22
Adei	Karapere	28, 51, 81
Tope	"	55, 59, 78
Keapu	"	21, 58
Oloa	Iapi	3, 80 (version 2)
Kabe	Koiari	23
Lopisa	Iapi	27
Pu	Karapere	40
Sokele	Iapi	44
Wabi	Karapere	52
Kusa	"	53
Loke	"	56
Rema	"	61
Pere	"	62
Nare	"	63
Yekipu	Koiari	64
Rube	Karapere	74
Waipa	"	79

B. Women

Name	Residence	Tales
Raminyu	Karapere	26, 34, 54, 60, 66
Alitapu	"	29, 37, 65
Ropainyu	"	43, 59, 70
Katainyu	"	25, 39
Yetoinyu	"	32, 69
Pipirainyu	"	42, 76
Yawame	"	46, 71
Raguame	"	6
Waipainyu	"	14
Kore	"	15
Nodo	"	33
Ladanyu	"	36
Polinyu	"	41
Koyame	"	75

Appendix 2

LIST OF SEQUENCES AND FUNCTIONS

Listed below are the functions for the eleven sequences, along with the tales in which the sequences are found. In some tales a particular sequence is missing a function or possibly two, and in some a pair of functions may appear in reverse order. For a more analytical presentation of this material, see *Fabricated World,* appendix 3.

1　TWO BROTHERS

        1i　　　　A brother benefits from a source of wealth.
        1ii　　　Another brother misuses the source.
        1iii　　There is an act of retaliation.
             Tales 1, 2, 3, 4, 5, 6, 7, 8, 9, 10

2　BROTHER AND SISTER

        2i　　　　One of the siblings acts improperly.
        2ii　　　The other sibling reproves the first or becomes
              distant.
        2iii　　The siblings separate.
        2iv　　　They rejoin.
             Tales 11, 12, 13, 14, 15, 16, 17, 18, 19

3　GHOST ATTACK

        3i　　　　A ghost attacks the hero/heroine.
        3ii　　　He/she receives aid, and escapes or kills the
              attacker.
             3A Tales (male ghost, male victim) 9, 10, 11, 15,
             16, 17, 18, 19, 52, 68, 73, 77, 78

3B Tales (male ghosts, female victims) 20, 27, 32, 33, 35, 38, 42, 60, 61, 62, 69, 70, 72, 79, 80

3C Tales (female ghosts, male victims) 4, 7, 8, 25, 64, 76, 81

3D Tales (female ghosts, female victims) 32, 34, 38, 54, 60, 71

4   BROTHER SISTER AND WIFE

4i	A brother marries a woman of special status.
4ii	His sister and wife are kept separate.
4iii	The sister and the wife engage in mortal combat.
4iv	There is an act of retaliation.
	Tales 11, 12, 20, 21, 22, 23

5   ABUWAPALE THE PROVIDER

5i	A young man unites with a woman of special status.
5ii	The woman gives him wealth, but under a condition.
5iii	He ignores the condition, and she dies as a result.
5iv	There is an act of retaliation.
	Tales 12, 24, 25, 26, 27, 28

6   GHOST MARRIAGE

6i	A youth (or his spirit form) visits a young woman.
6ii	Left behind, she journeys to meet him.
6iii	On her journey she meets kin of the youth's.
6iv	She joins the youth.
	Tales 29, 30, 31, 32, 33, 34, 35, 36, 37, 38, 39, 40, 41, 42, 43, 44, 45, 46, 47, 48
6Ai	The ghostsister of the youth helps her.
6Aii	Men capture the ghostsister.
	Tales 29, 30, 46, 47

7   POOR-MAN LITTLE-MAN OLD MAN

7i	A foe attacks a group.
7ii	The group's last surviving member overcomes the foe.
	Tales 49, 50, 51, 52, 53, 54, 55, 56, 57, 58, 59, 60, 61, 62

8   SKIN CHANGERS

8i   A young man's or woman's spouse has a
         disagreeable appearance.
8ii   During ceremonies the spouse appears very
         attractive.
8iii The young man or woman destroys the spouse's
         homely skin.
      Tales 28, 31, 63, 64, 65, 66, 67

9A   RESTORATIVE TRANSFORMATION

9Ai   A hero or heroine is attacked.
9Aii The victim's condition deteriorates.
9Aiii The victim is restored.
      Tales 4, 5, 6, 7, 8, 27, 66, 68, 69

9B   REGENERATIVE TRANSFORMATION

9Bi   A human substance is put in a concealed place.
9Bii People grow from the substance.
      Tales 14, 15, 30, 33, 49, 51, 67, 70, 71, 72

10   INTERDICTIONS

10i   A woman/man has the company of a man/woman.
10ii She/he is warned not to do something.
10iii She/he does not heed the advice.
10iv The inobservance has grave consequences.
      Tales 10A (interdictions given to women) 11, 22,
         23, 33, 35, 40, 41, 42, 44, 45, 48, 71
      Tales 10B (interdictions given to men) 12, 13, 17,
         24, 26, 27, 28, 36, 73, 74, 75, 76

11   RESULT

11i   Heroes or heroines cause or respond to death or
         injury.
11ii The characters' actions have lasting results.
      All tales except 27, 43